CAMBRIDGE LIBRARY COLLECTION

Books of enduring scholarly value

Religion

For centuries, scripture and theology were the focus of prodigious amounts of scholarship and publishing, dominated in the English-speaking world by the work of Protestant Christians. Enlightenment philosophy and science, anthropology, ethnology and the colonial experience all brought new perspectives, lively debates and heated controversies to the study of religion and its role in the world, many of which continue to this day. This series explores the editing and interpretation of religious texts, the history of religious ideas and institutions, and not least the encounter between religion and science.

Sermons Preached in India

Reginald Heber (1783–1826), second bishop of Calcutta, was appointed to the role in 1823, and had for a long time been interested in the Church of England's overseas missions. His diocese in the subcontinent had been established less than a decade before, in 1814, and included India, southern Africa and Australia. Heber travelled extensively throughout, visiting remote Anglican communities and later publishing journals about his travels. In addition, he was well-known as a hymn-writer. *Sermons Preached in India*, however, was published posthumously in 1829, and edited by his widow, Amelia. This volume also illustrates Heber's zeal to carry out his work across his diocese, the location of his sermons range from Delhi to Dum Dum. Missionaries would have been a significant part of his diocese, and these homilies reflect many of the difficulties faced by Anglicans living in a place that had its own strong religious beliefs.

T0382422

Cambridge University Press has long been a pioneer in the reissuing of out-of-print titles from its own backlist, producing digital reprints of books that are still sought after by scholars and students but could not be reprinted economically using traditional technology. The Cambridge Library Collection extends this activity to a wider range of books which are still of importance to researchers and professionals, either for the source material they contain, or as landmarks in the history of their academic discipline.

Drawing from the world-renowned collections in the Cambridge University Library, and guided by the advice of experts in each subject area, Cambridge University Press is using state-of-the-art scanning machines in its own Printing House to capture the content of each book selected for inclusion. The files are processed to give a consistently clear, crisp image, and the books finished to the high quality standard for which the Press is recognised around the world. The latest print-on-demand technology ensures that the books will remain available indefinitely, and that orders for single or multiple copies can quickly be supplied.

The Cambridge Library Collection will bring back to life books of enduring scholarly value (including out-of-copyright works originally issued by other publishers) across a wide range of disciplines in the humanities and social sciences and in science and technology.

Sermons
Preached in India

REGINALD HEBER

CAMBRIDGE UNIVERSITY PRESS

Cambridge, New York, Melbourne, Madrid, Cape Town,
Singapore, São Paolo, Delhi, Tokyo, Mexico City

Published in the United States of America by Cambridge University Press, New York

www.cambridge.org
Information on this title: www.cambridge.org/9781108093330

This edition first published 1829
This digitally printed version 2011

ISBN 978-1-108-09333-0 Paperback

SERMONS

PREACHED IN

INDIA.

BY THE LATE RIGHT REVEREND

REGINALD HEBER, D.D.

LORD BISHOP OF CALCUTTA;

FORMERLY RECTOR OF HODNET, SALOP; PREBENDARY OF ST. ASAPH; AND
PREACHER AT LINCOLN'S INN.

LONDON:

JOHN MURRAY, ALBEMARLE-STREET.

MDCCCXXIX.

TO THE

HON. SIR CHARLES EDWARD GREY,

CHIEF JUSTICE OF THE SUPREME COURT OF JUDICATURE IN BENGAL,

TO WHOSE AFFECTIONATE SYMPATHY AND KINDNESS

IN THE HOUR OF SORROW,

THE WIDOW AND CHILDREN OF HIS FRIEND

WERE SO MUCH INDEBTED,

THIS VOLUME

IS GRATEFULLY DEDICATED BY

AMELIA HEBER.

Bodryddan, St. Asaph,
    28*th* Feb. 1829.

PREFACE.

THE sermons contained in this volume are selected from those which the Bishop of Calcutta preached in India.

At the request of the Clergy of one of the Presidencies,—a request with which the editor has much gratification in complying—she has printed all the sermons preached within its limits, naming, both in the present volume and in that lately published, the station at which each was delivered.

The Bishop was much struck with the situation and beauty of the Church of St. George, at Madras, standing, as he expressed it, " embosomed in palms." As he intended taking a sketch of it on his return from his southern visitation, for the frontispiece of a volume of Indian Sermons, the editor, before she left Calcutta, requested a friend to procure her an accurate drawing of the building, which she has prefixed to the present series.

The Address on Confirmation will be read with
melancholy interest, from the circumstance of its
delivery having been the concluding act of her
husband's public life ; in less than two hours after
he had thus earnestly exhorted his congregation,
he was summoned to meet his Saviour !

CONTENTS.

2

SERMON XI.

THE CONVERSION OF THE HEATHEN.

[Preached at Bombay, on Whitsunday, May 22; at Colombo, September 18; and at Calcutta, on Advent Sunday, November 27, 1825; in aid of the Incorporated Society for the Propagation of the Gospel in Foreign Parts.]

ACTS ii. 38, 39.

SERMON XII.

THE OMNIPRESENCE OF GOD.

[Preached September 5, 1824, on the Consecration of the Church of Secrole, near Benares.]

GEN. xxviii. 16, 17.

SERMON XIII.

SIN AND GRACE.

[Preached at St. Mary's, Madras, March 4, 1826.]

ROMANS vii. 24, 25.

SERMON XVII.

THE

VALEDICTORY ADDRESS

OF THE

Society for Promoting Christian Knowledge,

DELIVERED BY THE

LORD BISHOP OF BRISTOL,

AT A SPECIAL GENERAL MEETING OF THE SOCIETY,

JUNE XIII. M.DCCC.XXIII.

TO THE

LORD BISHOP OF CALCUTTA,

PREVIOUSLY TO HIS DEPARTURE FOR INDIA:

TOGETHER WITH

HIS LORDSHIP'S REPLY.

At a Special General Meeting of the Society
for Promoting Christian Knowledge,
held at their House in Bartlett's-Buildings,
June 13, 1823, agreeably to public notice :

PRESENT,

His Grace Charles Manners Sutton, D.D. Lord Archbishop
of Canterbury, President,

His Grace William Magee, D.D. Lord Archbishop of
Dublin,

The Right Rev. William Howley, D.D. Lord Bishop of
London,

The Right Rev. Thomas Burgess, D.D. Lord Bishop of St.
David's,

The Right Rev. George-Henry Law, D.D. Lord Bishop of
Chester,

The Right Rev. William Van Mildert, D.D. Lord Bishop of
Llandaff,

The Right Rev. John Kaye, D.D.Lord Bishop of Bristol,

The Right Rev. Reginald Heber, D.D. Lord Bishop of Calcutta,

The Right Honourable George, Lord Kenyon,

The Right Honourable Thomas, Lord Lilford,

The Very Rev. Robert Hodgson, D.D. Dean of Carlisle,

Sir Thomas Dyke Acland, Bart. M.P.

Sir R. H. Inglis, Bart.

Ven. Joseph Holden Pott, M.A. Archdeacon of London,

Ven. John James Watson, D.D. Archdeacon of St. Alban's,

Ven. Charles James Blomfield, D.D. Archdeacon of Col-
chester,

Ven. Robert Nares, M.A. Archdeacon of Stafford,

Ven. Francis Wrangham, M.A. Archdeacon of Cleveland,

Ven. William Strong, D.D. Archdeacon of Northampton,

The Hon. & Rev. George Neville Grenville, M.A. Master
of Magdalen College, Cambridge,

And a large assemblage of Members of the Society,

His Grace the President, in the Chair :

The following Valedictory Address to the Right Reverend Father in God Reginald, Lord Bishop of Calcutta, previous to his departure for India, was delivered, on the behalf of the Society, by the Right Reverend Father in God John, Lord Bishop of Bristol.

My Lord Bishop of Calcutta,

Your preparations for the arduous voyage which you are about to undertake, being now so far advanced towards their completion as to preclude the expectation that you will again, at least for a long series of years, be enabled to attend the meetings of this Society, it has been resolved, and all must admit the propriety and expediency of the resolution, that a Valedictory Address should be delivered to your Lordship on the present occasion. The highly responsible and honourable situation, which you have been recently appointed to fill, is intimately connected with objects, to which the attention of the Society has, for more than a century, been directed. They would, therefore, subject themselves to a charge—of all others most abhorrent from their real character and feelings—a charge of indifference and inattention to the spiritual welfare of the inhabitants of Hindostan, did they not seize the opportunity, before your departure for those distant regions, of publicly expressing the deep, the intense interest, which they take in the success of your future labours.

But while I acknowledge the peculiar propriety of the resolution, I must be permitted to state my unfeigned regret that its execution has not been entrusted to abler hands. When it was proposed to me to undertake the office of delivering the present address, I was not insensible to the difficulty of the task in which I was about to engage. Every approach which I have since made to the subject, has confirmed me in the conviction of my inability to do it justice—to produce any thing which should not be alike unworthy of your Lordship's distinguished reputation, and of the reasonable expectation of the audience by which I am surrounded.

Happily, however, for me it is not requisite that I should enter upon the various important and interesting topics, which the occasion unavoidably suggests. In contemplating your elevation to the episcopal office, it is impossible to separate that event from the influence which it must necessarily have upon the spiritual interests of the subjects of our Indian empire ; of an empire scarcely inferior in extent to that of Rome in the plenitude of her power, and containing millions of our fellow-creatures, who are yet strangers to the saving truths of the Gospel. How grand, how overwhelming a subject is here presented to the contemplation ! A subject, in which the most exalted intellect may find a fit opportunity for the display of all its powers; but from which ordinary minds must shrink, oppressed by the humiliating consciousness of their own insufficiency! Great, therefore, is the relief which I have derived from the reflection, that the design of the present address neither requires, nor even permits, me to expatiate in this ample field. It would be no less presumptuous in me, than foreign from the intention of the Society, were I to occupy your time and that of this meeting in detailing my own opinions respecting the most effectual mode of communicating the blessings of Christianity to the nations of Hindostan, or in offering your Lordship my advice respecting the course which it is expedient for you to pursue in discharging the duties of your high station. My province is simply to express to you the feelings with which the Society regard your appointment to the superintendance of the Indian Diocese, and to bespeak your protection and support for the efforts which they have long made, and, with the blessing of Providence, shall never cease to make, to diffuse the knowledge of the Gospel throughout that vast continent.

Yet, I trust that you, my Right Reverend Brother, and that the rest of this respectable assembly will not charge me with improperly digressing from the immediate business of the day, if I briefly advert to the change which has been effected in the prospects of the Society, since a similar address was delivered in this place. Strongly as the Society were impressed with the conviction that the forma-

tion of a Church Establishment afforded the only
secure mode of communicating the blessings of
Christianity to our Eastern Empire—firm and
deeply-rooted as was their confidence in the zeal,
the discretion, the ability of him to whom the government of that Establishment was to be committed—they were, still, too sensible how short-
sighted are the views of man, and how frail the
nature of all his expectations, not to feel some
anxiety and apprehension respecting the success of
the newly-adopted measures.

Nine years have now elapsed since your lamented
Predecessor entered upon the discharge of his episcopal functions; and that, which then could only
afford a subject for conjecture and for hope, has
become a matter of retrospect and of certainty.
All the accounts which have reached the Society,
concur in stating that the new measures have been
attended with more complete success than from the
shortness of time, during which they have been in
operation, the most sanguine could have ventured
to anticipate. Many of the impediments which
directly or indirectly, retarded the reception of the
Gospel, have been removed. The establishment of
a visible Church has opened an asylum to the convert from the taunts and injuries of the professors
of his former faith. The progressive improvement
effected in the lives and conversation of the European settlers has deprived the natives of one of their
most powerful arguments against the truth of Christianity. They no longer look upon us as mere

conquerors, greedy only of wealth and of dominion; but as a virtuous and religious people, not less superior to them in moral goodness than in civilization and manners—in justice and benevolence than in arts and arms. Their attachment to their caste, which seemed to present the most formidable obstacle to their conversion, has been overcome. The mists, which enveloped their understandings, are fast dissolving before the irradiating influence of Sacred Truth. The superstitious dread, with which they regarded their deities, is giving place to juster conceptions of the Divine Nature; and the priests of the idol of Juggernaut are compelled to bewail the decreasing numbers and diminished zeal of his votaries.

What a variety of emotions is the cheering prospect which has at length opened upon us, calculated to excite! What gratitude to Almighty God for the blessing which He has been pleased to bestow upon the labours of the infant Church! What reverence for the memory of the distinguished Prelate, whose wisdom and piety have, under the direction of Providence, conducted those labours to so successful an issue! How powerful an encouragement does it hold out, how strict an obligation does it impose, stedfastly to persevere in the prosecution of these holy designs, till the triumph over the powers of darkness in our Indian empire shall be complete, and no other vestige of the ancient idolatry shall remain than the deserted temples of the divinities, who were its objects. Nothing now

2

appears to be wanting but that the number of labourers should bear a due proportion to the abundance of the harvest which is spread before them;
and our confidence in the enlightened piety of our
rulers forbids the supposition, that this want will
long remain unsupplied.   But, I must no longer
detain you from the immediate business of the
day.

My Lord, the Society for Promoting Christian
Knowledge desire to offer to your Lordship their
sincere congratulations upon your elevation to the
Episcopal See of Calcutta.

They derive from your appointment to this high
office the certain assurance, that all the advantages,
which they have anticipated from the formation of
a Church Establishment in India, will be realized;
and that the various plans for the diffusion of true
religion amongst its inhabitants, which have been
so wisely laid and so auspiciously commenced by
your lamented Predecessor, will, under your superintendance and controul, advance with a steady and
uninterrupted progress.   They ground this assurance upon the rare union of intellectual and moral
qualities, which combine to form your character.
They ground it upon the stedfastness of purpose,
with which, from the period of your admission into
the ministry, you have exclusively dedicated your
time and talents to the peculiar studies of your sacred profession; abandoning that human learning,
in which you had already shown that you were capable of attaining the highest excellence, and re-

nouncing the certain prospect of literary fame. But
above all, they ground this assurance upon the
signal proof of self-devotion, which you have given
by your acceptance of the episcopal office. With
respect to any other individual, who had been placed
at the head of the Church Establishment in India,
a suspicion might have been entertained that some
worldly desire, some feeling of ambition mingled
itself with the motives by which he was actuated.
But in your case such a suspicion would be destitute even of the semblance of truth. Every enjoyment, which a well-regulated mind can derive from
the possession of wealth, was placed within your
reach. Every avenue to professional distinction
and dignity, if they had been the objects of your
solicitude, lay open before you. What then was
the motive which could incline you to quit your
native land? To exchange the delights of home
for a tedious voyage to distant regions? To separate yourself from the friends, with whom you had
conversed from your earliest years? What, but an
ardent wish to become the instrument of good to
others? A holy zeal in your Master's service? A
firm persuasion that it was your bounden duty to
submit yourself unreservedly to His disposal—to
shrink from no labour which He might impose—to
count no sacrifice hard which He might require?
Of the benefits, which will arise to the Indian
Church from a spirit of self-devotion so pure and
so disinterested, the Society feel, that it is impossible to form an exaggerated estimate.

Nor has this act of self-devotion been the result
of sudden impulse; it has been performed after
serious reflection, and with an accurate knowledge
of the difficulties by which your path will be ob-
structed. You have not engaged in this holy warfare without previously counting the cost. So deeply
were you impressed with the responsibility, which
must attach to the episcopal office in India, that
you hesitated to accept it. With that diffidence,
which is the surest characteristic of great talents
and great virtues, you doubted your own sufficiency.
But upon mature deliberation you felt, that a call
was made upon you: a call—to disobey which
would argue a culpable distrust of the protection of
Him who made it. You assured yourself that the
requisite strength would be supplied by the same
Almighty Power, which imposed the burthen.
Amongst the circumstances which have attended
your recent appointment, the Society dwell upon
this with peculiar satisfaction; inasmuch as it forms
a striking feature of resemblance between your
Lordship and your lamented Predecessor; who,
like you, originally felt, and like you, subsequently
overcame a reluctance to undertake the adminis-
tration of the Indian Diocese.

Before that accomplished Prelate quitted his
native shores, which he was, alas! destined never
to revisit, this Society in a valedictory address en-
treated him to honour with his countenance and
protection their exertions for the propagation and
maintenance of the Christian Religion in the East.

They stated their exertions to consist in sending out missionaries; in procuring translations into the dialects of Hindostan of the Scriptures and the Liturgy of our Church, and distributing them throughout the country; and in encouraging the erection of schools for the instruction of children as well of Europeans as of natives.   They further invited his attention to the formation of Institutions in imitation of the Diocesan and District Committees, which had about that period been established in different parts of England and Wales.

In the designs recommended to his notice by the Society your lamented Predecessor was pleased to promise his cordial co-operation.   Under his fostering care committees were formed in the three Presidencies and in Ceylon, from the labours of which the most beneficial results have arisen.   The limits which the Society must prescribe to themselves in the present address, will not allow them to enter into a minute detail of their results.   Yet they cannot deny themselves the gratification of particularly referring to the re-establishment of the Vepery Mission Press through the interposition of the Madras Committee; a measure fraught with the most important benefits to the cause of the Gospel, since it supplies the means of diffusing through the whole of Southern India the word of knowledge and of life.

The same countenance, with which your Predecessor honoured their past labours, the Society now entreat your Lordship to bestow upon their future exertions. The nature of the objects to which those exertions are directed will, we are assured, of itself constitute, in your estimation, a sufficient title to your support. Yet we cannot but indulge the hope, that you will be induced to regard them with an eye of especial favour by the consideration that they proceed from the Society for Promoting Christian Knowledge. Though you have been precluded by the distance of your residence from the metropolis, and by more pressing avocations, from attending the meetings and taking an active part in the business of the Society, still ample proofs have not been wanting of your friendly disposition towards them. Your name has long been enrolled in the list of their members; and they feel both pleasure and gratitude, when they reflect that you condescended to close your ministerial labours in this country by a discourse delivered at their request, and, if they may be allowed to use the expression, in their service.

It now only remains to assure your Lordship, if such an assurance is indeed necessary, that in quitting your native land you bear with you the esteem and the regret of the Society. Though removed to a distant quarter of the globe, you will still be present to our thoughts. Every event which befalls you will be to us a subject of the liveliest interest: and with our prayers for the success of your public labours we shall mingle our petitions for your personal safety and welfare; humbly beseeching the Giver of all good gifts, that He will be pleased to shower his choicest earthly blessings on your head, till He shall at length call you, in the fulness of age and honour, to receive that eternal reward which He has reserved in His heavenly kingdom for those, who are the instruments of "turning many unto righteousness."

To this Address the Lord Bishop of Calcutta made the following Reply :

MAY IT PLEASE YOUR GRACE AND MY LORDS, PARTICULARLY MY LORD BISHOP OF BRISTOL.

IT may be easily supposed that the present is to me a very aweful moment—both when I consider the persons, in whose presence I stand ; the occasion, on which we have been called together ; the charge, which I have just received; and the Society, on whose part those admirable and affectionate counsels have been addressed to me. I cannot recollect without very solemn and mingled feelings of gratitude for the trust which has been reposed in me, and of alarm for the responsibility which I have incurred, how much I have been honoured by the kindness and confidence of the Society for Promoting Christian Knowledge, and the remarkable and most honourable interest, which this Society has always evinced in the welfare of the Indian Church. I cannot forget, that it was this Society which administered the wants, and directed the energies of the first protestant missionaries to Hindostan ; that, under

1

its auspices, at a later period, Schwartz, and Gerickè, and Kolhoff, went forth to sow the seeds of light and happiness in that benighted country; and that, still more recently, within these sacred walls, (for sacred I will venture to call them, when I consider the purposes, to which they are devoted, and the prayers, by which they are hallowed) Bishop Middleton bade adieu to that country, which he loved, and to that Church, of which he was one of the brightest ornaments. With such examples of learning and holiness around me, with such models of Christian zeal before me, I may well be acquitted of assumed humility, when I profess a deep and painful sense of my own insufficiency; and feel, that where so much has been done, and where so much remains to do, far greater energies and talents than mine will be necessary either to fulfil the reasonable expectations of the Christian world, or to avoid falling short, far short, of the achievements of my admirable Predecessor.

With such difficulties, and under such a responsibility my hope must be, and is, in the counsels and countenance of your Grace, and of the other distinguished Rulers of the English Church, whom I see around me; and it is therefore, that I could almost feel disposed to lament as a deficiency in the eloquent and pathetic Address of the Right Reverend Prelate, to whose kind notice of me I am so deeply indebted, that he has professedly waved all detailed explanation of his ideas respecting that line of conduct, which, in my situation, is most likely to conduce to, and accelerate the triumph of the Gospel among the Heathen. I regret this the more, since, in a recent admirable sermon by the same distinguished person, he has shown us, how remarkably he is qualified to offer counsels of such a nature. Most gladly, I am convinced, we should all, and most gladly, above all, should I have become his scholar in the art of feeding the flock of Christ, and teaching and persuading the things, which belong to the kingdom of God. But, though his modesty has withheld him from the task, I will still hope to profit by his assistance in private, for the execution of that awful and overpowering enterprize, which, (if I know my own heart) I can truly say, I undertake not in my own strength, but in an humble reliance on the prayers and counsels of the good and the wise, and on that assistance, above all, which, whosoever seeks it faithfully, shall never fail of receiving.

Nor, my Lord Archbishop, will I seek to dissemble my conviction, that, slow as the growth of truth must be in a soil so strange and hitherto so spiritually barren; distant as the period may be when any very considerable proportion of the natives of India shall lift up their hands to the Lord of Hosts, yet, in the degree of progress which has been made, enough of promise is given to remove all despondency as to the eventual issue of our labours. When we recollect, that one hundred years have scarcely passed away, since the first missionaries of this Society essayed, under every imaginable circumstance of difficulty and discouragement, to plant their grain of mustard-seed in the Carnatic; when we look back to those apostolic men with few resources, save what this Society supplied to them; without encouragement, without support; compelled to commit themselves, not to the casual hospitality, but to the systematic and bigoted in-hospitality, of the natives; seated in the street, because no house would receive them; acquiring a new and difficult language, at the doors of the schools, from the children tracing their letters on the sand; can we refrain not only from admiring the faith and patience of those eminent Saints, but from comparing their situation with the port which Christianity now assumes in the East, and indulg-ing the hope that, one century more, and the thou-sands of converts which our missionaries already number, may be extended into a mighty multitude, who will look back with gratitude to this Society as the first dispenser of those sacred truths which will then be their guide and their consolation? What would have been the feelings of Schwartz, (" clarum et venerabile nomen Gentibus;" to whom even the heathen, whom he failed to convince, looked up as something more than mortal,) what would have been his feeling had he lived to witness Christianity in India established under the protec-tion of the ruling power, by whom four-fifths of that vast continent is held in willing subjection? What, if he had seen her adorned and strengthened by

c

that primitive and regular form of government, which is so essential to her reception and stability among a race like our eastern fellow-subjects! What forbids, I ask, that, when in one century, our little one is become a thousand, in a century more, that incipient desertion of the idol shrines, to which the learned Prelate so eloquently alluded, may have become total, and be succeeded by a resort of all ranks and ages to the altars of the Most High; so that a parochial Clergy may prosecute the work which the missionary has begun, and " the gleaning grapes of Ephraim may be more " than the vintage of Abiezer ?"

There was one part of the Speech of my Right Reverend Friend, (if I may be allowed to call him so) which I cannot abstain, in gratitude, from noticing, though I confess, I allude to it with reluctance; I mean the obliging manner in which he has been pleased to speak of me. There is no man who knows better than myself, and this, my Lord, is no time for dissembling, how little these praises are deserved. Yet even these praises, by God's grace, I would hope may not be useless to me. They may teach me what manner of man the Society for Promoting Christian Knowledge desires as her agent and correspondent in India; they may teach me what manner of man a Bishop of Calcutta ought to be, what manner of man Bishop Middleton was, and what manner of man, though at an humble distance, I must endeavour, by God's help, to become.

I can only conclude by expressing, so far as words
can express, to your Grace, to the distinguished
Prelates around you, and to the Society for Promoting Christian Knowledge in general, my gratitude for the private and personal, as well as public
kindness and countenance, with which you have
honoured me ; my gratitude, and that of the Indian
Church, for the splendid bounty of which you have
made me the dispenser ; my gratitude for the patience and indulgence with which you have now
heard me ; my gratitude, above all, for those
prayers which you have promised to offer up, on
my behalf, to the throne of grace and mercy. Accept, in return, the blessing of a grateful heart ;
accept the settled purpose of my mind, to devote
what little talent I possess, to the great cause in
which all our hearts are engaged, and for which it
is not our duty only, but our illustrious privilege
to labour. Accept the hope, which I would fain
express, that I shall not altogether disappoint your
expectations, but that I shall learn and labour in
the furtherance of that fabric of Christian wisdom,
of which the superstructure was so happily commenced by him, whose loss we deplore ! I say
the superstructure, not the foundation, for this
latter praise the glorified spirit of my revered Predecessor would himself be the first to disclaim.
As a wise master-builder, he built on that which
he found ; but " other foundation can no man lay,"
nor did Bishop Middleton seek to lay any other
than that, of which the first stone was laid in

2

Golgotha, and the building was complete when the Son of God took His seat of glory on the right hand of His Father.

I again, my Lord Archbishop, with much humility, request your blessing, and the prayers of the Society. It is, indeed, a high satisfaction for me to reflect, that I go forth as their agent, and the promoter of their pious designs in the East ; and, if ever the time should arrive when I may be enabled to preach to the natives of India in their own language, I shall then aspire to the still higher distinction of being considered the Missionary of the Society for Promoting Christian Knowledge.

A

CHARGE

DELIVERED TO

THE CLERGY OF THE DIOCESE

OF

INDIA,

AT

Calcutta, May 27, 1824; at Bombay, April 29, 1825; at Colombo, September 1, 1825; and at Madras, March 10, 1826.

Σπουδασω δε και εκαστοτε εχειν υμας μετα την εμην εξοδον την τουτων μνημην ποιεισθαι.—2 Peter i. 15.

B

ADVERTISEMENT,

PREFIXED TO THE CALCUTTA EDITION.

THE Right Reverend Author, after holding his visitation at Madras, delayed the publication of his charge till the completion of his extensive journey to the south should have enabled him to speak, from personal observation, of the actual state of the several missions in the diocese. In the course of his laborious visitation of the several provinces of Upper, Central, and Western India, and subsequently of the Island of Ceylon, his attention had been anxiously directed to these inquiries; and the last weeks of his invaluable life were devoted to the minute and careful survey of the more cultivated fields of missionary labour in the Peninsula. And though, amongst the many circumstances which render the untimely loss of such a man a source of universal sorrow to the Church of India, this may well have been overlooked; it is yet no slight subject of regret to the Christian world, that he whose mind was most capable of appreciating those important labours, whose opportunities were most favourable for observing them, and whose high and sacred dignity gave weight and authority to his testimony, should not have been spared to record more minutely the scenes of infant Christianity which he had himself witnessed, and to communicate to the hearts of others the impressions of delight and gratitude which they had left upon his own.

A

CHARGE.

MY REVEREND BRETHREN,

ADDRESSING you, for the first time, in your collective and corporate capacity, I am happy to be enabled to announce the probable increase of your numbers to an amount more nearly adequate to the spiritual necessities of India; to the arduous and peculiar labours which the Indian clergy undergo; to the casualties of an enfeebling and devouring climate, and to that fair proportion which might be looked for between the ecclesiastical establishments of Fort William and its subordinate Presidencies.

The number of chaplains allotted to the former is increased, by a recent order of the Honourable Court of Directors, from twenty-eight to thirty-one, while the transfer of Mhow and Nagpoor to the establishments of Fort St. George and Bombay will enable the government of this Presidency to avail itself, in other quarters, of the services of the clergymen who now officiate there; and the change, which is further directed, of " station" into " dis-

B 2

trict" chaplains, may lead, I trust, to measures still
further increasing the effective nature of their ministerial labours.

For the munificent and parental care which has
prompted these measures, it would ill become me to
conceal the expression of my gratitude,—and it is
in the hope of so far exciting (by an unvarnished
statement of our wants) the zeal of our brethren at
home, as not to render vain the Christian care of
our rulers,—that I am induced to mention (what,
to those who hear me, is unhappily but too familiar) the very great deficiency, in numerical strength,
of the Clergy on the Indian establishment.

Of twenty-eight chaplains assigned by the Honourable Company to the Presidency of Fort William, fifteen only are now on their posts, and effective.   Five are, from ill health and other unavoidable causes, at present absent on furlough; while
of the remaining eight appointments, no fewer than
seven are represented as vacant, the clergyman
who fills the eighth only, being reported on his
voyage from England.

The consequence has been, that, even in Calcutta
and its vicinity, some Churches must have been
shut up but for the occasional help of clergymen
not in the Company's service; that at Cawnpoor, a
single labourer is sinking under the duty of a military cantonment about five miles in length, containing two places of worship, two burial grounds,
two distinct establishments of barracks, schools,
and hospitals, and for which the wisdom of govern-

ment had designated two resident ministers;—
while in the other mofussil provinces, some of the
most important stations are addressing to me, almost daily, their earnest (and, unhappily, their
unavailing) applications for that comfort and instruction which in our own country is accessible
to all.

This is a state of things, beyond a doubt, sufficiently lamentable. It presents the revolting spectacle of a nation almost without a priesthood to the
Romanists who dwell among us, and to the surrounding heathen. It has a tendency to increase
itself and its own evils by oppressing and overpowering the strength of those labourers who still
continue in the vineyard. And it excludes, in the
worst and most effectual manner, from the teaching and ordinances of our religion, the daily increasing multitude of our countrymen and their
descendants, of whom by far the greater part are
still ardently attached to the faith and worship of
their fathers.

In all which I have said, I am far from designing
to convey a censure on our rulers. Those rulers
have shown (I cheerfully bear them witness) a progressive attention, during many years, to the spiritual wants of their servants and soldiers in these
distant lands. Their endowments have been liberal; they have been careful of the comforts and
respectability of their clergy, and, in the general
exercise of their patronage, they have exhibited a
disinterestedness and an anxiety for the cause of

God and goodness, which few bodies of men have exhibited under similar circumstances. The inadequacy, the delay, the frustration of their measures for the spiritual good of India, may be ascribed, with more justice, to the general ignorance which prevails in England on most points connected with these important but distant territories ; to an apprehension, (certainly not an unnatural one,) on the part of the younger clergy, of an unhealthy climate, and almost a life-long banishment, and to their consequent backwardness in soliciting or accepting appointments, the duties of which are little understood, but the sacrifices incident to which are easily and generally appreciated.

And I have, therefore, thus strongly, but truly, depicted the condition of our Indian Church, both as it accounts, in no small degree, for that tardy progress of Christ's kingdom in the east with which our adversaries are not slow to taunt us ; and as it affords me an opportunity of bearing testimony to the diligence, the fidelity, the conciliatory and affectionate spirit, in which, so far as I have yet seen or known, the clergy of this diocese, to their power, and in some instances beyond their power, have laboured and are labouring.

Nor will I conceal my hope, that when our wants are more generally known, deserving candidates may more readily offer themselves to our rulers for situations, which, as they claim, undoubtedly, no common share of talent and diligence to discharge their duties effectually, so a greater and more im-

mediate return of usefulness is obtainable in them
than in almost any stations of ministerial labour
which have come within the compass of my experience.

It is, indeed, most true, that those men would be
much mistaken who should anticipate, in the fortunes of an Indian chaplain, a life of indolence, of
opulence, of luxury. An Indian chaplain must
come prepared for hard labour in a climate where
labour is often death; he must come prepared for
rigid self-denial in situations where all around him
invites to sensual indulgence; he must be content
with an income liberal, indeed, in itself, but very
often extremely disproportioned to the charities,
the hospitalities, the unavoidable expenses of his
station. He must be content to bear his life in his
hand, and to leave, very often, those dearer than
life to His care who feeds the ravens.

Nor are the qualifications which he will need,
nor are the duties which will rest on him, less
arduous than the perils of his situation. He must
be no uncourtly recluse, or he will lose his influence over the higher ranks of his congregation.
He must be no man of pleasure, or he will endan-
ger their souls and his own. He must be a scholar,
and a man of cultivated mind, for, in many of his
hearers (wherever he is stationed), he will meet
with a degree of knowledge and refinement which
a parochial minister in England does not often encounter, and a spirit, sometimes of fastidious and
even sceptical criticism, which the society, the

habits, and, perhaps, the very climate of India, has a natural tendency to engender. He must condescend to simple men, for here, as elsewhere, the majority of his congregation will, nevertheless, be the ignorant and the poor.

Nor, in his intercourse with this humble class of his hearers, must he anticipate the same cheering circumstances which make the house of the English parochial minister a school and temple of religion, and his morning and evening walk a source of blessing and blessedness. His servants will be of a different creed from himself, and insensible, in too many instances, to his example, his exhortations, and his prayers. His intercourse will not be with the happy and harmless peasant, but with the dissipated, the diseased, and often, the demoralized soldier. His feet will not be found at the wicker gate of the well-known cottage ; beneath the venerable tree ; in the grey church-porch, or by the side of the hop-ground and the corn-field ; but he must kneel by the bed of infection or despair, in the barrack, the prison, or the hospital.

But to the well-tempered, the well-educated, the diligent and pious clergyman, who can endear himself to the poor without vulgarity, and to the rich without involving himself in their vices; who can reprove sin without harshness, and comfort penitence without undue indulgence ; who delights in his Master's work, even when divested of those outward circumstances which in our own country contribute to render that work picturesque and

interesting; who feels a pleasure in bringing
men to God, proportioned to the extent of their
previous wanderings ; who can endure the coarse
(perhaps fanatical) piety of the ignorant and vulgar,
and listen with joy to the homely prayers of men
long strangers to the power of religion ; who can
do this, without himself giving way to a vain enthusiasm; and whose good sense, sound knowledge, and practical piety, can restrain and reclaim
the enthusiasm of others to the due limits of reason
and scripture ; to him, above all, who can give his
few leisure hours to fields of usefulness beyond his
immediate duty ; and who, without neglecting the
European penitent, can aspire to the further extension of Christ's kingdom among the heathen ;
to such a man as Martyn was, and as some still
are, (whom may the Lord of the harvest long continue to His Church !) I can promise no common
usefulness and enjoyment in the situation of an
Indian chaplain.

I can promise him, in any station to which he
may be assigned, an educated society and an audience peculiarly qualified to exercise and strengthen
his powers of argument and eloquence. I can promise him, generally speaking, the favour of his
superiors, the friendship of his equals, and affection,
strong as death, from those whose wanderings he
corrects, whose distresses he consoles, and by whose
sick and dying bed he stands as a ministering angel ! Are further inducements needful ? I yet
can promise more. I can promise to such a man

the esteem, the regard, the veneration of the surrounding Gentiles ; the consolation, at least, of
having removed from their minds, by his blameless
life and winning manners, some of the most inve-
terate and most injurious prejudices which oppose,
with them, the reception of the Gospel; and the
honour, it may be, (of which examples are not
wanting among you,) of planting the cross of Christ
in the wilderness of a heathen heart, and extending
the frontiers of the visible Church amid the hills of
darkness and the strong holds of errour and idolatry.

In what I have said, I feel that I have expressed,
almost without intending it, my opinion as to what
manner of man an Indian chaplain ought to be ;
and to such of you, my brethren, as fill that honourable rank, any further pastoral advice seems
scarcely necessary.   If there be any thing more, it
must relate to matters of detail and local expediency, which may be left to every man for himself,
according to his personal and particular experience.

Two such points there are, however, which I
would generally press on the notice of all, because
I can hardly conceive a situation in this country,
where an attention to both will not be both necessary and blessed.

The first is, a continued and earnest furtherance
of and attention to those powerful aids in your spiritual work, by the bounty of individuals, the parental care of government, and the pious munificence of the venerable Society for Promoting Christian Knowledge, in regimental or station schools,

wherever they exist or can be established; in the dissemination of religious tracts, of our excellent Liturgy, and the Holy Scriptures; and in the arrangement and conduct of those lending libraries, which should more particularly fall under the chaplain's care, and which I hope, by God's blessing, to see established throughout this land, wherever there is a barrack to receive, or an European soldier or invalid to use them.

The second point which I would recommend to every chaplain who is preparing himself for India, or who yet looks forward to a lengthened residence here, is the attentive and grammatical study of some one of the native languages. I mean not merely that jargon which a few weeks will bestow; which is picked up in our intercourse with the meanest of the people, and which suffices, perhaps, to order bread to be placed on our table, or to expedite our journey from stage to stage. Nor do I recommend, as a general measure, what is to most impracticable, and useful, perhaps, to few, an investigation of the abstruse elegancies and intricate machinery of the learned language of the brahmins. But I do earnestly recommend some further attention than the majority of chaplains in India are accustomed to pay, to those dialects which are intelligible to the great body of the Indian people, and which well-born and well-educated men employ in conversing with each other.

The duty, indeed, of endeavouring the conversion of his heathen neighbours, is to a chaplain, I

readily admit, an incidental duty only. It is a
duty, nevertheless, expressly contemplated in those
laws which send him hither; and the times may
yet return in which it may be expedient to remind
the opponents of Gentile conversion, that to acquire the languages and instruct the natives of
India is declared in the charter of these colonies, to
be a legitimate and necessary part of the labours
of every chaplain whom the East India Company
shall employ. I allow, nevertheless, that a Chaplain has other and more immediate cares. His
vocation is, in the first instance, to the scattered
flock of Christ in these lands, to the conversion and
renewal of all who are already named after our
Lord and Saviour. But God forbid that any among
us should forget that it is his duty, as occasion offers,
to labour after the good of all men; that he has no
commission from God but that which commands
him to preach the Gospel to every creature; and
that there are patterns before him, of men abundantly and exemplarily zealous in their duty to
their European charge, who have found leisure, nevertheless, for conveying the word of salvation to
those without these limits, and, to the praise of
presbyter, have added that of evangelist.

But this is not all. Even if you found no opportunity, or possessed no talent for convincing
the professed unbeliever, yet in every city, and
almost every cantonment of British India, a numerous and increasing population is found, the children of Europeans, and too often the monuments

of their vices, who, notwithstanding their English
descent, are accessible to instruction through the
languages of India alone, and who, though divested of the pride of caste, and, not a few of them
nominally Christians, have as much need to be instructed in the first rudiments of Christianity as
the inhabitants of Polynesia or Japan. On these
your labours must often be bestowed, for they are
an integral and essential part of that European
and military population for whose immediate benefit you are sent out hither. And, when the many
other ways are called to mind, in which a knowledge of the native languages will enable you to
forward the cause of Christ; by superintending
versions of the Scriptures and the Common Prayer,
by tracts, by schools, and by similar gradual and
peaceful methods of acquiring influence over the
Indian mind, and diffusing through the warm and
ripening mass an unseen leaven of godliness, it will
appear that this method of employing a clergyman's few leisure hours, is one of the most effectual means by which those hours may be made a
source of blessing.

Thus far, my reverend brethren, I have addressed myself to those of your number who may
be regarded in a peculiar degree as the parochial
and beneficed clergy of British India: but there
are others not comprehended under this description, and it is with no common thankfulness to
God, that I see the episcopal chair of Calcutta
now first surrounded by those who are mission-

aries themselves, as well as by those who are engaged in the important office of educating youth
for the future service of missions.

To the importance of that service no Christian
can be insensible : and I regard it as one among
the most favourable signs of the present times,
that, while Providence has, in a manner visible and
almost miraculous, prepared a high way in the
wilderness of the world for the progress of His
truth, and made the ambition, the commerce, the
curiosity, and enterprise of mankind, His implements
in opening a more effectual door to His Gospel, the
call thus given has been answered by a display of
zeal unexampled at any time since the period of
the reformation ; and America and England have
united with Denmark and Germany to send forth a
host of valiant and victorious confessors, to bear
the banner of the Cross through those regions
where darkness and death have hitherto spread
their broadest shadows.

Nor can it be a matter of reasonable surprise to
any of us, that the exertions of this kind, which the
last fifteen years have witnessed, should have excited a mingled feeling of surprise and displeasure
in the minds, not only of those who are strangers
to the powerful and peculiar emotions which send
forth the missionary to his toil, but of those who,
though themselves not idle, could not endure that
God should employ other instruments besides; and
were ready to speak evil of the work itself, rather
than that others who followed not with them should

cast out devils in the name of their common Master. To the former of these classes may be referred the loud opposition, the clamours, the expostulation, the alarm, the menace, and ridicule which, some few years ago, were systematically and simultaneously levelled at whatever was accomplished or attempted for the illumination of our Indian fellow-subjects. We can well remember, most of us, what revolutions and wars were predicted to arise from the most peaceable preaching and argument; what taunts and mockery were directed against scholars who had opened to us the gates of the least accessible oriental dialects; what opprobrious epithets were lavished on men of whom the world was not worthy. We have heard the threats of the mighty; we have heard the hisses of the fool; we have witnessed the terrours of the worldly wise, and the unkind suspicions of those from whom the missionary had most reason to expect encouragement. Those days are, for the present, gone by. Through the Christian prudence, the Christian meekness, the Christian perseverance, and indomitable faith of the friends of our good cause, and through the protection, above all, and the blessing of the Almighty, they are gone by! The angel of the Lord has, for a time, shut the mouths of these fiercer lions, and it is the false brother now, the pretended fellow-soldier in Christ, who has lift up his heel against the propagation of the Christian Gospel.

But thus it is that the power of Anti-Christ hath

worked hitherto and doth work.   Like those spec-
tre forms which the madness of Orestes saw in
classical mythology, the spirit of religious party
sweeps before us in the garb and with the attributes
of pure and evangelical religion.   The Cross is on
her shoulders, the chalice in her hand, and she is
anxiously busied, after her manner, in the service of
Him by whose holy name she also is called.   But
outstrip her in the race, but press her a little too
closely, and she turns round on us with all the
hideous features of envy and of rage.   Her hallowed
taper blazes into a sulphurous torch, her hairs
bristle into serpents, her face is as the face of
them that go down to the pit, and her words are
words of blasphemy !

What other spirit could have induced a Christian
minister, after himself, as he tells us, long labouring to convert the heathen, to assert that one hundred millions of human beings, a great, a civilised,
an understanding, and most ancient people, are
collectively and individually under the sentence of
reprobation from God, and under a moral incapa-
city of receiving that Gospel, which the God who
gave it hath appointed to be made known to all ?

What other spirit could have prompted a member of that Church which professes to hold out
the greatest comfort to sinners, to assert of a nation
with whom, whatever are their faults, I, for one,
should think it impossible to live long without loving them, that they are not only enslaved to a cruel
and degrading superstition, but that the principal

persons among them are sold to all manner of wickedness and cruelty; without mercy to the poor; without natural affection for each other; and this with no view to quicken the zeal of Christians to release them from their miserable condition, but that Christians may leave them in that condition still, to the end that they may perish everlastingly.

What other spirit, finally, could have led a Christian missionary, (with a remarkable disregard of truth, the proofs of which are in my hands,) to disparage the success of the different Protestant missions; to detract from the numbers, and vilify the good name of that ancient Syrian Church, whose flame, like the more sacred fire of Horeb, sheds its lonely and aweful brightness over the woods and mountains of Malabar, and to assure us, (hear Oh Israel !) in the same treatise, and almost in the same page, that the Christians of India are the most despised and wretched of its inhabitants; that whoever takes up the cross, takes up the hatred of his own people, the contempt of Europeans, loss of goods, loss of employment, destitution, and often beggary; and yet that it is *interest alone,* and a love of this world, which has induced in any Hindu, even a temporary profession of the Gospel?

And this is the professed apologist of the people of India! My Brethren, I have known the sharpness of censure, and I am not altogether without experience in the suffering of undeserved and injurious imputations. And, let the righteous smite

c

me friendly, I shall receive it (I trust in God) with
gratitude. Let my enemy write a book, so he
be my open enemy, I trust (through the same Divine aid) to bear it or to answer it. But whatever
reproofs I may deserve, to whatever calumnies I
may be subjected, may the mercy of Heaven defend
me from having a false friend for my vindicator!

My own experience in India is, I own, as yet but
little ; but the conclusions which I have been led to
form are of an extremely different character. I have
found, or seemed to myself to find, a race of men,
like other men who are not partakers in the rege-
nerating principle of the Gospel, very far gone, indeed, from God and His original righteousness ; but
exempt perhaps, by the fortunate circumstances of
their climate and habits, from some of those more
outrageous and appalling vices of which so dreadful
a picture is drawn in those nations to whom the
apostles preached Christ crucified.

I have found a race of gentle and temperate
habits ; with a natural talent and acuteness beyond
the ordinary level of mankind, and with a thirst for
general knowledge which even the renowned and
inquisitive Athenians can hardly have surpassed or
equalled. Prejudiced, indeed, they are, in favour
of their ancient superstitions ; nor should I think,
to say the truth, more favourably of the character,
or augur more happily of the eventual conversion
and perseverance of any man or set of men, whom
a light consideration could stir from their paternal
creed, or who received the word of truth without

cautious and patient inquiry. But I am yet to learn, that the idolatry which surrounds us is more enthralling in its influence on the human mind than those beautiful phantoms and honied sorceries which lurked beneath the laurels of Delos and Daphne, and floated on the clouds of Olympus. I am not yet convinced, that the miserable bondage of castes, and the consequences of breaking that bondage, are more grievous to be endured by the modern Indian than those ghastly and countless shapes of death which beset the path of the Roman convert. And who shall make me believe, that the same word of the Most High, which consigned to the moles and the bats the idols of Chaldee and Babylon, and dragged down the lying father of gods and men from his own Capitol, and the battlements of his " Eternal City," must yet arrest its victorious wheels on the banks of the Indus or the Ganges, and admit the trident of Siva to share, with the Cross, a divided empire ?

That the missionary to whose work I have referred, may have been, himself, unsuccessful in his labours, I certainly am not called on to deny or question. That those labours were honest and diligent I am extremely ready to believe, both from the acknowledged blamelessness of his life, from the time which he spent in the work, and the reputation which he enjoyed in Southern India. But the unsuccessful labours of one man, however diligent and able, are no argument against the hope that God, who alone giveth the increase, may

bestow more abundant blessing on other husbandmen.

And when we recollect that, by the rules of his
sect, the author of whom I speak was precluded
from the free dispersion, among his hearers and his
flock, of those sacred writings to which the first
preachers of Christianity appeal on all occasions,
or which those preachers themselves left behind
for the conversion and confirmation of after-ages;
when we recollect, that no translation of, I will
not say the Bible, but of any single Gospel or Epistle, was entrusted, for all that appears, by this missionary to his Indian converts;—it may occasion
the less wonder that they were but lightly affected
with a faith whose authentic documents were withheld from them.   And since, on his own showing,
it was his object, and that of his brethren, to allure
the Hindu from his ancient creed, by a display of
those gaudy vanities in which the Romish sect
most nearly approaches to the religion of Brahma,
what marvel will remain that the populace preferred those images to which they were accustomed, or that the more philosophic inquirer found
little apparent advantage in transferring his veneration from the legends of the Ramayana to the
almost equally doubtful names of St. Veronica, St.
Ursula, and St. George the Cappadocian!—But
we, my brethren, have not so learned Christ.
Whether our success be great or small, it is to
something very different from Hinduism that we
Protestants lead our converts; and though I am

1

far, Heaven knows, from placing on the same level
the Brahminical and the Romish faith ; and though,
as a form, though a corrupt form, of the knowledge
whereby men are brought to God, I rejoice in
every conquest which this latter has made among
the heathen, I would rather, should God so far
honour me, be the instrument of bringing one ido-
later to the worship of the one true God, and the
one Mediator between God and man, than to have
persuaded, like Xavier, my tens of thousands to
patter their rosary in Latin instead of Sanscrit, and
transfer to the Saints the honour which they had
paid to the Devetas.

But are any converts made to our sober and
less attractive ritual ?   Will not the homely truths
of Protestantism fail to attract attention where the
gorgeous rites of Romish splendour fail ?—Let me,
in the first place, express my sorrow, that so little
pains have yet been taken to bring Protestant
Christianity before the attention of the heathen in
its most comely and attractive form ; in that form
which blends decency of ornament with perfect
purity of worship, and has preserved the beauties
of the ancient liturgies without any intermixture
of more recent superstition.   The Common Prayer
has been translated into Hindustani, Cingalese, and
Tamil.   But how few places of worship for those
different nations are there, in which that excellent
ritual is regularly used with its striking and primitive appendages of surplice, font and altar !   Even
where Ministers of our own Church have officiated,

I have heard, in many parts of India, of a carelessness in these particulars. I am, therefore, the more
anxious to call the attention of those who hear me
to the advantage, and, I will say, the duty of con-
forming in external decorum, no less than in spirit
and doctrine, to a Church of which, I trust, none
of us are ashamed; and to that beauty and regularity of worship which both well becomes the
truth, and may cause the truth itself to be received
with less reluctance.

But are no converts made to Protestant Christianity? Bear witness to the contrary the Christians of Agra, of Benares, of Buxar, of Meerut, and
Chunar! Bear witness those numerous believers
of our own immediate neighbourhood, whom,
though we differ on many, and doubtless, on very
important points, I should hate myself if I could
regard as any other than my brethren! Let the
populous Christian districts of the Carnatic and
Tanjore bear witness, where believers are not
reckoned by solitary individuals, but by hundreds
and by thousands! Bear witness Ceylon, where
the Cross has, in a great measure, lost its reproach,
and the nobles of the land are gradually assuming
without scruple the attire, the language, and the
religion of Englishmen! And let him, finally, bear
witness whom we have now received into the number of the commissioned servants of the Church,
and whom, we trust, at no distant day, to send
forth, in the fulness of Christian authority, to make
known the way of truth to those his countrymen

from whose errors he has himself been gloriously delivered!

To perpetuate and extend these triumphs must be the endeavour of those around me, who, however small their success, are aware that, in thus endeavouring, they are fulfilling a solemn commandment of God, and who, though their visible success should be none at all, will at least, if they are faithful in their ministry, have saved their own souls, and laid up for themselves a good reward on that day when the Lord shall make up His jewels; a day for which no better preparation can be found than a patient and unwearied continuance in well doing, and in stretching out, like Him whom we serve, our consecrated hands to exhort, to heal, and to save, though it may be that, like His, our hands are stretched out to a gainsaying and unbelieving people!

From even the taunts of an adversary, however, a wise man will increase his wisdom. And, if we learn, from the volume which I have quoted, a greater moderation in our language and a greater circumspection in our deportment; more strict adherence to the union and discipline of the Church; and a more careful abstinence from every thing like exaggeration in those accounts of our progress in the work which are sent to our friends in Europe, it is apparent that some of those hindrances will be lessened which impede the progress of the truth, and that a more abundant blessing may be expected on our toils from Him who is the God of peace, of order, and of humility.

It is on these grounds that I would recommend to you, in your intercourse with the heathen, a careful abstinence from every thing which may enlist their angry passions on the side of errour; all expressions hurtful to their national pride, and even all bitter and contemptuous words against the objects of their idolatry.

In these respects, no better model can be found than the great apostle of the Gentiles, whose harshest words, in his addresses to the Athenians and men of Lystra, are of a kind to stimulate the curiosity, far more than to wound the zeal of the fiercest and least tolerant Pagan, and of whom at Ephesus, however boldly and successfully he had contended for the truth, no man was able to say that he was actually a blasphemer of their goddess. In no cause, indeed, however righteous, can abuse and insult hold the place of argument; and far nobler conquests may be gained in a friendly discussion with our adversary, than by adopting a tone which, in itself, gives him an additional motive to shut his ears against all which we urge to him.

The next topic which I would desire to impress on your minds, is the advantage and necessity (I speak both to chaplains and missionaries) of a constant and confidential communication of the more important occurrences of your ministry with each other and with your ecclesiastical superiors.

It was a wise rule of the ancient Church, " χωρις
ἐπισκοπου μη τι ποιειτε," not, certainly, that it is well
or worthy of the priesthood that any man or set of
men should systematically play the part of spies on
their Christian brethren, but because, by such a
system of confidence, the very existence of spies is
rendered almost impossible ; because the elders of
the Church, being acquainted with the views of
every man, and having opportunity, in the least
offensive way, to correct, to guide, to forward
them, became themselves a leading party in every
beneficial measure, and were enabled often to render measures beneficial, which would otherwise
have assumed a very doubtful character.

It is the misfortune of the modern English
Church, that the Bishop is too often regarded by
his clergy, not as the master-spring, but as merely
a controuling power ; a remora to check too ardent
zeal, rather than an agent to further improvement ;
a censor of measures already adopted, rather than
a guide in measures proposed. I rejoice to say
that, with such of my clergy as I have as yet personally known, I feel myself on a very different
footing ; and it is in order that this mutual confidence may become general throughout the diocese,
that I am anxious that all should be convinced
that, in their Ordinary, they have a fellow-servant
and a friend, actuated by the same general principles, confessing the same faith, and having the
same great objects continually in view ; who is
only desirous to forward their labours of love by

the aid of such experience as he possesses, and to prove to them, experimentally, that for the most ardent zeal, and for activity the most incessant, enough and more than enough of room is afforded by the closest principles of Church union, and the most cautious adherence to the canons and constitutions of that Church to which we profess allegiance.

Lastly, my brethren, whereuntosoever ye are called, and whatever may be the peculiar sphere of ministerial action marked out for you, let it be always in your minds, as the prevailing principle of your lives, that you are ministers of Christ, and devoted to his high and holy calling. *" Hoc agite !"* Let every man who hears you preach ; every man who witnesses your performance of your sacred functions ; every man who is admitted to your society and familiar conversation, be made aware that there is thus much distinction in your character, and that your main object is that of your profession.

Even if worldly estimation, if worldly popularity were our objects, it is conduct like this which (undisgraced by affectation and formality, and proceeding unfeignedly from the good treasure of the heart) would eventually most secure them. Consistency is, after all, that quality for which, even among worldly and carnal men, the most unfeigned respect is entertained ; and the man who is in earnest, whether they account him mistaken or no, is always esteemed the most, and listened to most willingly. But the world is not the master whom

7

I am desirous that you should seek to please; and the applause of the world is of very little moment to those whose industry is commanded in the words, " occupy till I come !" and whose labours will be rewarded with, " well done, good and faithful servant !"

It was by a more than usual attention to the consistency of his appropriate character, and to the paramount and indispensable necessity of his appropriate pursuits and duties, that the character of Bishop Middleton became that which you beheld, and that which he, for the example of us all, has left behind him. That great and good man, had his mind been attracted to secular objects, possessed much of every quality on which the world bestows its favour. But, though his memory was stored with all profane and civil literature, the application of his learning and talents was to ecclesiastical purposes only. He ranked among the very foremost critics of his age, yet it was to scriptural criticism only that his acumen was directed. He had, I am assured, an inexhaustible supply of lighter and more elegant literature, yet he sought to be remembered as a preacher and a theologian only. Nay more, when his life-long labours were at length drawing near their term, as if fearing the applause of men, even in those branches of study which were strictly appropriate and ministerial, he consigned, as a last sacrifice, his laboured manuscripts to the flames, content to live in the memory of those who personally knew, and loved, and ho-

noured him, and desiring no other reward than the
mercy of Him to whom his thoughts, his studies,
and his prayers, had been long and steadily dedicated.

One monument, however, he has left behind of
the zeal which prompted, the wisdom which planned,
and the liberality which largely contributed to it,
which must long preserve his name in the grateful
recollection of the Indian Church, and which bids
fair, under the Divine protection, to become eventually a greater blessing to these extensive lands,
than any which they have received from their
foreign lords, since the gate was first opened by
the Portuguese to the commerce and conquest of
Asia.

I mean the excellent institution of Bishop's College, which, notwithstanding every disadvantage
arising from scanty funds, from unfinished buildings, and the premature and irreparable loss of him
whose talents were, of all men's, best adapted to
contend with the difficulties which beset his infant
establishment, is already, I rejoice to say, made
available as a place of education, and already con-
firms the hopes with which its projector delighted
to contemplate it, as the probable future source
of sacred learning and religious instruction to the
Christian youth, whether of European or native
blood, through the whole of this vast empire, and
as the instrument, in God's good time, of making
plain His way through the wilderness of the heathen world, and giving light to the most remote,

the most obscured, and the most hopeless of the nations who sit in darkness.

But to the claims of Bishop's College on the assistance, the liberality, and the prayers, of all who love our English Church, or desire that it may be made an instrument of enlarging the general Church of Christ among mankind; to all which it now does, and the much more which with due support it may accomplish; and to the meritorious labours, I will add, of him who now single-handed supports the whole burden of the establishment, it is my hope, on some future day, more specifically to call your attention.

In the present instance, that attention, I am aware, must be exhausted, from the length of this morning's solemnity[1], and I feel myself less able to do justice to a subject of such importance, while I am suffering under the recent loss[2] of a distinguished and excellent friend; from whose eminent talents, from whose amiable temper, from whose high religious principles, and his repeatedly ex-

---

[1] The visitation at Calcutta, to which alone these two paragraphs relate, was lengthened by the addition of an ordination service, that of the native catechist of Schwartz, Christian David, of Tanjore, who is alluded to in the earlier part of the charge.— *Calcutta Editor.*

[2] The friend whose sudden loss is thus feelingly alluded to by the Bishop, is the Honourable Sir Christopher Puller, Chief Justice of Bengal, who had but recently arrived in the country, and died, after a short illness, May 25, 1824, but a few hours before the delivery of this charge in Calcutta.—*Calcutta Editor.*

pressed intention of devoting his ample means and
powerful mind to the service of that God from
whom he had received them, I had anticipated the
most important aids in securing the prosperity of
the Indian Church, and furthering the triumphant
progress of that Gospel in which his hope and
heart were laid up, and in which, while he yet
lived, his life was hidden.

A few days only are gone by, since, with anima-
tion on his benevolent countenance, he expressed
to me his gratitude to the Most High for the many
blessings which he had received, and his desire to
dedicate' to God, through Jesus Christ, an increased
proportion of his time, his means, and his influence.
A few hours only are past since those good resolutions are-gone thither, where they are treasured by
a gracious Master whom he had served from his
youth, and who, when his noon of life had scarcely
begun to decline, saw fit to call him to his repose
and his reward.   In him India—in him the Anglo-
Indian Church—in him the cause of missions here
and throughout the world—in him the poor of
every caste and country have lost a fearless, a
kind, a bountiful, and unpretending friend ; but he
will not have died in vain if the consideration of
his sudden mortality induces us to ponder the
worth of this world in regions where, more remarkably than on any other part of its surface, the present moment is all that we can count on, where
the sublimest and most awful phenomena of nature
remind us every instant of our uncertain tenure,

and the still breath of pestilence, and the louder warnings of thunder, adjure us to apply our hearts to wisdom.

Finally, brethren, farewell ! Be patient and watch unto prayer ; for your flocks and for yourselves, that ye may be diligent in the discharge of your stewardships, for behold He cometh quickly, and blessed is that servant whom his Lord, when He cometh, shall find so doing !

And " Oh, Almighty God ! who hast built Thy Church on the foundation of the Apostles and the Prophets, Jesus Christ Himself being the chief corner-stone, grant us so to be joined together in unity of spirit by their doctrine, that we may be made an holy temple acceptable unto Thee, through Jesus Christ our Lord. Amen."

SERMON I.

ST. JOHN i. 20.

He confessed and denied not, but confessed " I am not the Christ."

ABOUT the middle of the long reign of the Roman Emperor Tiberius, when all mankind were in hushed and anxious expectation of that Great Deliverer whom both Jewish and Pagan prophecies had foretold as about this time to make his appearance upon earth; a new and mighty teacher of morality appeared in the wilderness of Judæa. His dress, his voice, his aspect, were the image of austere holiness, and of the then almost forgotten severities of the ancient prophets and penitents. His hair and beard, unshorn, after the pattern of the Nazarites, hung wildly over his breast and shoulders; his half-naked body was macerated with frequent fasting; his raiment was the coarse hair cloth which covered the Arab's tent; his food, the insects of the air and of the field; and his luxury, the honey left by wild bees in the sun-burnt rocks of Arabia Petræa.

D

He was recognized as John, the son of a Jewish priest, whose birth had, some thirty years before, been announced by repeated miracles; foretold by an angel, preceded by a miraculous dumbness and followed by a miraculous cure; whose boyhood and youth had, from the first, been strange and solitary, and who had fled from the amusements natural to his age, and the pursuits appropriate to his station, to the dismal and dangerous retreat of the waste and howling wilderness: till now, in the full vigour of his mind, and sublimed and purified by a life of meditation, he took his station at the ford of Bethabara, and, in words full of power and dignity, called on his countrymen to escape from the wrath to come.

The ford of Bethabara, which he selected for this first appearance, was a place of all others best calculated for the double purpose of a popular teacher and a severe and habitual ascetic. Only six miles from Jericho, and in the high road from Jerusalem and the sea coast to the wealthy cities of Gadara and Aræopolis, a celebrated prophet was, in such a situation, seldom likely to want an audience; while the waters of Jordan, its marshes, and the adjacent wilderness, not only suited his mission as a Baptist, but were favourable also to the austerities and occasional secessions from the world which became the character of one who mourned for the world's transgressions.

Nor was the ford of Bethabara recommended by such considerations only. With St. John and with the Jews it might, probably, weigh still more, that it was by this very passage, which was regarded as a figurative baptism, that their ancestors under Joshua, (himself, both in name and office, the type of a more illustrious Teacher,) had gone through the stream of Jordan, and, not without a miracle, had entered into their promised Canaan. And, as the scene of Elijah's occasional residence and miracles, as the visible instrument in the cleansing of Naaman, and as the favourite retreat, during the independence of the Israelitish state, of the most popular prophets and their scholars, there is reason to believe that both the river and the lake of Tiberias had acquired a sort of sacred character, and that the pilgrimages which Christians make thither are little more than the relics of a similar practice among the Jews.

The time, moreover, of St. John's appearance was no less favourable to his renown than the station which he had chosen. I have said that all mankind, and not the Jews alone, were at this period in still and anxious expectation of a mighty sovereign and conqueror to be born in the land of Judah; and I repeat the observation, because there are few facts in history more certain (though many of much less consequence are far more generally attended to,) than that amongst the heathen also, and more particularly in the Roman world, there were extant books of supposed divine authority, and which, so far as we have any account of them, gave an almost similar description of the future

Messiah with that which is read to the present
day in the prophetic writings of the Old Testament.

I am well aware, indeed, that the work which
now bears the name of the Sibylline prophecies, is
marked by many strong internal proofs as a forgery
of far later date than the reign of Augustus or
Tiberius, and composed when the worship of the
cross and the other superstitions of the middle
ages, had already made considerable progress. But
that books were in existence, under the name of
the Sibylline Oracles and the Prophecies of Hy-
daspes, which spoke many strange and many true
things of Christ and of His kingdom, is proved, by
the testimony of the most ancient apologists for
Christianity, as allowed by the heathen themselves
to be ancient and inspired documents, and yet in
favour of the Christians. It is in part confirmed
by Cicero, who, when, for a political purpose, de-
preciating the authority of the Sibylline books, observes as a reason why they were not to be followed, that they contained doctrines contrary to
the established systems of idolatry and polytheism[1].
And it is still more confirmed by that well known
and remarkable Eclogue of Virgil, which so
strangely corresponds with the leading chapters of
Isaiah, and which, whatever its immediate occasion
may have been, and however the flattery of the
poet may have led him to apply to one of the Cæ-

---

[1] Cic. de Div. lib. ii. s. 54.

sarean family expressions of a nobler import, has
avowedly borrowed its ornaments and metaphors
from traditions or prophecies then actually current
among his countrymen [1].

The subject is one not easily exhausted, and it
is one to which I may hereafter recur. It is important in many respects, not only as, so far as it
extends, a confirmation of Christianity, but as pre-
sumptive evidence, (when coupled with the prophecy of Balaam, the Epiphany of the Persian
Magi, and the many circumstances in the Brahminical creed, which strangely border on our own,)
that the coming of Christ was more widely made
known, and the manifestation of the Spirit less
limited in ancient times than Jews and Christians
are apt to believe, and that the mercies of God
through His Son, as they were intended for all, so
they were made effectual to many, for whom, in the
midst of their heathen darkness, our human wisdom would be at a loss to provide security.

But my present reason for mentioning the fact,
is to point out the advantages with which the son
of Zacharias began his mission, and the facilities
which he possessed (had he thought fit to employ
those facilities) for assuming any title or character
which the wildest ambition might have dictated.

All Judea, in fact, (we learn it from profane as
well as from sacred authorities) was excited and
alarmed at his appearance. The priests and

---

[1] Virg. Buc. IV. v. 4. et seq.

scribes, the pharisees and sadducees, the publicans and the soldiers, (it appears from Josephus that Herod had sent an army across the desert against his father-in-law, Aretas king of Arabia Petræa) were alike moved by his eloquence, and added numbers to his audience and his disciples[1]. Nay, Herod himself, till incensed by the severe honesty of his counsels, appears to have held him in honour, and yielded obedience to many of his injunctions as one in whom the Spirit of God in no common measure abode, and whose favour and prayers were not below the notice even of a politician and a conqueror.

Nor can the enemies of our faith pretend that the facts which I have urged, are founded on the representations of Christian and partial authorities only. They are confirmed, circumstantially confirmed, by the last historian of the Jewish nation, who in a passage of undoubted authenticity[2], has attested the popularity, the virtues, the influence, and the untimely end of him whom our Lord designates as the most distinguished among the sons of women[3].

All things appear to have *favoured*, all things may be said to have *solicited* his assumption of the Messiah's name and character. The messengers from Jerusalem, we find actually pressing it on him, and, by a mixture of cross-examination

---

[1] Antiq. Book XVIII. c. v. §. 1.
[2] Antiq. Book XVIII. c. 5. §. 2.   [3] St. Matt. xi. 11.

and entreaty, persuading him to profess himself
that which they so earnestly desired he might be
found to be. " Who art thou? Art thou the
Christ? Art thou Elias? Art thou that Prophet?
Why baptisest thou then, if thou art not? Who
art thou, that we may give an answer to them that
sent us[1]?" Surely to the meaning of interrogatories
like these, an imposter or a fanatic could hardly
have remained insensible, any more than to the
command of money and of men which the publicans and soldiers might have furnished, and the
important position within his grasp, as occupying
the ford of Jordan.

Place Mahomet in such a situation, and consider
what answer he would have returned; contrast
that answer with the answer sent by John, and
enquire of your own hearts whether this last
do not contain the words of truth and soberness.
He describes himself not as the expected King of
Israel, but as a harbinger sent before to smooth
and prepare His way; he disclaims the title both of
Elias and Jeremiah (the latter of whom was, by many
of the Jews, expected to rise again), and instead
of smooth and flattering language to those whose
good will it was most necessary to conciliate, he
exhorts his hearers, one and all, to practical holiness and individual amendment of life ; reproving
the pharisees for their hypocrisy, and Herod for
his uncleanness; the soldiers for their rapine, and

[1] St. John i. 19—22.

the publicans for their extortion; while, instead
of warming the hearts of men with the hopes of
national greatness and political freedom, he fore-
warns them that the axe was already laid to the root
of their tree, and predicts, in no doubtful terms, the
approaching rejection and ruin of their church and
people [1].

Is it urged that St. John was sensible of the
dangers which might arise from assuming the foremost and most conspicuous place in a religious revolution; that he preferred the safer rank of vizier
to the new Messiah, and was anxious, therefore, to
point out to the curiosity and reverence of the
multitude, some other head on which might rest
the task of redeeming Israel from bondage, the
splendours and the dangers of sovereignty?

On whom did his election fall? Did he fix on
some well-known character, some powerful and
popular leader, who was best qualified to promote
his views and to ensure success to his predictions?
Herod was at hand, corresponding to all these characters, and would no doubt have done many
things, nay, every thing which a reputed prophet
could have asked, who undertook to clothe him
with the title of Messiah, and Son of David. The
Parthian was on the frontier, with the gold and
the horsemen of the east at his command, waiting
only for such a demonstration on the part of the
Jews to rush forward with all his archery. Ro-

---

[1] St. Luke iii. 7—20.

man generals might have been found (as Josephus afterwards found Vespasian) to listen with greediness to the tale that, from the east, a monarch of the world was, about this time, to issue[1] ; or, if he preferred a native Jew, and a leader of humbler origin, the neighbouring mountains were filled with popular and warlike chieftains, who had resisted thus far the mandates of the Roman conqueror, and to whom, in their last unavailing struggle for liberty, the nation of Israel at length committed their cause.

But on none of these did the choice of the Baptist fall. He chose an unknown young man, of royal blood indeed, but of obscure and narrow circumstances; the reputed son of a carpenter in a provincial town of Galilee. Him he approaches with the reverence due to a superior being; in terms of the deepest abasement he describes his own inferiority to Him, and points Him out to the multitude of his disciples as the Son of God, the Saviour of the world, the Person who, though his junior by mortal birth, had, in Heaven, existed before him; the latchet of whose sandal he was himself unworthy to loose; but for the manifestation of whom to Israel he had been sent to baptise with water.

And, here again, the opponents of Christianity have no ground for objecting that our facts are taken from the Gospel alone. The disciples of St.

[1] Jos. Bell. Jud. lib. III. c. 8.

John, a sect of Jews still existing in considerable
numbers in the north-eastern parts of Arabia, who,
by a strange perverseness, while professing themselves the Baptist's followers, reject, in all essential points, his testimony concerning Jesus; have
preserved, nevertheless, amid the fable and allegory
of their mystical books, an account of how St. John
baptised the True Light, the holy Son of God, in
the Jordan, with the strange addition, in which,
however, some circumstances of truth are mingled,
that the person thus distinguished was seen by St.
John no more, but that His Spirit rested on him,
while He Himself returned to His Father.

They thus, as may be seen by a reference to the
passage itself in Michaelis [1], identify St. John with
the Messiah, whom he foretold, and incorporate
him with the Second Person in the Godhead. It is
strange how such a perversion of the truth should
have found place among men who approach so
nearly to the truth; but their very blindness makes
their testimony, so far as it goes, more valuable,
inasmuch as it is, in a certain degree, the testimony
of an adversary.

Nor, by those who are constrained to admit the
leading facts of our Saviour's intercourse with St.
John, will the appearance of any previous or subsequent collusion between them be pretended. They,
indeed, were distant kinsmen; but the habits of

[1] Michaelis, vol. III. pp. 295—302. For the Christians of
St. John, see also Taylor's Calmet, fifth edit.

St. John's early life had effectually divided him from one who, till thirty years of age, had remained patiently subject to the domestic discipline and humble toils of His earthly parent. St. John himself declares, and there is every appearance of truth in the declaration, that he knew not the man, save by a miraculous and public sign, who was to baptise with the Holy Ghost and with fire. Instead of taking advantage of the zeal of the assembled multitude, which, had any concert existed, the Messiah and His forerunner would scarcely have neglected to do, our Saviour wanders forth alone, without waiting to receive their homage, and lingers for six weeks in the depths of the adjoining wilderness. On His return, though again hailed by the Baptist as the Lamb of God, He resumes no intercourse with him; each proceeds on his course of laborious preaching, of painful wandering, but our Lord alone, of blessed and most mighty miracles; the one laying claim to an existence and authority eternal, supreme, and infinite; the other, even in bonds and death, rejoicing in the success of the younger prophet, and cheerfully sacrificing his own importance and supremacy to *His* superior claim on whom the hopes of Israel rested, and of whom all the prophets of ancient time had spoken.

It is plain that St. John, while acting thus, could have no motive for deceiving others. But might he be himself deceived? was he an honest but visionary enthusiast? Many reasons may be urged against our entertaining such an opinion of him.

In the first place, the character of an enthusiast is almost always strongly marked by pride. Such a person is extremely unlikely to descend, as St. John did, to take the second place, or to rejoice so consistently and unaffectedly in the decay of his own popularity.

Secondly, the practical tenour of John's preaching, the repentance which he inculcated, and which he made, as we see in his answers to the soldiers and publicans, to consist not in superstitious forms, not in abstraction and contemplation, but in the discharge by every man of the plain and appropriate duties of his condition, is of a character too honest, too sensible and sound, for a heated temper or a diseased imagination.

And, above all, the coincidence of his choice with the circumstances and character of Jesus, is a decisive proof that such a choice was not determined by chance, nor built on the dictates of a capricious and casual fancy. If men drew lots for a king, it would be strange indeed if, out of a mighty and promiscuous multitude, the lot should actually fall on one of royal blood, of unexceptionable character, with every private and every public quality which could fit him for a ruler or a conqueror. But what are the qualifications of an earthly king, to those marks which were to distinguish the Messiah, who was not only to be a descendant of David, but the son of a virgin; who was not only to speak as never man spake, but to do the works which never man did; to heal the sick, to cleanse the leper, to cast out devils, to preach the Gospel to the poor, to raise the dead, yea, and Himself to arise from the dead, having first poured forth His soul to death, and made His life an offering for many? Was it a casual or enthusiastic choice which rested on a Man, whose bidding the waves obeyed? Was the fig-tree in the plot, which dried up at the word of Jesus? or were the earth and moon and sun confederates in the forgery, which quaked, and became dim, and hid their glories in the hour when the Lord was crucified? Verily "John did no miracle; but all things that John spake of this Man were true [1]:" and the truth and the life is in Him.

A confirmation, then, of our faith, is the first and most obvious lesson which we are to learn from the Baptist's history. But there are other circumstances in which the son of Zacharias was sent for the instruction of the world, and in which he was given as a sign for many. I say a *sign* and not a *pattern*, inasmuch as, for the particular austerities which he practised, we have no warrant in the example of our Lord, nor in the earlier days of the Church, nor could such austerities be usually practised without a neglect of more important duties. But when we see the son of Zacharias in the wilderness, a mournful solitary man, can we refrain from observing, how insignificant in the sight of God are the advantages of

[1] St. John x. 41.

1

worldly wealth and greatness, since the most illustrious of His saints and His only Son Himself, had
of this world's goods so extremely small a pittance?
Or, can we avoid observing, that as St. John, the
reprover of sin, preceded Jesus, the messenger of
pardon; so Christ, it is plain, can be only effectually approached by the gate of repentance, while
repentance is of no avail, unless, like St. John, it
leads us to Christ?

Some days yet remain of that season which the
Church has devoted to the consideration of our
Saviour's advent, and a preparation for the feast of
His nativity. In those days, let St. John be in your
thoughts; during those days let the Son of God be
the object of your devotions; and intreat His grace
that you may be so prepared to partake in His
sacraments, that at His second coming in might
and majesty ye may be found fit to enter into His
joy. Blessed is that servant whom his Lord when
He returneth shall find thus doing!

SERMON II.

OFFICE OF CHRIST.

[Preached at Trichinopoly, April 2, 1826.]

1 St. John v. 6—8.

This is He that came by water and blood, even Jesus Christ;
not by water only, but by water and blood; and it is the Spirit
that beareth witness, because the Spirit is truth. For there
are three that bear record in Heaven, the Father, the Word,
and the Holy Ghost, and these three are one. And there are
three that bear witness in earth, the spirit, and the water, and
the blood, and these three agree in one.

To understand the meaning of these difficult words
of St. John, it will be necessary to consider the
tendency of his general argument, and for that purpose to go back to the former part of the chapter
whence they are taken, in which he is at once en-
forcing the practical duties of a Christian, and the
motives and principles and gracious aids from which
those duties must proceed, and by which alone our
weakness is enabled to perform them. We are
called upon, he first tells us, to prove our love of
God by the active discharge of our duty; and this
duty is rendered easy to us by the change which is
wrought by God's grace in every one who truly
seeks His mercy through the merits of His Son,
which, to express the total alteration caused by it
in our desires and habits, is called regeneration, or

being born afresh, and, to signify the degree of
God's power to which we are thereby admitted, is
here called by St. John, the being " born of God."
" This is the love of God," he tells us, " that we
keep His commandments, and His commandments
are not grievous; for whatsoever is born of God
overcometh the world[1]." As if he had said, the love
of God can only be proved either to God or man,
by our keeping those commandments, which God
Himself hath given us. But how are these commandments to be kept? How is it that, weak as
we are, the lovers and servants of sin, we shall be
enabled to do all which God requires at our hands
as proofs of our love? How shall we be able to
deny ourselves and our sinful lusts, to renounce the
world, the flesh, and the devil; to give up our sins,
though those sins be dearer to us than a right hand
or a right eye; to bear with cheerfulness the scorn
and persecution of men; to be contented to incur
the names of fool and hypocrite and madman, rather than do those things which God has forbidden?
The world and its temptations are set against the
kingdom of Christ, and who are we that we should
be able to struggle with the world? Be not afraid
of your own weakness, or the world's terrour. In
yourselves you have no power, but through Christ's
merits power shall be given you; and he that is
born of God, we have God's own word for it, shall
be able to overcome the world. But wherewith
are we to be thus enabled? What shall be our wea-

_____
[1] 1 St. John v. 4.

pon in this great battle? through what feelings,
what hopes, what inward power, shall we be able to
resist such enticements, to withstand such terrours?
The objection is foreseen, the answer is ready;
" This is the victory that overcometh the world,
even our faith; who is he that overcometh the
world, but he that believeth that Jesus is the Son of
God¹?" In other words, our knowledge and belief
in Christ and in His promises, our hopes of Heaven,
our fears of hell, our deep and unaffected thankfulness towards Him by whose merits Heaven is
opened to us, and by whose sufferings we are redeemed from everlasting misery; these hopes, this
fear, this love, are so much stronger than all with
which the world can tempt us, that if we resolutely
maintain this faith as our comforter under distress,
and as our warning guide when urged by pleasure
or by interest, there is no distress, no pleasure, no
interest which can be sufficient to separate us from
our duty and from our love which is in Christ. It
is always thus, when a stronger motive is offered to
the mind, and so offered that the mind is really
made sensible of it, those weaker objects which before impelled or attracted us lose their effect on
our will, and give place to the more powerful hope
or apprehension. When the sun is absent from
the earth, and the Heaven is obscured with clouds,
a candle from a cottage window shines far and wide
like a star through the darkness. But let the moon

¹ V. 4, 5.

E

rise and the stars of Heaven appear, the candle is
seen no longer, and both the moon and the stars
grow dim when the glorious light of day walks forth
from his eastern chamber.   Exactly so, in the natural state of man, the meanest trifles are sufficient
to entice or agitate us; one man seeks for happiness in pleasure and sensuality; another gives his
whole mind and care to the gathering together of
wealth, all which in a few years he must leave behind; with a third, ambition is the ruling passion.
But if an angel were to lift up one of these men, as
St. Paul was caught up in vision, if he were to hold
him by the hair of his head between hell and Paradise, if he were to show him from the middle of that
great gulph whereby the seats of pain and blessing
are divided, the tormenting flames, the bitter tears,
the hopeless agony which dwell in the first; and
the trees of life, the groves of palm, the golden city,
with its gates of pearl and crystal streets, which
God hath prepared for them that love Him[1]; if he
were told, " from those torments Christ hath died
to save thee, and to these habitations of blessing
His grace will bring thee if thou dost not cast away
thy soul:" and if, while the man yet saw these opposite prospects, he were at that very moment to
be tempted by the choicest of the things which he
had followed after, do you think that they would
have power to move him?   Oh no; his heart
would be full of other thoughts, of Heaven and hell,
of blessing and cursing, of his natural danger and

---

[1] Rev. xxi. 21.

his hope in Jesus Christ, and all that once could rouse his passion most would fall as idly on his senses, as music on the deaf ear, or beauty on the blinded eye. But that effect which the actual sight of Heaven and hell is supposed to produce on a man so circumstanced, the faith that Heaven and hell are really what they are represented in Scripture, will be able, if we keep it constantly in mind, to produce on our hearts and behaviour. By this we are more than conquerors, and by this we shall triumph not only over the world, but over the devil and ourselves, if we continue to believe that Jesus is the Son of God and to receive the Gospel, which He hath given us, and to bear by His grace this faith in our souls, and to recall it to our minds whenever temptation comes upon us.

In the former verses, then, of this portion of St. John's Epistle, we are taught the necessity of good works, and the manner in which faith, if sincere and constant, will produce the answerable fruit of good works in our life and conversation. And the apostle then continues to explain in very few and somewhat mysterious words, the nature of that faith which we are to maintain respecting the person and office of our Saviour. We are to believe that " Jesus Christ is the Son of God," that He " came by water and by blood, not by water only, but by water and blood," and we are to believe this on the testimony of God's infallible Spirit. " It is the Spirit that beareth witness, and the Spirit is truth."

It is not my intention to enter on the long controverted subject of the authenticity of that particular verse which follows, in which mention is made of the Three Heavenly Witnesses; that verse, undoubtedly, teaches nothing which a trinitarian can admit to be at variance with the general tenour of Scripture. I am, however, little inclined to seek support for an aweful truth from materials of suspected soundness, or (while the doctrine of a Trinity in unity is taught in so many other texts of Scripture) to lay a stress on one of which it is not ascertained that it is in Scripture. And I am, in the present instance, yet more disposed to avoid entering into the discussion, since the particular verse in question, so far as the main purpose and connexion of the apostle's argument are concerned, is illustrative and ornamental only. The number and unity of the Celestial Witnesses are only alluded to on account of their analogy, in these particulars, with the triple and accordant evidence of " the spirit, the water, and the blood." It is to these last, then, and to the testimony which they bear, that I am anxious to direct your attention; and, in so doing, it shall be my endeavour, first, to ascertain what doctrine that is for which St. John is here contending; secondly, who those witnesses are which he describes as effectually supporting it; and, thirdly, in what manner it becomes us to lay their testimony to heart, and apply to ourselves, our hopes, our fears, and the conduct of our mental and external habits, those aweful and comfortable

2

truths which the inspired reasoner enforces with so much earnestness.

It is obvious, in the first place, that the doctrine refers to some peculiarity in the person of Christ, and in the mission which He came to execute on the part of His Heavenly Father. In the preceding verses of the chapter, which, together with my text, have been read to you this morning from the altar, St. John had been establishing the necessity of good works, as an evidence of our love for God, and the necessity and efficacy of that faith without which a life of consistent holiness is impossible.

" This is the love of God that we keep His commandments; and His commandments are not grievous; for whatsoever is born of God overcometh the world: and this is the victory that overcometh the world, even our faith. Who is he that overcometh the world, but he that believeth that Jesus is the Son of God [1] ?"

As if He had said, " It is vain and worse than vain for men to pretend to love God, unless they do those things which they know to be well-pleasing to Him. Nor, for the neglect of such things, is the weakness of our human nature an apology. Weak as we are in ourselves, there is, in our regenerate nature, a principle which enables us to be more than conquerors over the most terrible of our spiritual enemies, and the shield by which we may quench their darts is the faith which we cherish that Jesus is the Son of God."

[1] St. John v. 3, 4, 5.

But then, as if apprehensive of our resting in this bare and general confession, he proceeds to explain who that Christ is, in whom he would have us firmly to believe, and what grounds are afforded to us for receiving the peculiarities which he here ascribes to Him. " This is He," (that he is speaking of Christ the Son of God there can, I conceive, be no controversy) " This is He that came by water and blood, even Jesus Christ; not by water only, but by water and blood, and it is the Spirit that beareth witness, because the Spirit is truth; and there are three that bear witness in earth," (I pass the controverted clause) " There are three that bear witness in earth, the spirit, and the water, and the blood, and these three agree in one." It remains, then, that I should prove to you what the peculiarity is which St. John asserts of Christ, and to which he represents these three as witnesses.

There are three remarkable events in the history of our Saviour while among men, to some or all of which the apostle may be thought to have alluded. They are, first, His own baptism in the river Jordan, in which, as He commenced His mission and public ministry, so He may be fairly said to have come to us, in His official character, by water. Secondly, that violent death in which only, so far as we know, He was, in any sense, implicated with blood. And, thirdly, that remarkable effusion, after death, of both blood and water trom His side, which St. John has thought fit, in its proper place, to record with such solemnity of asseveration, and to which he here again recurs with an earnestness so remarkable as to convince us that he regarded it as something far more than a natural phenomenon.

Now, if we were asked why these things were so solemnly and circumstantially recorded of Christ; why it was decreed in the counsels of God, that Christ should undergo these things; that He should submit to a baptism for which, in His innocence, He had no need; that He should endure a most painful death to which, in His perfect righteness, He was not justly liable; or that, lastly, a miracle should be wrought after His death, to produce a stream of blood first, and afterwards water from His body? I apprehend no answer could be so reasonably given, as that these things had some further and some mysterious meaning, that they were done for our advantage or for our instruction. And when we find these things so accurately and solemnly recorded, when our attention through the whole New Testament is so often called to them, and when, as in the present passage, we find an inspired apostle insisting on a faith in these things and in all of them, " not the water only, but the water and blood," as essential to " the victory which overcometh the world;" we must be still more confirmed in the opinion, that this meaning, whatever it be, must be one extremely important to us all, and that the actions thus recorded are something more than merely curious and interesting as proofs of our Saviour's humility, His fortitude, or the sincerity of His preaching.

But further, and as a probable guide to the import of such circumstances in the Messiah's life, it must be remarked that the Messiah was a Jew, that the prophecies, and the ceremonies of the ancient covenant were all in a strange and pre-ordained analogy with His life and character; that in Him the laws of Moses were fulfilled, inasmuch as of Him they were only shadows; that His mission, though its benefits were to include all nations, was, in the first instance, addressed to the Jews; and that all which He taught, and all which He performed had, as its primary motive, their instruction, their conversion, their reconciliation with His Almighty Father. Whatever meaning then attached to these actions and circumstances of His life, it was one, in all probability, conformable to the ancient Jewish laws, and such as was obvious to a Jewish understanding; and there is, therefore, no way so likely to arrive at the truth, as to examine what sort of impression they were likely to make on a follower of Moses and the prophets.

And here it is very remarkable that water and blood were, in the religion of Moses, the two necessary tokens of atonement for sin, and purification from all guiltiness before God. Without these, by the law, no justification could be obtained. And these were inseparably united with the notion of an expiatory sacrifice; a sacrifice, that is, in which the death of one innocent being was accepted by the Divine justice, instead of the death of many guilty ones.

In every such ceremony both the victim and the priests were sprinkled with water before the former was slain or its blood was offered up to the Most High ; and, the sacrifice completed, water was again sprinkled over all those who had partaken in the devotions. The first of these forms was, evidently, to represent that repentance which was required to cleanse the heart before the offering could be accepted or acceptable. The second was to show that by God's acceptance of the blood, He had washed us clean from our sins, and from all their dismal consequences. And so well were these circumstances understood, that it has been at all times a sort of proverb among the Jews, that " without water is no sacrifice," and that " the law begins with water and ends with water [1]."

If, then, a Jew had found it written in some of his ancient prophets that the Messiah whom he looked for was to come " by water and by blood," he would naturally suppose that these expressions referred to some great atonement which the Messiah was to offer up for the sins of His people. And, if he were induced, from other arguments and from the greatness of our Saviour's miracles, to acknowledge that our Lord was, indeed, the Messiah which should come, I know not how he could have reconciled the type and antitype any otherwise than by supposing that the whole ministry and death of Jesus was one mighty sacrifice for men ; that as a necessary preparation for this sacrifice He was

[1] Grotius in loc.

baptized by St. John in the river Jordan; that the
sacrifice was accomplished when He poured out His
own blood for us on Calvary; and that from His
dead side the Father Almighty thought fit to cause
water to flow, in token that the expiation was accepted and entire, and that from Him alone who
had atoned for our sins by His blood, were we to
seek for and to receive that purity of life whereof
water is the expressive symbol.

But that meaning which a Jew would have assigned
to the passage in question, if it had occurred in one
of the ancient prophets, we certainly are bound, on
every principle of good sense and rational criticism,
to apply to the same words as employed by one of
our own sacred writers. It makes no difference
whether they were predictive of a future, or de-
scriptive of a past occurrence. In the latter case,
still more than in the former, we are sure that they
refer to Jesus; and as St. John was a Jew, and expresses himself, in the present instance, in terms
expressly appropriate to the Jewish expiatory ceremonies, I really cannot see how an unprejudiced
enquirer can escape from the conclusion, that a
faith in the atonement for sin by the actual sacrifice of our Lord was, in his mind, an essential part
of that faith whereby we are saved. The historical
faith which acknowleges that, eighteen hundred
years ago, a person named Jesus was born and
founded a sect, lived about thirty years on earth,
and was crucified; the unitarian faith which re-
ceives Him as a prophet sent from God, as the Son

of a virgin, as a teacher of pure morality, as raised
again by His Father from the dead in order that,
in His own person, He might afford an illustrious
precedent of the resurrection,—both these, however one may in its clearness and its approach to
truth far surpass the other, yet both fall short,
very short of the apostle's estimate. It is not
enough to acknowledge that He was the Son of
God, unless we confess also that He came " by
water." It is not enough to say that He baptized
us to repentance, unless we add that He came with
His own most precious blood, both to purchase for
us a power to repent and to make our imperfect
repentance acceptable. Nor, lastly, would it be
sufficient to acknowledge the sacrifice of His blood
alone, unless we acknowledged that our further
sanctification depends on Him from whose torn side
the blessed stream flowed forth to the cleansing of
the nations.

To this doctrine the Spirit of God bare witness
from the mouth of the apostles and in the many
mighty works which showed forth themselves in
them. To this doctrine the Spirit yet bears witness
in those writings of the New Testament where its
truth is described, as with a sun-beam, in language
which the wilfully blind alone cannot see, in the
Epistle to the Hebrews, in the Epistle to the Romans, and in the passage which I have this day, to
the best of my power, explained to you. To this
doctrine the water and blood bear witness; the
water in which we are baptized in Christ's name,

1

and the cup ln which is a symbol of His sufferings;
of which both the one and the other would be altogether unmeaning or unintelligible unless we desired, in the one, to be "buried with Him by baptism into death[1]," and, in the other, to be made
partakers in the benefits of His cross and passion.

The victory then, whereby we overcome the
world, is a faith in the atonement for sin by our
humbled and crucified Saviour.   But, on the other
hand, if our faith falls short of this illustrious victory, it is plain that our faith is imperfect, or that,
from some fault in ourselves, it has failed to produce its proper effect on us.   To those for whom
Christ's blood was shed, to them from His side the
waters of regeneration flowed.   Those whom He
saves, He also sanctifies.   If we believe that His
death has obtained pardon for our sins, we must
also believe that His grace has quickened us to a
life of holiness.   And, if our actions do not show
forth our faith, if our hearts be not right before Him,
we may be sure that, so far as we are concerned,
His sacrifice hath not yet taken effect, and that the
curse of God is in force against our souls, pronounced against all them that work iniquity.

How greatly, then, does it concern those who
detect in their own consciences the stain of unre-
pented and habitual transgressions, instead of flattering themselves with vain hopes of safety through
a Saviour whom they put by their evil deeds to

---

[1] Rom. vi. 4.

open shame, to cry out for mercy while mercy may yet be found, and to seek by earnest prayer and diligent endeavours after righteousness, that purifying grace of the Most High which must quicken us, in the life which now is, before we can reasonably expect in the life to come, to be quickened from death to glory.

Nor do I know any way in which Christ and Christian holiness may more effectually be sought after, than by a constant recurrence to those solemn witnesses which He has left us of Himself, those Scriptures which are the express dictates of the Spirit of life and truth ; those Sacraments which are so many renewed and repeated images of His death, His atonement, and His resurrection.

In our infancy we bare witness, by water, to the necessity of a new birth from sin ; in our riper years, and more particularly in the last most solemn season of the Christian passover, we have most of us, I will hope, renewed our covenant with the Lord, and offered up to His service our bodies and souls, as redeemed by His blood from pangs unutterable and endless.

What now remains but a constant and earnest recollection, that the privileges and the duties of a Christian go always hand in hand; that the greater the mercies received, the more need is there of showing forth our thankfulness; that we do not cease to be the servants of God, when we are admitted to the privileges of His children; but that from these last, on the other hand, a more illustrious obedience is expected, the service of love, the free-will offering of the heart, the ardour which endeavouring to do all, thinks all too little to repay the benefits received, and express the affection felt, and which, after a life spent in the service of its Lord, lays down at length its tranquil head to slumber beneath the cross, content to possess no other merit than His blood, and presuming to expect no further reward than His mercy !

SERMON III.

CHARACTER OF CHRIST AND HIS RELIGION.

[Preached at Madras, March 12, 1826.]

ST. MARK viii. 9.

And He sent them away.

IT is with these words that St. Mark concludes
his account of the second occasion in which our
Lord displayed His Almighty power, by multiply-
ing a very small quantity of food into nourishment
for many thousand persons. He had before, with
five loaves and two fishes, satisfied the hunger of
five thousand men; He now, with seven loaves and
a few small fishes, afforded a sufficient meal for
four thousand. And, having thus by a miracle relieved their bodily necessities, as He had by His
preaching nourished and strengthened their souls
with the bread of life, the evangelist informs us
that " He sent them away;" a circumstance which
I have chosen as the subject of our morning's contemplation, because, simple as it may seem, we
may draw from it, by God's help, in the first place,
a very important confirmation of the dignity and

disinterestedness of our Saviour's character, and of
the truth of His Gospel ; secondly, a striking illus-
tration of the spirit and principles of that religion
which He brought into the world ; and, thirdly, a
useful guide to our behaviour in the daily course
of our lives, and an additional motive to the diligent practice of those duties, the discharge of which
is the end and object of all religious knowledge.

" In those days the multitude being very great
and having nothing to eat, Jesus called His disciples
unto Him, and saith unto them, I have compassion
on the multitude, because they have now been
with me three days, and have nothing to eat ; and
if I send them away fasting to their own houses,
they will faint by the way, for divers of them came
from far.　And His disciples answered Him, from
whence can a man satisfy these men with bread
here in the wilderness ?　And He asked them, how
many loaves have ye ?　And they said seven.　And
He commanded the people to sit down on the
ground, and He took the seven loaves and gave
thanks, and brake, and gave to His disciples to set
before them, and they did set them before the
people.　And they had a few small fishes, and He
blessed and commanded to set them also before them.
So they did eat and were filled ; and they took up
of the broken meat that was left seven baskets.
And they that had eaten were about four thousand.
And He sent them away."

I have repeated to you the whole history that
you may be the better able to judge of the meekness

and moderation of our Saviour, and how greatly
His conduct differed from that which would have
been pursued by a fanatic or an imposter. Supposing it, for the sake of argument, to have been
possible that in these miracles of loaves and fishes,
He could have been Himself deceived by enthusiasm
or credulity, or, could by subtlety or magical arts,
have deceived the enthusiasm and ignorance of His
followers; supposing, I say, this to have been possible, which few men in their senses will suppose,
yet is such a supposition in the present case rendered absurd by the total and evident absence of
any interested or ambitious design which could
have led Him to deceive others, or of any pride or
vanity by which He Himself could have been de-
luded. If He had either designed, as His enemies
accused Him of designing, to make Himself a
worldly king, or if He had derived a vain and selfish
pleasure from the number of His disciples, and the
hosannas of a surrounding multitude, how little
would He have been disposed to send that multitude away, instead of taking advantage of the favourable moments while their hearts were yet
warm with the recollection of the miracle, to have
secured the zeal and active services of those whom
He had the power of thus strangely feeding. A
leader who either possessed, or was believed to
possess such a power might have filled his ranks
with all the idle and needy of the land; and the
multitude would have flocked into the wilderness
for the bread which he distributed. But the views

F

of Christ were different; to His views His conduct was answerable; nor were either the one
or the other different from what we should have
expected in a Being superior to man; a Being
trusting in Himself and in His Father alone, whom
neither the blame nor praise of man could reach,
alike above the mark of his hatred and his services.
So far from priding Himself on the number and
greatness of the miracles which He wrought, He
does those miracles as things of course, and with
the same degree of unaffected indifference with
which a service of the most trifling kind is rendered
by one man to another; He displays, almost uniformly, His Divine Power in works of mercy and
loving kindness; and instead of collecting an army
among His followers, and causing Himself, as He
well might haye done, to be proclaimed king over
Israel, He actually dismissed two armies, one after
the other, who were not only flushed with hope
and inspired with the fullest confidence in Him,
but were actually inclined, as we read in another
chapter, to make Him king whether He would or
no. Such a conduct as this is what no deceiver
would have followed in his own person; nay, it
may be pronounced with equal certainty, that our
Saviour's character and behaviour, as described by
the four Evangelists, are such as, if the Evangelists
had been deceivers, they could not possibly have
described or imagined. His is, in fact, a character
of such perfect excellence and purity as no writer
has elsewhere described either in history or fable,

and which it is absolutely absurd to suppose, that
the Evangelists, being, as they were, unlearned
men, and writing, as they did, separately and without collusion, could have conceived or painted, if
the same original had not been before them all.
If, then, the history which has been read to you
be true, it is certain that Christ was, what He professed, the Son of God Most High ; and that it is
true we may be sure from the want of power in the
Evangelists to describe such a person as our Lord
from fancy, or to agree in imputing to Him a conduct so consistent with itself in every part, and in
every part so different from that of other men.
And this is the first observation which may be
grounded on the words which I have read to you,
namely, that they confirm our belief that Jesus was
the Son of God, that all things which He hath
spoken unto us from the Father are true, and that
in Himself there is no falsehood at all.

The second observation relates to the tendency
and character of the religion which He taught.
That religion, above all others, which have been at
any time offered to the world, is distinguished by
its peculiarly practical nature ; by its not drawing
men away from the interests, the charities, nor,
when used within due bounds, the enjoyments
and pleasures of the present life ; but by being a
system of which it is the leading object not to take
us out of the world, but to fit us for lives of innocence and usefulness in the world. It was the
boast of ancient philosophy, and it has been the

boast of false religion and of the power of Anti-
christ, under whatever disguise presented to mankind, to withdraw men as much as possible from the
cares and duties of a worldly and industrious life;
to teach them to place their ideas of perfection and
their hopes of salvation in a total retirement from
mankind, or in an inactive and unprofitable round
of ceremonies and superstitions, commanding to
abstain from labour, which is the common condition
of our kind; from marriage, whereby we contribute to the common stock of happiness and of pro-
ductive labour, the enjoyments and toils of our
children; from meats, which God Himself hath
given to be received with thankfulness; from conversation, whereby the bonds of charity are kept
alive, and the common fund of religious and useful
knowledge extended and preserved.   But the religion of Christ, as taught by Christ Himself, and the
apostles who were inspired by Him, not only does
not command, but expressly discourages all heed-
less singularity or solitude.   If He calls us into the
desert for a time to hear the words of life, He calls
us only that we may return to the world better
qualified to perform our parts in it; the more industrious in our lawful business, in proportion as
we are the more fervent in spirit; and so much the
better sons, the better parents, the better husbands, brethren, subjects, fellow-citizens, or friends,
by how much we are the better Christians.   It is
in this manner that the connexion so often spoken
of between faith and works is made abundantly cer-

tain and manifest; because in the Christian religion
there is no single article of faith which does not
immediately lead us to a necessity of some answerable practice. We believe in God, but this faith is
not to be shown forth by us, as by many of the
pretended wise men among the Indians, by sitting
still, day after day, in the silent and fixed contemplation of that glorious Being, whose essence and
attributes surpass the utmost reach of our minds.
Our faith in God is an active faith, which leads us
to pray to Him, and strive to please Him. Our
faith in Christ is to be shown forth by loving Him,
and, for His sake, loving each other; our faith in
the atonement, which He has made for sin, is to be
proved by our honouring His name not only with
our lips but with our lives; our faith in a judgement to come is to be proved by being such men
in all godly soberness as we desire the Lord of all
things to find us at His return. We have promised,
indeed, in our baptism, to renounce the sins and
vanities of the world, but to renounce a due and
temperate use of the world itself is neither desirable nor possible. Our business is to pass through
its temptations and engagements like air through
water, whose bubbles, though buried in the mass,
still rise rapidly upwards, and keep themselves distinct from the surrounding element, till they find
that Heaven to which they are tending. But to
leave the world is not ours till death has set us free,
and to each regenerate Christian, Christ seems to
say in His Gospel, as He said of old to the restored

lunatic of Gadara, " Canst thou hope that thy new
religion is to set thee free from thine ancient duties ? Tarry not here under an idle pretext of
serving me more entirely, but return to thine own
city and thine own house, and by a diligent discharge of thy duties there, show forth how great
things God hath done for thee[1]."

In a certain sense, then, the words which St.
Mark applies to that mighty multitude whom Christ,
after miraculously supporting their feeble natures,
" sent away" to their respective cities, will apply to
the situation of us all, when dismissed from the
house of God, to put in practice the lessons which
we have there learnt, in the bosom of our families,
and amid the larger or smaller circles of our kindred, our friends, our neighbourhood. Each of us
may consider himself as having repaired to this
holy place to learn the will of the Most High, and
to obtain His saving help towards its performance,
and each of us, when he retires from the temple, is
returning, it may be hoped, with an increased
knowledge of his duty, and an increased power of
performing it, to those familiar scenes where the
course of his duty lies, and wherein his behaviour
must determine whether he has truly profited or
not, by his visit to God's house.

Let me entreat you, then, my brethren, to suppose yourselves for a moment in the situation of
those persons who had been instructed by the

---

[1] St. Luke viii. 39.

preaching of Christ, and miraculously fed by His bounty, and whom, having thus imprinted on their minds the sense of their own duty and His own divinity, He " sent away" to their respective habitations. With what feelings, think you, would you, under such circumstances, have left the presence of the Son of God ? Would the marvellous things which you had heard and seen, the proofs of power, the lessons of holiness, have been dismissed from your minds as a mere aweful spectacle to please the eye, a most sweet sound of the harp or the organ which, though pleasant for a time, left no instruction behind it ? Would you have allowed your former sinful habits immediately to renew their sway, and have deferred all serious thoughts, all holy words, all actions of faith or prayer, till the time of solemn worship should again come round, and you should again meet Christ in the wilderness ? Or would not your consciences have rather told you, that now the time was come to show forth the progress which you had made in His lessons ; that as you hoped for His future preaching, it became you to prove that you had profited by that help which you had already received, and that it would have been better never to have consulted the Heavenly Physician, than, having affected outwardly to do so, to act contrary to all the directions which He gave.

My Christian friends, you have this day attended the worship of Christ, and have heard His Gospel read, and, so far as His ministers have been able,

sincerely and faithfully expounded to you. You
have heard the solemn commandment of the Most
High, and joined in prayer for strength to keep
His laws.   And I am persuaded that such as have
asked faithfully and humbly for that merciful support and guidance, have obtained as really, though
not so perceivably, the help and nourishment and
comfort of God's grace, as the multitude, of whom
you have heard this day, had their bodily wants
assisted.   All this has been done for you by Christ
Himself, who, according to His promise, has been
no less truly present in the midst of us, than if we
had beheld Him seated on His rocky throne, dis-
pensing, as to this multitude in the wilderness, the
precious manna of the Gospel.   We shall shortly,
as His ministers, and in His name, pronounce His
blessing on you, and " send you away." But is this
all ? does your duty end here ?   Oh no ! We send
you away that you may ponder in your hearts the
truths which you have heard, and improve, by daily
prayer and watchfulness, the grace which you have
received.   We send you away that you may show
forth in your lives those principles which we have
endeavoured to impress on your memory ; we send
you away as it were soldiers from their review, to
prepare yourselves for actual service, and for a
vigorous and victorious battle against the world, the
flesh, and the devil.   We send you away, but in
the hope that you may return again, after a week
spent in the upright and persevering discharge of
your different duties of parents, masters, children,

servants, friends, neighbours, husbands and wives;
that you may return again with joy to renew your
spiritual strength at the fountain of all power and
godliness; and to bless that God who hath preserved you from a lost captivity to the power of
sin, and hath covered your head in the day when
you sustained the assaults of your ghostly enemies.
We send you away, that by a daily practice of
every good gift you may improve your principles
and confirm your habits of holiness, that the work
of salvation which you now begin in much weakness
and trembling, may be brought to perfection by
Him who mightily worketh in our infirmity, and who
knoweth, even from the mouth of babes and suck-
lings to still the enemy and the avenger. Depart
then in peace, and in the favour of the Lord; and
that these our hopes may be realized, return not at
once into the bustle and burden of life till, either
publicly or privately, you have renewed your vows
and your petitions. Give up some little space of
this sabbath afternoon to the serious consideration
of your condition, your hopes, your fears, your
duties; into the examination of what sins they are
to which you are most inclined, and against which
you should, therefore, be on your guard more particularly; what company, what pursuits you have
found most injurious to your souls, and how best
they may be avoided or rendered harmless, giving
up, in earnest prayer, yourselves, your interests,
and affections to the service of God, and entreating
Him that this coming week, at least, may be spent

without offending Him. So shall the dawn of each
returning day bring increase of knowledge ; so,
when another Sabbath shall call you to these holy
walls, you shall return in the increased favour of
God and the clearer light of His countenance; and
so, at length, when the last great Sabbath of nature is arrived, and He, who once fed the poor of
the flock in the wilderness, shall return in His Father's glory to rule over Heaven and earth, He shall
" send you away" no more, but cause you, world
without end, to dwell in His Tabernacle, and before His face, that where He is, you may be also !

SERMON IV.

CHRIST PREACHING TO SINNERS.

[Preached at Dacca, July 4, 1824.]

St. Luke xv. 10.

I say unto you, that there is joy in the presence of the angels of God over one sinner that repenteth.

It was an accusation very frequently brought against our Saviour by the ruling party of the Jewish nation, that He showed in His preaching and daily habits an undue indulgence to sinners; that many of His disciples were taken from among men of this description; and that in meals and in conversation, He did not disdain the society of those whom the more rigid Pharisees condemned as impure and unholy. It does not, indeed, appear, however they might by loose and injurious revilings, attempt to stigmatize His character, that they ever brought against Him any definite charge of having partaken with sinners in their evil ways. The practice to which they objected was the simple intercourse, the act of conversing and breaking bread with sinners; and, in order to understand

2

the force and nature of their objection, it is necessary to take into account some of the peculiar prejudices of the Jews as to the touch or society of
particular persons, as also who those persons were
against whom these prejudices were directed.

In this country, I need scarcely mention, that it
is a custom with those who pretend to any degree
of holiness, to shrink from the touch of persons of
a different religion, or of a character less devoted
to the practice of contemplation and piety. Among
the Mahommedan fakirs there are few who will
willingly suffer their hands or their garments to be
approached by a Christian, while the institution of
castes is, with the Hindoos, carried to the height of
absurdity, superstition, and inhumanity. Even the
Jews, oppressed and degraded as they are in outward circumstances, show still, in all parts of the
east, a considerable anxiety to withdraw from such
contact or salutation.

The generality of this prejudice forbids our
ascribing its origin to a source so circumscribed as
the ceremonial law of Moses ; nor, indeed, with all
the precision of that law in declaring certain objects
unclean, and prescribing a certain form of purification as necessary to every one who came in contact with them, is there any hint in the Pentateuch
of such rules being applicable to opinions or moral
habits, nor any justification of that intolerant fancy
which led Simon the pharisee to doubt our Lord's
prophetic character because He suffered a penitent
sinner to embrace His feet and moisten His garment

with her tears [1]. The name of unclean is applied
in Leviticus exclusively to objects in themselves
disgusting, or which, for the sake of health, it was
convenient to esteem so; the practice of the ancient
Israelites, as displayed in the books of Kings and
Chronicles, was very far from erring on the side of
too great aversion from their idolatrous neighbours; and the custom of which I speak may be
suspected to be of a later and far less holy origin; to
have returned with the Jews from their captivity,
and to have been strengthened during the Macedo-
nian persecution; to have been borrowed from the
semi-Indian creed of their Persian and Chaldean
sovereigns, or to have been a natural consequence
of that gloomy period of their history when, under
the rod of Antiochus, and ill-treated by all mankind, the names of enemy and foreigner became to
them, in the strictest sense of the word, synony-
mous.   It is evident, however, that with persons
who boasted their abhorrence of sin, it was by no
means unnatural to apply to moral those rules
which had been given for cases of physical pollu-
tion; to cry out to their fellow-creatures, " come
not near, I am holier than thou," and to apprehend
that the approach of a wicked, like that of a leprous
person, made them unfit, for a time, to enter into
a place of worship, or to offer up, even in private,
acceptable devotions to the God of purity.   Nor
need we wonder that the Pharisees, in a tradi-

[1] St. Luke vii. 38.

tionary precept quoted by Drusius, are said not to
have allowed " the people of the world to touch
them," or that the disciples of the wise are forbidden in the Mechilta, to enter into the company of
a sinner, even in order to pray with him or to study
the Scriptures together [1].

Nor was it only to persons of notoriously im-
moral lives that this name of sinner was appropriated.   The Heathen, the Samaritan, partook in
the same opprobrium, and any transgression either
of the law or of the traditions of the elders, which
drew down on the individual so transgressing the
penalty of being excommunicated, drew down on
him at the same time the name of sinner, and an
exclusion from the touch and fellowship of the
godly.   The publicans too, or collectors of the
Roman taxes, were not only hated as the agents of
a foreign tyrant, but accounted unclean from their
habits of intercourse with the heathen ; and every
Israelite who had not joined himself to some particular sect or religious party, who had not, to use
their own expressions, wallowed in the dust of the
schools, and been initiated into those refinements
on the Mosaic religion which the Essenes or the
Pharisees inculcated, was regarded by both these
sects with an intolerant pride, as " the people of the
earth," and, as in the present instance " sinners."

It followed as a necessary consequence that, as
other causes besides immorality might produce

<hr/>

[1] Drusius de iii. sectis. L. ii. p. 83.   Mechilta, f. 37. 2.

ecclesiastical censures, as though many of the publicans were unjust and impious, that character did
not necessarily or universally belong to them ; and
as the simplicity of the secular and unlearned Jew
might be perfectly compatible with the most essential duties of industry, integrity, and piety; it
followed that many were thus branded with an opprobrious epithet, who were, possibly, better men
than those who affected to despise them. And it is
certain that this description of persons contributed
more than any other among the Jews to the number of our Saviour's followers. Such as were already
cut off from the synagogues and people of Israel,
had nothing to hold them back from embracing
the truth whenever and by whomsoever offered to
their acceptance. Those who surrendered no privilege, who broke no ancient tie, who deserted no
long loved society, had a lighter cross to bear in
the Messiah's kingdom, and found the narrow gate
far wider than they who were folded gorgeously
and warm in the trappings of self-love, and the
distinctive mantle of a sect or a party. They who
were unused to any notice from persons of a religious character, and who were abandoned, by the uncharitable contempt of their graver countrymen, to
infamy, impenitence and despair,—it was likely that
they would flock with joy to any door which should
be opened to their restoration, and be willing to
recover their lost self-esteem by any sacrifice which
the Messiah might enjoin them. And our Lord,
whose errand it was to reconcile the differences

and heal the intestine feuds of the house of Israel, appears to have taken delight in displaying His superiority to these unfounded traditions, and in kindly extending His charitable notice to those who needed it most and received it most gladly.

When taunted by the Pharisees for this line of conduct, He sometimes replies that He came "to save that which was lost," and that " they that are whole need not a physician, but they that are sick[1]." Sometimes, as in the case of Zaccheus, He reminds them that these sinners and publicans were children of Abraham as well as themselves, and partakers with them in God's promises. And sometimes, as in the parable of the prodigal son, and in that from which my text is taken, He lays down the broad, and to the Jews, the unusual principle, that not only is the penitent prodigal accepted by His Almighty Parent, but that he is accepted with joy; not only that he is admitted on his return, but that he is sought for during his wanderings; and that when found, there is more joy in Heaven on account of his repentance, than over the salvation of very many just persons to whom repentance was comparatively needless.

He appeals to the natural feelings and daily experience of every man, whether that which is lost does not, on that account, acquire an additional value in our hearts; and whether that which is recovered is not many times more dear to us than

---

[1] St. Matt. xviii. 11. St. Luke v. 31.

if we had always continued its possessors. " What
man of you," are His words, " having an hundred
sheep, if he lose one of them, doth not leave the
ninety and nine in the wilderness, and go after that
which is lost until he find it? And when he hath
found it, he layeth it on his shoulders rejoicing;
and when he cometh home, he calleth together his
friends and his neighbours saying, rejoice with me,
for I have found my sheep which was lost! I say
unto you that, likewise, joy shall be in Heaven over
one sinner that repenteth, more than over ninety
and nine just persons, which need no repentance [1]."

The instruction contained in this parable is of
two kinds, and addressed to two different classes
of hearers.

The first are those happy characters whom our
Lord designates by the name of the righteous, " the
just persons who need no repentance." Not that any
have existed, save Christ alone, to whom in some
sense or other, and that a very cogent one, repentance has not been necessary. But they who have
escaped the greater and more glaring crimes, who
have, through good education or timely repentance,
overpowered, in some considerable degree, the principle of evil within them; whom the habit of successful resistance' has rendered superior to the
ordinary assaults of Satan; and whom the grace
of God, both prompting and helping their endeavours, has marked out, amid the wickedness of the

[1] St. Luke xv. 4, 5, 6, 7.

G

multitude, as faithful, at least, though not perfect
followers of their Saviour; these just persons, so
happy in their good name and their good conscience, may learn from the present parable and
the occasion on which it was spoken, to cherish
new feelings, and to observe a new conduct towards
those unfortunate wanderers from the fold of virtue and happiness who are described as lost sheep,
and the objects, on that account, of an especial
solicitude on the part of their owner. They will
learn from His conduct, who is our hope, our example, and our God, that far from shunning such
persons as unclean, or abhorring them as heirs of
perdition, it is their duty, as servants of Christ, to
exert their utmost influence to snatch them from
the intolerable dangers by which they are at present surrounded; and that they can no better prove
their love for Him by whom they are redeemed,
than by forwarding His gracious purposes concerning those whom it was the main object of His
coming into the world, to enable to an effectual
repentance.

Nor is this a task confined to any peculiar order
or profession. It is the duty of the layman as well
as of the priest, of the catechumen as well as of
the teacher; and all who can supply a word of private warning against sin, or of private encouragement to repentance; all who have a prayer or a
tear to give for the soul of a wicked neighbour, are
as much bound to do their best to snatch that
neighbour from sin and its consequences, as they

would be called on to pluck him out of the fire, or to prevent his walking down a precipice.

It is not, indeed, the prevailing fault of the present times, that the contact of sinners of a common degree is abhorred or shunned by those who think themselves righteous. Yet there is a smooth insincerity which carries itself alike with all; there is an indifference as to the moral condition of those with whom we live; and there is a readiness to desert and despair of those who have advanced beyond a certain point in the broad and beaten track which leads to perdition, as distinctive, perhaps, of the present day, as the superstitions which I have noticed were of the later Jewish republic; and as hurtful to the souls of men, and as opposite to the obligations of Christian charity, as the intolerance of the modern Turk, and the stiffness of the ancient pharisee.

We see our neighbour wasting his goods, impoverishing his family, destroying his health, and flinging himself, body and soul, into intolerable and everlasting misery, without a word or a look which can show we disapprove of his conduct, or a single entreaty to consider what he is doing and retrace his steps in time. We smile on his progress as he wades further in sin and ruin, and when, at length, he plunges out of his depth, and the stream hurries him away beyond those bounds of vice which the custom of the world has marked out as tolerable, then those who sport in the shallows of the torrent, and they that linger by its side,

alike grow zealous in the cause of morality and of
insulted Heaven, alike begin to " shake their heads
and whisper much, and change their countenances[1],"
and call all mankind to witness their indignation
against vice, and thank their God that they are not
such as this man is, who went, if the truth should
be told, but a few paces further in wickedness than
themselves.

Many a man whom the neglect or flattery of his
neighbours has consigned to incurable destruction,
might, if those neighbours had, in the beginning of
his wanderings, stepped in with their advice, their
entreaties, their prayers, have been preserved for
ever in the sheepfold. And many a man, and still
more, many a deceived and miserable woman, who
had been given up by her former, and, perhaps, less
strongly tempted associates, to infamy and to perdition, might yet have been recalled, when their situation appeared most desperate. A little unexpected
notice from persons of unblemished character, a
little advice conveyed with meekness and affection,
a little confidence shown, and some little help or
countenance given to enable them to begin their
lives anew; these, or less than these, if administered
with prudence and good will, and in a manner of
which the motives admitted of no doubtful interpretation, would have opened many a heart which
unkindness and despair had dried up and withered,
and (unless they were entirely hardened and for-

___
[1] Eccles. xii. 18.

saken by God as well as by men) would, under His blessing and with His assistance, have preserved a member to society, delivered the soul of a fellow-creature from torment unspeakable, recovered a servant to his Lord and ours, and occasioned a day of joy in Heaven.

If any of those who hear me have an opportunity to try their generous zeal in such a task as I have now marked out for them, let me express an earnest hope that no unreasonable timidity, no culpable indifference will be allowed to interfere with a work so holy! Suffer not, I would say to a person thus situated, suffer not your unhappy brother to perish if your advice can save him. I do not call on you to become a public teacher, an intrusive and unauthorized censor of other men, occupied in detecting their faults, and vexing society with morose and needless admonition. But, in the moments of private intercourse, amid the confidence of private intimacy, there are times to be found, by whoever looks for them in sincerity, when the honest and affectionate counsels of a friend are worth more than many sermons. And do not, above all, when a wretched fellow-creature is given up as irreclaimable and not to be endured by that very world whose example first led him into transgression, when his heart is sick and can find no physician, and they who might help him lift up their voices against him, or pass by on the other side, do not, if you have any chance of re-

claiming such a creature, do not be hasty to abandon him.

St. Paul the apostle, during his abode as a pri-
soner at large in Rome, is related in ecclesiastical
story to have met with the runaway slave of one of
his friends who had robbed his master.   Instead of
giving up this unfortunate man immediately to justice, instead of hardening him by reproaches, or
shunning him as pestilential or dangerous, the
apostle undertook, it is said, the care and conversion of the reprobate; he received him into his
house, and by the counsels and comforts of the
Gospel, awakened in him a sense of his errours, and
a faith in the great Redeemer of mankind.   He
did more ; he persuaded him, as a proof of his
sincerity, to return to his injured master, whom he,
at the same time, induced to receive him again by
that letter which is read in our Churches under
the name of the Epistle to Philemon.

Onesimus, for this was the fugitive's name, did not
disgrace his recommendation; he became a sincere
Christian and a faithful servant, and in process of
time, for his distinguished piety, was chosen a minister of the Church; he died a bishop and a martyr.

The means and language to be employed in the
holy work which I have been recommending, must
naturally vary according to a thousand various circumstances.   Some may be " saved with fear, pull-
ing them out of the fire [1];" over some a winning

------

[1] St. Jude 23.

softness may possess greater influence; continued
admonitions and patient discussion may be necessary to subdue a third; while even the apparent
displeasure and expressive silence of a respected
and holy person may, with a fourth, be sufficient
evidence of his danger. In general, however, it
may be laid down as a rule, that gentle means and
gentle language are much more likely to save a soul
than menaces or harshness. These rather serve to
harden men in sin than to draw their steps aside
from it; they may provoke, they may terrify, but
they seldom work an effectual or lasting change in
any one. Better is it to imitate the conduct of the
Heavenly Shepherd who, while He was found in
likeness as a man, did not spurn the sinner at His
feet, or reproach the publican at His table; who
describes Himself as seeking His lost sheep diligently, but without anger or clamour; and as not
driving, but affectionately carrying it on His shoulders to the sheepfold.

Do not, however, mistake me; when I recommend gentle means, I do not recommend guilty
compliances. We must not humour our brethren
in their sins, nor deceive them by the hope that
their state is more secure than the truth will warrant. Far less must we, in order to gain their good
opinion, become the companions of their evil deeds,
or, even in appearance, countenance their false
principles. By acting thus, we shall be so far from
saving a soul, that we shall be the occasion of two
souls perishing; our neighbour's, by confirming him

in his bad habits, and blinding him to the greatness
of his danger; our own, by our deceitful flattery,
and the infection of his sinful example. So long as
the sheep is a wanderer it cannot be in favour with
its shepherd; till it is found, there can be no rejoicing.

We should also be religiously careful lest our
own conduct should bring our sincerity into question, since the sight of all mankind is keen to detect inconsistency in their monitors; and since, if
our actions belie our words, it is vain to hope that
our advice will be heard with conviction. And more
than all, and for the sake not of our friend only,
but of our own salvation, we should use the utmost
care and diligence lest, while we give instruction
to others, we ourselves should be cast away; and
lest, while we boast ourselves the instructors of the
weak, the dispensers of spiritual wealth to the
needy, and the guide to them that sit in darkness,
our own eyes may labour under a greater infirmity
than that of which we undertake to heal our brother; and while we say we are rich and in need of
nothing, we may find ourselves too soon in the presence of our Judge, both " poor and miserable, and
blind and naked."

Of the instruction which the same parable con-
veys to sinners, a very few observations may be
sufficient. The first which I shall offer is the great
danger of sin, and the exceeding terrour of its natural consequences, which can so excite the pity of
the Most High, and the sympathy of the holy and

happy inhabitants of another and a superior state of existence. That must be no common misery to rescue us from which the Almighty did not withhold His only Son ; those effects of our wanderings must be strange and terrible, which can draw down on us the attention of the armies of Heaven, and call forth their lively joy at the rescue of a lost fellow-creature. The glory of the Most High might well spare the children of the world from the hallelujahs of Paradise ; the happiness of angels is already complete without the addition of such beings as ourselves to their glorious company. It is only our misery which leads them to think of us at all; it is only our danger which makes our escape a subject of rejoicing. And if, with them who best know the value of a soul, our souls are thus valued; if to them who best know the fruits of sin, those fruits appear so terrible, how great is our infatuation who slumber on the brink of a precipice at which the far-seeing cherubims shudder, who defy the threats, who despise the warnings, who render vain the indulgence, the sufferings, the gracious influences, the patient and persevering kindness of the Almighty.

Nor are they our fears alone which are thus embattled against our continuance in sin ; our hopes and our kindlier feelings are, at the same time, encouraged to a speedy and effectual repentance from the interest which the angels take in our success, and from the merciful solicitude which the God of angels and of men has Himself expressed

for our safety.   For our race, when we had wan-
dered aside from the paths of peace and happiness,
for our race the Heavenly Shepherd left His ancient
and faithful flock, the spirits who kept their first
estate, the sons who were ever with Him.   It was
us whom He sought in the wilderness of the world ;
it was our nature, our infirmities, the punishment
of sins which dwelt in our bodies, which He bare
on His shoulders through the valley of the shadow
of death, that He might bring us back to His Father's kingdom.   And think you there will not be
joy in the presence of His angels hereafter, when
His toils shall receive their full reward in the restoration of countless millions, and when the sheep
who have been lost and found again, shall return
under His care to that fold from whence they never
more shall wander ?   Or do we shrink back in
hopeless despair of a prize so much beyond the
limits of our natural weakness ?   " Fear not, little
flock, for it is your Father's good pleasure to give
you the kingdom [1]."   That repentance of a sinner
in which the angels rejoice, that repentance which
God Himself delighteth to behold, God, we may be
sure, well knows how to bring to pass, and He will
bring it to pass, unless the sinner refuses to be
healed.

Day by day He calls us, saying, why will ye die ?
Day by day His Spirit is at hand, and to be found
of all that diligently seek Him.   Day by day He

---

[1] St. Luke xii. 32.

prompts the desire which leads us to His mercy-seat, the effectual prayer whereby we seek Him. Let us but fan that holy flame, which the breath of the Lord hath kindled; let us but seek His help where it hourly solicits our acceptance; let us but endeavour to forsake those evil ways of which death is the appointed issue, and that which the angels desire, and that which the Lord desireth, shall be surely and speedily accomplished, if we will but add our hearty desires to theirs, and meet, by our fervent prayers and penitent resolutions, the hopes and promises, and helps and consolation of Heaven.

SERMON V.

THE LAW AND THE GOSPEL.

[Preached at Calcutta, November 30th, 1823.]

GAL. iii. 19.

Wherefore then serveth the law ? It was added because of transgressions, until the seed should come to whom the promise was made.

THE main scope and purpose of St. Paul in his Epistle to the Galatians, has been by many men so greatly misunderstood, and so dangerously perverted to purposes entirely foreign to the apostle's intention, that we cannot too closely bear in mind that the dispute between them was, whether the law of Moses was of perpetual obligation or no, and whether the observance of its ceremonies and sacrifices was necessary to obtain pardon for the sins of mankind ? The Galatians and the great body of Jewish Christians, supposed that circumcision, that the refraining from swine's flesh, that the wearing their beards long, and a blue fringe on their garments, were observances with which, as they had been once commanded by God, no man had power to dispense with ; and that expiation and forgiveness of the sins of the world were to be sought for

1

universally, through the means of the sacrifice ordained by Moses.

St. Paul, on the other hand, was taught by the
Holy Ghost, that the laws of Moses were calculated
only for a certain space of time and a particular
race of mankind; that the distinctions which had
formerly served to separate them from the Gentiles,
became of no use whatsoever so soon as the Gentiles and the Jews were united in the bands of
Christianity as " one fold" under " one Shepherd[1];"
and that the sacrifices and ceremonies, which were
only shadows of good things to come, became void
and without obligation or effect when the One
most pure Lamb of God had been offered for the
sins of the world.

The nature of the dispute is grievously misunderstood by those who apply it to the value of
good works in their modern and more exalted
acceptation. The Jews were not weak enough, in
general, to believe (though some vain and conceited
pharisees among their number might have fancied
it,) but the great body of the nation had not so
extravagant notions of themselves as to believe
that their own good works, or their observances
of the moral law, were either so valuable in themselves, or so perfectly and steadily performed, as
to purchase for them the inheritance of Heaven, or
even a freedom from the anger of the Almighty.
They had been taught by their own prophets that

---

[1] St. John x. 16.

" there is no man that sinneth not [1]," and they
only erred in supposing that pardon for their sins
might be procured by a diligent observance of the
various ceremonies which Moses ordained, without
regarding, or, at least, without fixing their entire
attention on the One great and all sufficient sacrifice for sin through the blood of Jesus Christ our
Saviour.

In answer to this mistake St. Paul was earnest
in his endeavours to convince them, both from the
nature of the law itself (which had, plainly, no
value of its own, since the blood of bulls and goats
had no natural power to remove sin,) and from
the curses against disobedience contained in the
law, (which the weakness of our unassisted nature could not escape, inasmuch as without some
further divine help than the law afforded, no man
could hope to keep the entire law unbroken,) and
from the plain and undoubted reference which the
ceremonies of the law possessed to a future Redeemer, that the law had, in itself, no power to
save any man except through the imputed merits
of a Saviour.   And, on the other hand, that as
Abraham himself had been declared righteous by
God, through the same merits, before the law was
given, it was plain not only that without those
merits the law could not save, but that with those
merits the law was not needed to save us. And it followed not only that the Jew had, no less than the
Gentile, great need of the Christian atonement,

1 Kings viii. 46.

but that the Gentile, through Christ's atonement, might be in a state of salvation though he were altogether regardless of those ceremonies and sacrifices of the law on which the ancient Jew relied for pardon and acceptance.

But to this argument a natural objection was raised. " If the law be unnecessary, why was it given at all? If the promise to Abraham had reference to Christ and was sufficiently answered, both to Jew and Gentile, in His birth, sufferings, and resurrection, why did God think fit to publish the law to the children of Israel, and to publish it under circumstances of such exceeding majesty and terrour as are related in the nineteenth and twentieth chapters of Exodus? God doth nothing in vain; an unmeaning or useless law He certainly would not have laid on us. Wherefore then serveth the law ?"

To this St. Paul makes answer, that the law " was added on account of transgression until the seed should come to whom the promise was made." This is an answer which may seem to require explanation, and which will be found very amply to repay the pains of the most attentive enquiry that can be bestowed on it. It contains, as you will observe, two implied assertions : first, that the law was, in some way or other, called for by the transgressions of mankind ; and, secondly, that it was only thus called for during the time which passed before the coming of our Lord, from whom, when He came, the offences complained of were to re-

ceive a better and sufficient remedy.   Both these
points I shall now endeavour to explain to you ; and,
first, in what manner was the law of Moses added
" on account of transgressions."

There are three respects in which it may be said
to have been thus appointed.   First, as a rule of
life and additional sanction of duty.   Secondly, as a
sacramental means of grace, whereby the former
generations of faithful Israelites might be made
partakers of that salvation which, in after times,
the Almighty purposed to raise up to their children.
Thirdly, as a looking-glass wherein our human
nature might see reflected its own weakness and
deformity, and so be brought, with deeper humility
and warmer and stronger love, to lay hold on the
merits of the Redeemer.   All these I shall notice in
their order.

First, the law of Moses was " added" to the
world " on account of their transgressions," as a
rule of life and an additional sanction of duty.   The
first men and early patriarchs appear, indeed, to
have received repeated revelations from God of
His being, His nature, and His attributes ; and in
the institution of sacrifices, and the prophecy that
the seed of the woman should bruise the serpent,
they were not left altogether without some knowledge of the means whereby sin was to be, in after
times, subdued and expiated.   But, except in two
instances, that of eating the blood of living animals,
and that of murder of their own species, no rule
that we know of was given for their conduct in life,

except that law of nature, that moral sense of right and wrong, that inward voice of conscience and of reason by which the heathen are, even now, as St. Paul expresses it, " a law unto themselves," and by which whoever is guided may learn " to do as he would be done by," and to govern his lusts and passions.

But that both the revelations which God had made of His own nature, and the feelings which He had implanted in the bosom of man, were insufficient to subdue the unruly wills and affections of our species, or to keep them from adding vanity and will-worship to the pure religion which they had, at first, received from their Maker, is certain both from the sin and misery which, in every heathen country, abound to a far greater degree than is suspected by Christians ; and, secondly, from the fact that, so early as the time of Abraham, not only the greater part of mankind, but even the father of the faithful himself, before God had called him, were given up to the worship of false gods besides the True, and honoured the sun, the moon, the stars, and other creatures, instead of and more than the Almighty and ever blessed Creator.

For all these sins and for all this darkness of ignorance, God had, indeed, provided a cure in that blessed Mediator who was the Lamb slain from the beginning of the world, and in the light of that glorious Gospel which He was, in the fulness of time, to reveal. But in the mean time, and while the wheels of salvation tarried in their course, it

pleased Him to abate at least, if not entirely to
remove the nuisance, by giving a law which, though
not perfect in itself, was well suited to the manners
and circumstances of that age and nation for whose
use it was principally intended; and, if it did not
effect that which it was reserved for Christianity
to accomplish, the purifying of " a peculiar people
zealous of good works[1]," yet separated, at least,
one nation from the grossest and most grievous of
those sins and errours into which the Gentiles had
fallen; and sanctified them to Himself as guardians
of His name, and the depositories of those promises and prophecies which were, to the universal
world, the charters of future salvation.   As purifying, then, the Israelites from idolatry ; as keeping
them if not free from sin, yet comparatively free
from the worst and most hateful practices of their
neighbours; and as supplying a somewhat stronger
ground of virtue than the law of nature could supply, the law of Moses may be truly said to have
been " added because of transgressions," and to
have answered the object of God as a temporary
check to the overflowing of the offences of mankind.

Again, the law was added " on account of transgressions" as a sacramental means of grace, and a
pledge of that great atonement whereby all the
repeated transgressions of men were, at length, to
obtain their pardon.   We believe indeed that, from

---

[1] Titus ii. 14.

the first martyr, Abel, down to the good old Simeon,
who prayed for his release from life on the birth of
his Lord, and thirty years, at least, before the sacrifice for sin was offered on Mount Calvary, we
believe that the blood of Christ had power to
cleanse from sin those who looked forward to it, in
faith, beforehand, as well as those who now, in
faith, look back to it. And it is equally true that
the sacrifices and purifications of the law had, in
themselves, no power to put away sin, nor any
value but what they obtained by a reference to the
blood of the Messiah. But still they were seals
and pledges of that mercy; still they were tokens
whereby God assured the penitent sinner of His
resolution to wipe away the guilt of the world; and
the mercy of God which had determined Him to
pardon such a sinner, led Him also to comfort
and support him beforehand with the assurance of
future pardon. Nor is this all, for as God hath
ordained that the grace whereby Christians forsake
sin should be sought for and received by them
through certain actions, as baptism and the Lord's
Supper, commemorative of Christ's death; so He
also thought fit that the same necessary spiritual
aid should be obtained by the house of Israel
through ceremonies and sacrifices whereby that
great sacrifice was prefigured. Thus it was then
that the ceremonies of the law were to the Jew
what the sacraments of the Gospel are to the
Christian, a public expression of his faith in Christ's
blood, " a means of grace and a pledge to assure

him thereof;" and this grace and this pledge were
rendered necessary " because of transgressions."

Thirdly, the law of Moses was given " because
of transgressions," as a looking-glass wherein our
human nature might see its own weakness and deformity, and thus be brought, with deeper lowliness
and warmer love, to lay hold on the offered merits
of the Redeemer.   In the law was shown forth the
anger of God against sin ; in the law were exhibited
the purity and holiness which were necessary to
purchase His approbation ; and the difference which
every man felt between his own character and this
perfect model ; and the impossibility which he could
not but feel in himself to equal or resemble it, while
they were sufficient to have driven him to despair
if no atonement had been provided for sin, made
him cling with ten thousand fold more of joy, and
love, and thankfulness to that wonderful and precious atonement which God had prepared in His
Son.   The Jew, on looking on the law, perceived
its spiritual nature, and that he himself was carnal,
sold to sin.   He felt another love in his members
warring against the law in his mind [1] ; he felt that
he was unable of himself to merit Heaven or to
escape the wrath of God ; and when he was now
ready to cry out, " Oh wretched man that I am,
who shall deliver me from the body of this death [2] ?"
he found on a sudden his condemnation withdrawn,
his ransom paid, his chain of sin unloosed by the

[1] Rom. vi. 23.   [2] Rom. vii. 24.

meritorious life, the redeeming sufferings, and the
sanctifying grace of Jesus Christ our Lord! Well
might his thankfulness be proportioned to the dangers from which he was set free, and blessed was
that knowledge of himself and his condition which
the law supplied "because of transgressions."

But all these ends which the law so excellently
answered, these ends were temporary only, and
lasted no longer than "till the seed should come
to whom the promise was made" that in Him all
the nations of the earth should be blessed. The assurance and certainty of everlasting life and of a
just and equal judgement after death which Christ
declared to all men, and of which He gave an
ample proof by His own resurrection, are a far
more powerful sanction to the law of nature and
conscience, and the purity of Christ's example is a
far more perfect rule of life than any which were
supplied by the law of Moses. The sacrifices for
sin, which were "a shadow of things to come[1],"
faded away at once when those realities were present which they only prefigured; and the forms
which were proper as types of an expected Saviour
were fitly replaced by that feast of thanksgiving,
which became those who rejoiced in an atonement
already offered.

The anger, lastly, of God against sin, and the
purity which were required to please Him, were
shown forth more strongly than ever in the dread-

---

[1] Col. ii. 17.

ful expiation which the sins of the world required, and the aweful fact that it was His own beloved Son, in whom *only* He was well pleased.

If then, we are asked, why the law of Moses was given by God? the answer will be, " It was added because of transgressions, until the seed should come to whom the promise was made." If we are asked, whether we are bound to keep that law? we should reply that it was not given to us nor to our fathers, and that we live under a better covenant, and have, in the example of Christ, a better rule of life before us. If it should be further enquired, why, then, do we read the Scriptures of the Old Testament? we may answer, that we read them to confirm our faith in Christ by learning all that wonderful chain of prophecy which, from Adam to Moses, and from Moses to Malachi, fixed the attention of the world on Him before His coming; that we read it to increase our thankfulness, by comparing the glorious light which we now enjoy, with the dim and blunted rays which were cast from the veiled countenance of Moses; that we read it to quicken our godly jealousy, and make us more active in the service of the Lord, by observing the zeal which, with far less advantages than ourselves, the ancient patriarchs exhibited. If, lastly, the enquirer should ask what obligation we have, since the law of Moses has no weight with us, to the practice of moral and religious duties? let our answer be given, not only with our lips but in our lives, that the greater the benefits bestowed, the

7

more we are bound to show forth our thankfulness by doing, to the utmost of our feeble power, whatever may please our Benefactor; that the greater the pardon which we have received, the more should we fear to fall again into those sins which rendered it necessary; that the greater the salvation offered, the more offence and peril there must necessarily be in neglecting it. There is no privilege conferred in Scripture which does not carry along with it its corresponding duty. Christ only made the law of Moses unnecessary by furnishing us with stronger motives of hope and fear to the practice of the law of nature; He died for our salvation that He might, by the example of His love and the privileges which He has purchased, purify unto Himself a peculiar people zealous of good works, and while He has given, both in His life and in His preaching, a perfect pattern of Christian holiness, He hath declared that not those who say Lord, Lord, but those who do the will of His Heavenly Father, shall enter into the Kingdom of Heaven!

SERMON VI.

THE CHRISTIAN'S FAITH AND FEAR.

[Preached at Dum Dum, Dec. 4, 1825.]

ISAIAH li. 12, 13.

I, even I, am He that comforteth you. Who art thou, that
thou shouldest be afraid of a man that shall die, and of the
son of man which shall be made as grass ; and forgettest the
Lord thy Maker, that hath stretched out the Heavens, and
laid the foundations of the earth ?

THE chapter from which these words are taken, is
part of a prophecy intended to support and comfort the faithful worshippers of God in the kingdom
of Judah, under the weight of those calamities
from which, on account of the many sins and pro-
vocations wherewith the greater number of their
countrymen had offended the Almighty, the nation
at large, and even the few righteous among the
many wicked, were to suffer. It is this small minority of humble and holy men whom the prophet
calls upon in the first verse of the chapter. " Hear-
ken to me ye that follow after righteousness !"
whom he exhorts to take example by the uncon-
querable faith of their great forefather Abraham,

from whose loins, as from a quarry in an everlasting
rock, their city and their nation had been upbuilded;
who, (when the Lord had promised to make him,
in his old age, the father of a mighty nation, and
to give him for his inheritance a land wherein,
while yet living, he only possessed ground enough
for a grave) yet, having received these promises,
believed against probability, hoped against hope;
and disregarding all which man might reckon difficult or impossible, fixed his attention, his faith,
and his earnest thankfulness on His power only
who had spoken the word, and who both could
and would, undoubtedly, bring to pass the thing
which He had declared.

In like manner Isaiah encourages the faithful
Israelites, in the midst of those most grievous calamities which, as he himself foretold, were about to
overtake their nation,—however great and hopeless those calamities might seem, however unlikely
or impossible the world might think it that the
kingdom should ever again be restored to Israel,
or Jerusalem be again raised from its ruins, or the
people who had been carried into captivity be again
brought back from their prison-house in the land
of Shinar; yet, not for all these discouraging circumstances,—to be cast down or dismayed, but to
believe and be persuaded that the Lord would still
comfort Sion, that He would still make her waste
places to be inhabited, and the courts of her ruined
temple to ring once more with thanksgiving and
the voice of melody.   Nor is it only this restora-

tion of their people and political freedom, of which
he bids them be thus confidently hopeful. He
goes on to assure them that, in the restoration of
Judah to their own land, there are other nations
besides Judah concerned, that it was in the city,
and among the people thus to be rebuilded and
brought back again, that the Lord would bring
forth to light that great salvation of the Messiah,
the Son of David, (whose kingdom is so gloriously
described in the seventy-second psalm) whose
power was to extend to the most distant islands of
the sea, to whom prayer and daily praises were to
be offered up by all nations, on whose arm the
Gentiles were to trust, and whom the Almighty
had hid in the hollow of His hand, (or His mysterious and secret providence) as an instrument
wherewith He was to renew His covenant with
Sion, and to plant (as we read in the sixteenth
verse,) on the ruins of a worn out and sinful world,
a new Heaven and earth wherein righteousness
should dwell for ever.

These are the gracious and glorious promises
which the prophet Isaiah, by the command of God,
intermixes with his threatenings against the people
of Judah. With these he would have them comforted though desolation and destruction, and the
famine and the sword should come unto them ;
though their sons should faint and lie at the head
of their streets like wild bulls in a net ; though
their nation should be afflicted and drunken, with
a worse drunkenness than wine, with evil passions,

with political fury, and the dregs of that cup of infatuation, trembling, and astonishment, which Divine justice pours forth to all those whose ruin is
determined.

Notwithstanding these things he bids them hope
for eventual deliverance. Notwithstanding these
things he assures them " I, even I, am he that
comforteth you!" And he gently chides them in
the words of my text, " who art thou, that thou
shouldest be afraid of a man that shall die, and of
the son of man which shall be made as grass, and
forgettest the Lord thy Maker that hath stretched
forth the Heavens and laid the foundations of the
earth ?"

Having thus explained the connexion of my text
with the rest of the chapter in which it is found,
as well as the general meaning of that chapter, the
first observation which I am desirous of making on
it is, that the grace of God is never so far withdrawn from mankind as that, in any nation or great
body of men, however the wicked may exceed the
good among them in number, in power, and in for-
wardness ; and however far gone this numerous,
and powerful, and active majority may be in wickedness and defiance of God, there will not still
remain a certain number of sincerely pious and
faithful worshippers shining forth as a light in a
dark place, and, however despised or overlooked
by the worldling's eye, yet neither forgotten nor
forsaken by Him who seeth in secret, and who
hears the whispered prayers, and reckons up the

secret alms of those who seek to please Him only.
It is thus that, when in a time of what appeared
a universal abandonment of God, the prophet
Elijah complained that he only was left alive of
Jehovah's worshippers, he was told by that still
small voice which visited him in Horeb, " Yet I
have left me seven thousand in Israel, all the knees
which have not bowed unto Baal, and every mouth
which hath not kissed him¹." It is thus that Isaiah
allows that in the land of Judah, amid the multitude that went astray, " the Lord of Hosts had left
a very small remnant²;" and that he now addresses
this remnant with words of comfort, as " ye that
follow after righteousness." And it is thus that
Christ has promised that, amid the different offences, divisions, and apostacies by which the Christian world has been and is still to be afflicted, He
will still keep to Himself a faithful Church with
whom His Spirit shall to the end of the world
abide, and against whom, however small in number
or humble in circumstances, " the gates of hell
shall not prevail³."

A due consideration of this truth will be, in many
respects, most useful to us. It will give us a better
and more comfortable trust in the goodness and
protection of Providence to know that, however to
mortal apprehensions " the whole world lieth in
wickedness⁴;" however the tares which the enemy
hath sown may overspread and overshadow the

¹ 1 Kings xix. 18.   ² Isaiah i. 9.
³ St. Matt. xvi. 18.   ⁴ 1 John v. 19.

fields, there still is good corn there which is known
to the Lord of the harvest, for whose sake His
dews may still fall, and His suns still shine, till
the day of harvest be come, and the wheat and
the weeds shall be separated from each other everlastingly.

It will teach us, also, a more comfortable and
more charitable opinion of our fellow-creatures and
fellow-servants, of whom, even under the most un-
favourable circumstances, we learn that a certain
proportion is always favourably regarded by the
Most High; and instead of looking, as good men
are sometimes tempted to do, on our neighbours
and fellow-countrymen as profane, as worldly, as
outcasts from grace, to hope the best of every
man, and to regard every man either already a
child of God, though we may not know it, or as
one who may yet be made so by our kindness, our
advice, our good example, and our prayers. And,
above all, the reflection that we are not alone or
friendless in the great battle which we are called
on to wage against the powers of evil, that there
are others who strive by our side, though the darkness of our present condition may prevent our dis-
covering their numbers, that the same afflictions
which we pass through are also " accomplished of
our brethren that are in the world [1];" this reflection, I say, may strengthen our feeble hands, and
confirm our weary resolutions ; and we may feel

[1] 1 Peter v. 9.

ashamed to shrink from temptations and trials
which others around us, with no more advantages
than ourselves, have felt and are feeling, have endured and are enduring, have conquered and are
conquering.

That the world then, bad as it may seem, and
bad as it would be if left to the consequences of its
natural corruption, has yet, through grace, been
never left without a certain proportion of those,
who, if not sinless, were yet faithful and accepted by
God, is the first consideration which arises from the
perusal of this chapter of Isaiah. Another is the
fact that, however this small number of righteous
persons are sharers, to a certain extent, in the
general calamities which the sins of the many draw
down on the communities to which they belong,
they are not less the beloved of the Lord, and
have, from Him, their many peculiar comforts in
which the world does not partake, and with which,
as a stranger to their hopes and principles, the
world does not intermeddle.

It is probable, indeed, (and this is the reason of
my saying that the righteous are only to a certain
extent sharers in the general calamity of a wicked
nation) it is probable that in very many instances
the calamities themselves are tempered, as they fall,
by God's providence in their particular cases ; that
His blows when they seem most undistinguishing,
nevertheless strike those the hardest whose sins
cry loudest for punishment, and that the sword of
the destroying angel, though it does not spare

entirely, yet passes more lightly over the houses of the humble and the penitent. Thus Jeremiah, and thus Daniel, still more, though captives like the rest of their countrymen, found favour in the eyes of their conquerors, and thus when Jerusalem, after Christ's decease, fell a sacrifice to the sword of the Romans, the Christians who were in the place were so wonderfully delivered that not a hair of their heads perished. And thus in the greatest danger of our life of every day, the angel of the Lord is said to encamp about those who fear Him, to preserve them, if not from every evil, yet from the worst of those evils to which, without His help, they are liable.

But besides this greater share of God's mercy and protection in this life, (which is then of most value when the judgements of God are visibly walking abroad), besides this private and personal ground of comfort, the righteous have a still more blessed consciousness in the season of public distress and danger, inasmuch as their example, their prayers, and the acceptable service which they render to the Almighty, is often useful to others besides themselves, and may contribute in no small degree to the preservation of their families, their friends, and their country. If there had been ten such in Sodom the city would have been spared; and in the greatest and most terrible calamity that ever befell, or ever will befall a nation, the siege and ruin of Jerusalem, already mentioned, we know from Him who cannot lie, that not only the Christians were themselves preserved, but their unbelieving countrymen, for their sakes, were punished with a less enduring misery. " Except that the Lord had shortened those days, no flesh should be saved ; but for the elects' sake whom He hath chosen, He hath shortened those days[1]." Nor can a stronger inducement, in its class of motives, be offered to any man who loves his friends and country to apply himself to lead such a life as God approves of, than the hope that his earnest endeavours after holiness may give his prayers for them a value in the sight of that pure and holy Being, with whom the " fervent prayer of a righteous man availeth much[2];" who gave a favourable answer to Daniel on the banks of Ulai, and who granted to St. Paul the lives of all them that were shipwrecked with him.

There is yet a consideration which must naturally tend to give courage and hope to the righteous in a season of general calamity, the recollection, namely, that all things which befall them are ordained by a wise and most merciful God, who knoweth what is best for His creatures, and can at any time, when He sees good, deliver them from the troubles by which they are now surrounded, or make those troubles themselves work to them for good, and to the bringing forth of an exceeding weight of future happiness and glory. Nor is this all ; for as the faithful Israelite looked forwards, in

---

[1] St. Mark xiii. 20.   [2] James v. 16.

the labours of his Babylonian slavery, not only to that appointed deliverance and return to their native land which God had promised to his tribes, but to the still more glorious deliverance which the Almighty should accomplish for his nation and all other nations of the world in the coming and triumph of the Redeemer, so has the faithful Christian, whose ransom from sin is already paid, and who awaits but the second coming of the Lord for his full and perfect release, so has he abundant reason to count all things as nothing which he may in this world endure, in comparison with that glorious hope which the Gospel holds out to him of " a treasure in the heavens that faileth not [1]."

It was this second life, indeed, to which, though with a dimmer light and a hope less sure and certain, the ancient Jew looked forwards,—as well as ourselves,—when, under the calamities of his nation, he fled to the promises of God for comfort. Without this hope the very promise which was held out of deliverance from captivity and of the glories of a future Messiah, would have little power in comparison to support the afflicted under the present burthens of his lot, or make the just rejoice on his death-bed.

I do not deny that the lover of his country might be glad to learn that her slavery was not to be perpetual ; that the father of a family might feel considerable comfort on finding that, though he and his

---

[1] Luke xii. 33.

I

sons were to live and die in bondage, the chains of his grand-children would be broken; that the lover of mankind would be happy in the prospect of a Saviour to be born in after-times from the nation of the Jews and the family of David, who should undeceive those millions who had, till then, been fettered with the errours of a false religion, and the ceremonies of a foul and bloody idolatry. But there is evidently something more personal, something closer to the heart, and more immediately interesting to the feelings in that hope which Isaiah holds out as arising from the consideration of Christ's coming, and which was to support the righteous under the severest weight of national misfortune. And what could this be but the expectation that, lay down their lives in God's cause when they might, they should not lay them down for ever; that whether their bones were laid to rest in the distant land of their captivity, or consumed to dust amid the ashes of their burning temple, those bones should be clothed anew with flesh, and that dust should wake into life at the call of the promised Messiah; that fall where they might, their spirits should rest in peace, and that they should see their Redeemer for themselves, and " stand in their lot at the end of the days [1]."

But, if such was their hope on the promise of God alone, a promise less declared, less explicit, less positive and clear by far than those assurances which

[1] Dan. xii. 13.

are made to us in the Gospel, how much more
should we depend on those stronger and clearer
revelations of a life after death which the Gospel
contains, supported as they are by the greatest
proof which God could give of His power and will
to perform them, in giving up His Son Jesus to
death, that the debt of our nature might be paid in
His blood, and in raising Him up from the dead as
a proof that His atonement was accepted?

There is only one observation more which I shall
make on the present chapter, and that is the moral
consequence which, in the words of my text, is
drawn from all the considerations of God's power
and promises wherewith the prophet comforted his
countrymen. I mean the fitness of an unshaken
faith in God, and a fearless discharge of our duty
under whatsoever calamities and against whatsoever opposition. It is a glorious thing to have a
courage independent of chance or change ; a breast
from which the arrows of danger fall blunted, and
which neither the rage of the people nor the frown
of the mighty can turn from the line of wisdom and
of duty. But this is, on every ground both of
reason and Scripture, most likely to be the portion
of him whose heart is right with God, who is firmly
persuaded that all things are governed by Divine
Providence, and who extends an humble but reasonable hope that his own life, his own best interests, his only happiness in this world and in the
world to come, are the objects of Divine protection.
" I fear God," it was the noble saying of a foreign

writer, " and I have, therefore, no other fear [1]."
Such a courage indeed is often laid claim to in
Scripture as the usual and distinguishing privilege
of the truly religious. Of the wicked it is said in
the book of Proverbs, that they " flee when no man
pursueth, but the righteous are bold as a lion [2]."
" Are not two sparrows," saith our Lord, " sold for
a farthing, and one of them shall not fall on the
ground without your Father. Fear ye not, therefore, ye are of more value than many sparrows."
" Why are ye fearful, Oh ye of little faith?" were
the words of the same Divine Person to His disciples in the tempest [3]. " I, even I am He that
comforteth you," said God through His prophet to
the pious Israelites. " Who art thou that thou
shouldest be afraid of a man that shall die, and of
the son of man which shall be made as grass?"

Still, however, " fear," it will be said, " is a natural and unavoidable passion. The protection of
Heaven, though it is doubtless promised to the
righteous in such a degree and such a manner as
that all things shall eventually work for their good,
and that they may be delivered from many evils
which must otherwise befall, or supported in many
which must otherwise overwhelm them, yet are
they no where promised an exemption from all mi-
series, from their fair proportion of the natural evils
of mortality, from pain, from poverty, from oppres-

---

[1] Racine, Athalie, Acte i. scene 1. " Je crains Dieu, cher Ab-
ner, et n'ai point d'autre crainte."

[2] Prov. xxviii. 1.   [3] St. Matt. x. 29. 31. viii. 26.

sion, or from death. There are some sufferings, in themselves sufficiently terrible, to which the righteous in their present state of mortal imperfection are exposed as well as other men ; there are some, if Christ's words be true, to which, even more than other men, and out of their very righteousness, and for the sake of Christ and His Gospel, the righteous are liable. And so long as God gives power to the oppressor to kill, diseases to vex, and hunger and cold to torment us, the mere present suffering which will arise from such causes is, in itself, a sufficient ground for fear in the breast of every one whose body is sensible to pain and privation."

I allow the reasonableness of the objection ; I am ready to admit that it is only comparatively and not absolutely that the religious man can hope to be free from fear of worldly evils, and that the degree of his fear must in a great measure depend not only on the strength or weakness of his religious principles, but on the state of his nerves, and the degree to which he has been already accustomed to danger and suffering. But, if he cannot hope to get rid entirely of his fear of worldly calamities, he may make that very fear an argument for a still greater fear of Him by whom all good or evil are, in this life, ordained, and on whom depend the far greater and everlasting good or evil of the life which is to follow. Are we by our nature or habits so sensible to the loss of worldly comforts, that the dread of approaching poverty is enough to

make us melancholy, the dread of approaching disgrace to drive us mad? let us reflect how we shall
one day endure the want of a drop of water to cool
our tongues; with what patience we shall one day
bear the scoffs and mockery of devils, and the eyes
of the whole world and of all the angels of God,
when our secret sins are made known in the day of
judgement!

Are we so sensible of pain that we tremble at the
bare apprehension of its infliction now? Let us
ask ourselves how we shall like to dwell with everlasting burnings? Let us consider whether it be
not an inconsistency, a madness even beyond the
madness of Bedlam, to be thus alarmed at the
smaller and so indifferent to the greater danger, to
be "afraid of a man that shall die, of the son of
man which shall be made as grass, and forget the
Lord thy Maker, that hath stretched out the
Heavens and laid the foundations of the earth?"
"Be not afraid of them that kill the body, and after
that have no more that they can do!" but if ye
must fear these, forget not that there *is* One who
is more terrible than them all. "I will forewarn
ye whom ye shall fear! fear Him which after He
hath killed hath power to cast into hell! Yea, I
say unto you, fear Him [1]!"

[1] St. Luke xii. 4, 5.

SERMON VII.

THE CHRISTIAN'S TREATMENT ON EARTH.

[Preached at Calcutta, Nov. 1825.]

1 St. Peter iii. 13, 14.

Who is he that will harm you if ye be followers of that which is good? But and if ye suffer for righteousness sake, happy are ye!

This epistle was addressed by St. Peter to men under great tribulation, the converted Jews in different parts of the east, " the strangers," he calls them, " scattered throughout Pontus, Galatia, Cappadocia, Asia, and Bithynia [1]." Strangers indeed they were, as dwelling in foreign lands and remote from their beloved Jerusalem ; strangers they were, still more, to whom the world was an uneasy pilgrimage, who were the objects, if Tacitus is to be believed, of the common hatred of the human race, shut out in no small degree from the defence of the laws, and exposed on the slightest pretences, or on no pretence at all, to the heaviest lash of their severity.

Of the dangers and distresses to which the pri-

[1] 1 St. Peter i. 2.

mitive Christians were liable, it would be long,
and with my present audience it would be needless
to enter into a detail.   But this notice of them was
required to put you in possession of the general
drift and tendency of St. Peter's arguments, which
were directed, through a considerable part of both
the Epistles which bear his name, to counteract
and conquer the peculiar temptation to which a
community thus situated were liable.   For such
men it was, in the first instance, a just and natural
apprehension that their faith would fail under the
weariness of hope deferred; that their courage
would yield, and their spiritual sight grow dim,
amid the calamities to which they were exposed,
and the dangers which threatened their progress.
Secondly, since every thing they did was taken in
a bad sense by those around them, it might be
feared, lest this want of a good name should make
them careless of their actual behaviour; lest they
should begin to neglect appearances in utter despair of persuading mankind to think well of them,
and be tempted really to become the wretches they
were accused of being.   But, in the third place, the
probability perhaps was greater still that, though
their morals might remain unimpaired, their tempers might be soured and rendered churlish; that
they whom the world hated, might begin, at length,
to hate the world; and that they might endeavour
to revenge their own sufferings on all around them,
either by a general moroseness and peevishness, or
by availing themselves of some of those opportuni-

ties which the disorderly state of the remoter Roman provinces supplied, to break forth in violence and rebellion.

The two former of these temptations St. Peter opposes in by far the greater part of his Epistles, where he encourages the converts to steadiness in their calling by pointing out the greatness and certainty of the promised recompence ; where he extolls the blessedness of that celestial aid which the grace of the Most High affords to all that daily seek it; and where he reminds them, that their hope was for ever rendered vain unless the daily tenour of their lives refuted the calumnies of their adversaries.

The third temptation is that which he chiefly combats in the present chapter ; wherein he exhorts them not only to be courteous and kind to men of the same persuasion with themselves, but to be gentle and forgiving even towards their worst and bitterest persecutors, in the confidence that they would thus not only secure the protection of the Almighty, but that, in very many instances, the hearts of their enemies themselves would be subdued by their persevering virtue and gentleness. " The eyes of the Lord are over the righteous, and His ears are open unto their prayers ; but the face of the Lord is against them that do evil. And who is he that will harm you if ye be followers of that which is good ? But, and if ye suffer for righteousness sake, happy are ye ; and be not afraid of their terrour, neither be troubled, but sanctify the Lord God in your hearts."

In this latter argument it is plain that there are two distinct but not inconsistent propositions; first, that, even in this world, the probability is that the faithful and peaceable follower of Christ will not be molested; secondly, that if it should so happen that we are molested for the sake of our righteousness, we have, on this very account, an additional reason for gratitude to God, and for reliance on His help and blessing.

The first of these assertions (so far as the mere abstract probability of the case extends) might seem at first sight to be a thing so clear as to require very little argument to prove it. Few, even in comparison, are found of a temper so utterly devilish as to desire to injure their neighbour without some received or fancied provocation. But as the consistent follower of righteousness gives no just ground of provocation to any; as, on the contrary, his life, so far as his means extend, is occupied in doing good to all, it might be reasonably hoped that his innocence would, amid the strifes and ambuscades of the world, be his helmet, his sword, and his shield; and that he who was the friend of all would, at least, have no one for his enemy. It is plain, however, from the words of St. Peter himself, that this statement of the case must be taken with very considerable exceptions; since, even while he asks the question, " who is he that shall harm you?" he hypothetically subjoins, " but and if ye be persecuted." Nay more, when he adds, " if ye be persecuted for righteousness sake," he admits that they, to whom he was writing, might be exposed to violence and injustice, not only in spite of their innocence, but actually in consequence of it.

It is, indeed, not more strange than true, that there is a principle in every man's nature, which induces him to dislike whatever differs from himself; and that this dislike is stronger in proportion as we doubt the wisdom of our own choice, and suspect that we are wrong in those circumstances, whereby we are distinguished from such as are of a contrary opinion. It is this which has made many men intolerant towards other and new religions, who all the while have been conspicuously and glaringly negligent of their own; it is this which, even where the forms of belief have been the same, has continually led the worldly man to revile and detest the superior strictness of his pious neighbour, and to exclaim, in the words of the eloquent author of the apocryphal book of Wisdom, " He is not for our turn;" he is grievous " unto us even to behold, for his life is not like other men's; his ways are of another fashion[1]." " If ye were of the world," said He who well knew what was in man, " if ye were of the world, the world would love its own; but because ye are not of the world, but I have chosen you out of the world, therefore the world hateth you[2]." Nor can it be a subject of wonder, that from these and other similar passages in the Holy Scriptures, very many have been led to believe that every sincere Chris-

[1] Wisdom ii. 12. 15.   [2] St. John xv. 19.

tian is inevitably exposed to the scorn and malice
of his unconverted neighbours, and have conse-
quently been compelled to explain away, in a most
unsatisfactory manner, the expectation expressed
by St. Peter, that, even in the present life, and in
the present evil world, our following that which is
good, is likely to preserve us from injury.

This belief, however, when entertained without
due qualification, is, I am convinced, not only a
mistaken but a mischievous one. It has led some
good and humble men to doubt, very causelessly,
of their own spiritual state, and their acceptance
with the Almighty, because they have not been
able to say with truth, that they were either so unhappy or so much hated among mankind as they
conceived to be a necessary evidence of their conformity with the Son of God.   It has led some of
a more sanguine turn to make much of little sorrows, and glorify themselves as martyrs under little
or imaginary grievances, while others whose own
imprudence or inconsistency have been the cause
of the rough treatment they have met with, have
been encouraged in their errours, and hardened in
their unruly temper, and have appealed to the opposition which they encountered as a proof that
they were the genuine followers of the meek and
gentle Jesus. And I am anxious, on these accounts,
to examine the grounds of an opinion so uncom-
fortable, and which tends to throw a fresh and unnecessary difficulty in that path of life which is, of
itself, sufficiently steep and thorny.

One main part of the errour appears to arise from a too strong estimate of the corruption and depravity of mankind. That mankind are, indeed, in a forlorn and fallen condition, that they are, by nature, strangers to God, and very far gone from that glorious likeness of Himself in which He first created them, is, unhappily, most true, and God forbid that we should ever lose sight of it in our sorrowful and daily recollections.

But that, in this depravity of the natural man, no kind or amiable quality remains, that he is so far sunk below the beasts that perish, as that pity cannot move, nor justice awe, nor kindness conciliate him, that he universally, or even usually, delights in evil for evil's sake, and that where no prejudice or interest intervenes, he is unkind, uncourteous, or ungrateful, is certainly that which I find no where written in the Book of Truth, and against which, the book of nature and experience appears to bear abundant testimony. The very weakness of man indeed (and his weakness is, in this instance, a blessing) forbids his being consistent and uniform in vice any more than in virtue. And there are many countervailing circumstances, such as the weight of public opinion, the vacillation of men's own opinions, the feelings of worldly prudence, and the approbation, often involuntary, of whatever in other men is disinterested, kind, and lovely, which will very often be the means, under God's providence, of making the enemies of the righteous man his friends, and keeping the followers of that which is good from being materially harmed by any one.

I say under God's providence, because it must be further borne in mind that, however wicked man may be, and however entirely his heart may be bent on mischief, still that heart is in the hand of the Lord, the same Lord whose eyes are over the righteous, and His ears open unto their prayers, whose defence and shield may well be trusted for the safety and happiness of them that love Him. It is His apostle, it is His Holy Spirit who speaks to us in the words which I have quoted, and, with whatever exceptions these gracious assurances may possibly be qualified, the righteous man may yet found on them a probable hope, even in this life, of seeing good days, and being safe from those that would harm him.

I know it will be answered, that both reason and Scripture are, on the whole, against our conclusion. In private life even the best of men have their enemies, their slanderers, their revilers; and the general history of religion we find to be made up of little else than a series of horrours and cruelties inflicted by the wicked on the righteous; and sometimes on no other account, so far as man can discern, than that silent reproach which their good examples have given to the opposite lives of their persecutors.

The first murder which the world ever saw was occasioned by a difference of this kind. The prophets of ancient times, of whom the world was not worthy, were scourged, imprisoned, sawn in sunder, and slain with the sword. St. John the Baptist lost his head because he persisted in warning Herod of his wickedness; and the best and wisest of beings, the Son of God Himself, who went about doing good, and against whose pure and perfect character the malice of His enemies could find no colourable aspersion, was taken in His innocency and doomed to a death of torture. Accordingly the same Divine Lord has left as a legacy to His disciples the painful reversion of His stripes, His thorns, His agony, His bitter tears, and commanded each of us, as a pledge of our sincerity in His service, to " take up the cross," before we can presume to account ourselves His followers.

I answer, that these cases of persecution for righteousness sake are exceptions, and very great and aweful ones, from the general rule which St. Peter lays down; but still they are exceptions only They apply to a body of persons numerous, indeed, in themselves, but, thank God! very small in proportion to the total number of that mighty multitude who are redeemed from sin and misery by the blood of the Lamb, and the sanctification of the Holy Spirit. Of these by far the greater number will be found to have gone down to their graves in peace and in favour with both God and man; too happily obscure for the axe, the sword, or the fire, or protected from such dangers by the prevalence, the nominal prevalence at least, of those very doc-

trines, to plant which their heroic precursors thought
their blood a trifling sacrifice.

Even in the age when martyrs were most numerous, a few thousands out of the whole populous
family of Christ, afford no very formidable aggre-
gate ; and how many ages have since passed away
in which martyrdom has been unknown, and the
mighty of the earth have, from the oppressors, been
transformed into the nursing fathers of Christ's religion! It is, doubtless, true, that Christ speaks of
His cross, in general terms, as that condition of His
service which we must be all of us prepared to encounter, and bear with us boldly and cheerfully.
And it is also true that the uniform manner of our
Lord (as it would be the manner and the duty of
every experienced person preparing another for the
duties and dangers of a new profession) is to state
those duties broadly and strongly, to the end that
no one might treasure up disappointment for himself by too flattering and easy a picture of the
arduous undertaking before him. But if I were
preparing a young seaman or soldier for the toils he
must expect to undergo, if I were painting to him
the various bitter accidents of flood or field, the
wounds and the watchings, the hunger and cold,
the toil and thirst, the storms, the rencontres, the
defeats and the captivities, the

—— dura navis,
Dura fugæ mala, dura belli,

would it be fair to understand me that all these or

1

THE CHRISTIAN'S TREATMENT ON EARTH. 129

any of these calamities were necessarily to befall the individual whom I was addressing ; that no seas were ever calm, no voyages ever prosperous, and that no military man was known at any time to descend to his grave in peace, and with his children weeping around him ? Such visitations, like the persecutions foretold in Scripture, are spoken of as impending over all, because they are such as may happen to any, and because all should, therefore, be prepared, if they come, to meet them boldly. But it would be a strange seaman who, during a prosperous voyage over an untroubled sea, should cry out before every ruffle of the elements as if it were St. Paul's euroclydon. And it is, surely, a strange and unthankful trifling with God's mercies and our own experience to talk of afflictions in His cause, when no man, on that account, either makes us afraid or troubles us, and when those lions have, by His Providence, been long since chained, which used, in ancient days, to scare the pilgrims in their journey to the New Jerusalem.

" But does not," it will be rejoined, " in common life, and in those smaller distresses which every day brings forth, and which determine the general character of our journey far more than the greater but less frequent dangers to which you have alluded; does not experience shew that genuine religion is still, to the generality of mankind, the object of dislike, and, so far as the present circumstances of the world will admit, of persecution ? Is not the child who prays to God, and reverences its parents,

K

exposed too often to mockery from its idle companions? The young man who is sober and chaste,
is he not ridiculed for want of spirit? is not the devout man of riper years too often charged with
hypocrisy? and are not many of every age to be
found who have been disliked or ill-used on account
of their piety?"

I answer that all this is very true, and a treatment like this may very possibly befall any one of us
in his journey through the wilderness of the world;
but still these are exceptions from St. Peter's general rule, and such exceptions will be found less
numerous than they at first appear, if we distinguish those sorrows and vexations which good men
endure on account of their religion, from those
which they might have experienced whether they
were religious or no; and those, still more, which
they bring on themselves, not by their religion, but
by their imprudence and their failings. Christ's
kingdom is not of this world; and no promise that
I can find in Scripture has been made to His followers, that they should have less than their share
of the common accidents of their nature; that a
ruin tottering to its foundation should necessarily
remain suspended while a Christian passed beneath;
that a Christian should not slip, where another man
should break a limb; or that a Christian should
not be stripped by robbers, or torn by wild beasts,
like any other man who might pass from Jerusalem
to Jericho. Christians are men, and sinful men,
and they require, no less than their fellow trans-

any of these calamities were necessarily to befall the individual whom I was addressing ; that no seas were ever calm, no voyages ever prosperous, and that no military man was known at any time to descend to his grave in peace, and with his children weeping around him ? Such visitations, like the persecutions foretold in Scripture, are spoken of as impending over all, because they are such as may happen to any, and because all should, therefore, be prepared, if they come, to meet them boldly. But it would be a strange seaman who, during a prosperous voyage over an untroubled sea, should cry out before every ruffle of the elements as if it were St. Paul's euroclydon. And it is, surely, a strange and unthankful trifling with God's mercies and our own experience to talk of afflictions in His cause, when no man, on that account, either makes us afraid or troubles us, and when those lions have, by His Providence, been long since chained, which used, in ancient days, to scare the pilgrims in their journey to the New Jerusalem.

" But does not," it will be rejoined, " in common life, and in those smaller distresses which every day brings forth, and which determine the general character of our journey far more than the greater but less frequent dangers to which you have alluded ; does not experience shew that genuine religion is still, to the generality of mankind, the object of dislike, and, so far as the present circumstances of the world will admit, of persecution ? Is not the child who prays to God, and reverences its parents,

K

owned, will not be sorry to bring down his character to its own low level.

But do our opponents appeal to the experience
of mankind ? To that experience let them go !
Let them ask themselves whether, among their
own acquaintance, their own neighbours, the public
men whose lives and circumstances are known to
them, there is any considerable appearance of
such persecution as they apprehend, such affliction
for conscience sake as is implied in their gloomy
anticipations ? Is the sober, the honest, the religious labourer less employed by his superiors in
rank, or less thriving in the world than his godless
neighbour ? Among merchants, among statesmen,
I will add, among the followers of the naval or
military profession, will it usually be found, (for
some detached and remarkable instances are no
sufficient proof of the general rule) that a man's
religion has done him any harm ? Why, then,
should we dress up the confession of our faith with
these unreasonable and unnecessary terrours, or
doubt that, even in this world, as well as in the
world to come, and in the necessities of the present
life, as well as in the one thing eternally needful,
the Lord of all things may, if we seek His help,
make our very enemies to love us, and those, of
whom we fear that they should carry us captive,
to take pity on us ?

As, however, situations may arise, in which we
may be called upon, we know not how soon or how
suddenly, to prefer our duty to our interest, and to

suffer for righteousness sake, it is fit to keep our hearts in constant readiness for such a trial by the assurance, which should be deeply impressed on them, that such afflictions as, on this account, befall us are, by the concurrent assurances of God's words, among the surest earnests of His favour. " Blessed are ye when men shall revile you, and persecute you, and shall say all manner of evil against you, falsely, for my sake! Rejoice, and be exceeding glad,—for so persecuted they the prophets which were before you[1]!" " Rejoice," saith St. Peter, " inasmuch as ye are partakers of Christ's sufferings, that when His glory shall be revealed, ye may be glad also with exceeding joy[2]."

And the reason for such joy a little consideration will suggest to us. In the first place, such persecutions, wherever they recur, are so many fulfilments of our Saviour's prophecy that men should thus deal with His followers for His name's sake; and they are, in consequence, so many confirmations of our faith in Him, and so many fresh grounds of hope that, as the sorrows which He foretold have come true, the far greater joys which He has promised, will, in like manner, come true also. No other religion which the world has known was announced with such forebodings. The pretenders to inspiration have usually, if not uniformly, amused their followers with hopes of unmixed success and

---

[1] St. Matt. v. 11, 12.   [2] 1 St. Peter iv. 13.

universal extension ; and the failure of their hopes has demonstrated the folly of their assumptions.

Our Lord promised His people affliction first, and weight of glory afterwards.   The affliction has arrived, yea, in a great measure, has passed away ; the glory will therefore follow !

Secondly, since God has shown afflictions to be so precious in His sight, as to conduct His only Son through the same thorny passage to His present exaltation of Majesty, we may well feel ourselves honoured in being made to resemble Him, even in the circumstances of His humiliation ; and that we are thought worthy to be His companions in working, by the same means, the same glorious will of His and our Almighty Father.   The soldier who sleeps on the bare field of battle, feels elevated in his spirit so that his general lies no softer ; and shall not we in our necessities, sometimes think with a holy joy that, even in these things, God hath made us like His Son ?

Thirdly, when we recollect, that the greater our sufferings are now, and the more courageously we pass through them, the more our faith is proved, our love rendered brighter, and the more exceeding weight of glory and reward is, for Christ's sake, laid up for us hereafter, may we not rejoice in our distress as a pledge of God's gracious designs in our favour, as a gate to greater eminence and far higher seats in His kingdom, than are to be attained by an easier entrance ?   Strange things are told in the early Christian writers of the glories and the nearer and more immediate access to the Lord, which those who were killed for His name's sake should receive from Him. And be these as they may, yet, doubtless, a more than common happiness is laid up, not for the martyr only, but for every one, in proportion to his losses and trials in the cause, who, though he has borne a lighter and less illustrious cross, has still borne cheerfully whatever cross his Master has given him to carry. We know of men in hard and dangerous professions, who rejoice when sent on services of still greater danger and hardship, as knowing that where peril is, promotion may also be found; and the sufferer for conscience sake may, much more, exult in his trials, as knowing that, in the strength of God's grace, He will come off even more than conqueror.

But, fourthly, lest all these hopes should fail us in the hour of danger, it is wise, nay it is most needful, to accustom ourselves to frequent self-denial, even in lawful indulgences; to obtain, by frequent exercise, a complete mastery over ourselves; by a constant study of God's word to store our minds before-hand with a deep sense both of His threats and of His promises, and by daily meditation and prayer to accustom our thoughts to the constant spectacle of Christ on the cross, entreating His grace to frame our minds into the likeness of His Heavenly temper.

So shall we fear God; and, fearing Him, be fearless of all besides :—so shall we love God; and, for His sake, count all the world as dross in com-

1

parison of His services ;—so, amid the changes and
chances of this mortal life, shall our hearts be there
fixed where unfailing joys are to be found; and
where all which now distresses us shall appear but
as a painful dream when we awake from sleep refreshed and thankful, and the light of Heaven's
great morning beams in through the windows of
the sepulchre !

SERMON VIII.

THE PHARISEE AND THE PUBLICAN.

[Preached at Ghazeepoor, August 29, 1824.]

St. Luke xviii. 14.

I tell you that this man went down to his house justified rather than the other: For every one that exalteth himself shall be abased; and he that humbleth himself shall be exalted.

The parable of which these words form the conclusion, was spoken by our Saviour, as the Holy Scripture itself tells us, in reproof of certain persons who " trusted in themselves that they were righteous and despised others;" and of the persons, accordingly, whom He sets before us, the first is of a class of men who, more than all others among the Jews, enjoyed the reputation of a strict and scrupulous piety; while the second was from a description of persons, many of whom were, really, of depraved and infamous behaviour, and all of whom, from the prejudices of their countrymen, were regarded, whether justly so or no, as depraved and infamous. " Two men," are our Lord's words, "went up into the temple to pray; the one a pharisee, and the other a publican."

The pharisees, it may be here necessary to observe, were a party among the Jewish nation whose
name is taken from a Hebrew word signifying divi-
sion or separation, because they had divided themselves in many circumstances of dress and manners and society from the generality of their brother Israelites, and of those who worshipped the
same God with them in the same temple, on pretence of superior holiness, and of keeping themselves altogether unspotted by the company, the
amusements, and even the touch of carnal and
worldly persons. They were famous among their
countrymen for their dislike of all diversions, however innocent, for the length of their prayers and of
their graces both before and after meat, for their
rigid observance of the Sabbath and fasting days appointed by the law of Moses, and by the zeal which
they showed for not only the slightest observances
recommended in that law, but for many other additional rules and restrictions which, though the
law said nothing of them, they professed to have
received from the tradition of the elders. Thus
the law respecting the Sabbath, in itself strict, they
straitened still more by forbidding men so much as
to heal the sick on that day, to take physic themselves, or to give physic to others. On fasting days
they not only refused to eat all food before the
appointed hour, but if they took a draught of water
took care to strain it through a cloth, lest any
thing solid might lurk in it, and be accidentally
swallowed. The blue fringe which it was the cus-

tom of the Jews in general to wear on their clothes, the pharisees wore twice as large as other men, in order to prove that they were not ashamed of their religion; and their wrists and foreheads were usually bound round with strips of parchment written over with texts of Scripture, " to keep," as they said, " the law of God before their eyes, and to prevent its ever escaping from their memories."

On the whole, as their manners and appearance were formal, grave, and melancholy, so they chiefly lived among their own members, calling themselves in their books and in their general conversation, " the godly," " the elect," " the wise," and the " disciples of the elders;" and shunning not only the company, but the touch and the neighbourhood of those who did not belong to their own little circle, and of whom they therefore spoke as " the men of the world," " the unclean," and " the vulgar," or " unenlightened."

With all these pretences to piety, many grievous crimes, as it appears from Scripture, prevailed among them. Many of them were extremely covetous; and even made their outward piety a means of obtaining wealth and legacies from their countrymen; " devouring widows' houses under the pretence of long prayers;" and " making clean the outside of the cup and the platter, while the inward part was full of ravening and wickedness [1]."

But though such faults were but too common

[1] St. Matt. xxiii. 25. St. Luke xi. 39.

among them, and though our Saviour, therefore,
reproves them perhaps more sharply, and certainly
more frequently than any other party among the
Jews, (possibly because from their numbers they
oftener fell in His way ; and possibly because, with
all their faults, they were more within the ordinary
reach of grace than their wicked and godless rivals
the Sadducees,) yet they had, when compared with
these last, many favourable circumstances in their
character, and many among them were really good
and godly men who, when their prejudices were
once removed, became sincere and humble followers of the Messiah.　They had kept entire the
ancient and true doctrine of a resurrection from
the dead, which the Sadducees ventured to deny;
they were really zealous, though not according unto
knowledge, for the honour of God's name and the
observance of His Sabbaths ; they were commend-
ably anxious in spreading a knowledge of the law
of Moses among the heathen and their own ignorant countrymen ; and they were accordingly held
in great reverence by the common people; and the
scribes or teachers of the law of Moses, as well as
the rulers or elders of the people, were most frequently of their number.

　Of the publicans it is enough to say that they
were collectors of taxes for the Romans, who, some
time before, had conquered the Jews and held
them in the same state of subjection, though of a
far less just and gentle kind, than that in which
the English now hold the inhabitants of India.

And it is easy to suppose not only that any Jew who undertook such an office would be extremely unpopular among his countrymen; but that, in fact, the more respectable Jews would, generally speaking, be slow to hold an office which at the same time made them hated by their own brethren, and exposed them to lose caste by living and eating with their heathen masters.

When, therefore, our Lord fixed on two persons of these different descriptions as going together to the House of God to pray, He fixed on characters the most different that His countrymen had seen, the most popular and respected and the least esteemed, the most outwardly careful of their religious interests and the most outwardly and generally neglectful of them; the class who were supposed in general to be most dear to God (and who certainly supposed themselves so) and those who were considered the greatest strangers to Him. And if we ourselves had been, with the same feelings and prejudices, among the number of our Saviour's hearers, and had been asked by Him, which of these two persons was in our opinion most likely to obtain a favourable answer to his prayers, and to conciliate the mercy of Heaven, we should have probably supposed, as the Jews no doubt supposed, that the advantage was decidedly with the pharisee.

" The pharisee, (however, the story then proceeds,) the pharisee stood and prayed thus with himself, God, I thank Thee that I am not as other men are, extortioners, unjust, adulterers, or even

as this publican. I fast twice in the week, I give
tithes of all that I possess. And the publican
standing afar off, would not lift up so much as his
eyes unto Heaven, but smote upon his breast, saying,
God be merciful to me a sinner! I tell you," adds
our Lord, " that this man went down to his house
justified rather than the other!"

What, then, is the cause of this difference ? What
of the pharisee being rejected, what of the publican being, in comparison, preferred by the Almighty
searcher of hearts ? Was the pharisee a hypocrite,
who laid claim to virtuous habits to which he had
no pretension ? Was it untrue that he was really
strict beyond most of his countrymen in the morti-
fication of his appetites, and the payment of a part
of his substance to the service of God and the
ceremonies of religion ? *That* it would be hard to
believe, nor have we any reason to believe it from
the words of Scripture. He was, it will be observed, praying, and praying in words which no-
body heard—" he prayed thus *with himself.*" But
no man is weak enough to believe that he can tell
a lie to God; no man, who is not a madman, can
dare to insult his Maker by laying claim, when
that Maker only hears, to virtuous actions which
he knows to be imaginary. Or is God indifferent
whether our actions be good or evil ?—are prayers,
or fastings, or a careful concern for the decencies
of religion offensive to Him, or worthless in His
eyes ? On the contrary, our Saviour Himself has
laid down rules for His disciples when they fast;

He has Himself set us an example of religious fasting; and He has Himself said, when blaming the pharisees for their neglect of the weightier matters of the law, that, while they sinned greatly in leaving these undone, it behoved them also by no means to neglect the others[1].

Or was the publican, in reality, a person of exemplary conduct who afflicted himself unnecessarily on account of his spiritual state, and was, in truth, already a saint while he condemned himself as the worst of sinners. Neither of this is there any appearance. The pharisee, who seems to have known him, probably spoke the truth when he described him as a man of bad character. And it is remarkable, that neither does our Lord, notwithstanding his expressions of repentance, speak of him as of one, at present and absolutely in a justified state, but only that he was justified *rather* than the other, that his character, with all its faults, was less displeasing to God than the vain self praise and uncharitable censure of the pharisee. The publican might be, and probably was, a real sinner; the publican might be, and probably was, of a character offensive to God; and yet the pharisee might, in God's eyes, be still less accepted and acceptable. What then was his fault? He trusted in himself that he was righteous and despised others; and thus he threw away at a single stroke all the blessings which God might else have had in

---

[1] St. Matt. xxiii. 23.

store for his abstinence, his purity, his justice, his
attention to the religion of his Father ; and by a
little foolish self-love, and by a little ill-natured
comparison of himself with his neighbour, made
vain the endeavours of, perhaps, a long life, and,
while he thought that he was standing firmly,
made that very flattering thought the occasion of
a dismal fall !

Is it necessary that I should go on to explain
and vindicate the justice of such a sentence ? Will
not the common sense of those who hear me teach
them, that for even the best of men to boast himself before his Maker, must be to that Maker most
offensive, inasmuch as, however good he may be,
it is God to whom he owes it all ? The pharisee
himself, indeed, acknowledged this. He was not
so vain, he was not so silly as to be ignorant that
of himself he was able to do nothing ; and he
therefore gives, in words at least, the glory to God,
and thanks Him that he was not like other men,
an extortioner, unjust, or adulterous. But in this
very enumeration of God's favours to him, he
shows that he allowed himself to take a pride in
them : that, instead of endeavouring after a further
progress, he was idly amusing himself with viewing
the progress which he had already made ; uncon-
scious all the while how much ground his rivals in
the race were gaining on him. How much more
blameable then, how much more ridiculous (if any
thing could be a matter of ridicule in which the
souls of men are concerned), must their pretensions

be who reckon up their own good deeds, not as reasons for thankfulness to God, but as claims to reward or pardon from Him ; who talk of the good which they have done, or the harm which they have not done, as if, by its own value, it gave them a title to Heaven, and to come into the presence of their Maker not like His servants but His creditors !

Let us examine this matter a little further! Whoever prides himself on his own good deeds in the sight of God, must suppose one or both of two things ; either that those good deeds have of themselves some power to gratify or benefit God, so as that God *owes* him Heaven in repayment for the advantage which He has received from him, or that those actions for which he expects rewards were, at least, in his own choice to perform or to neglect, and such as if he had neglected them God could have had no reason for punishing him.   But how different from the truth are both these suppositions !   In the first instance, so highly exalted is God above all our actions and their consequences, that it is plain He needs none of our services ; that the obedience of such worms as we are is as nothing in His sight, whom all the cherubim and seraphim serve in their bright and burning stations, who " hath measured the waters in the hollow of His hands," and to whose call the lightenings answer, " here we are [1]."   It is only from His

<hr />

[1] Isaiah xl. 12. .Job xxxviii. 35.

love to us, for our own sakes, and in order to our
happiness, that He has made us at all, or has laid
any commands upon us.   He bids us love each
other, and do good to each other, because, by this
means, we each of us shall make the other happy
or relieve the other's distress.   He bids us be
sober, be honest, be chaste, be industrious, because
it is by an observance of these rules alone that we
can keep ourselves in health, in cheerfulness, in
plenty, and worldly prosperity.   He bids us pray
to Him, and give Him thanks, and serve Him, because He thus opens to us a fresh source of strength
for the discharge of our duties ; of hope and comfort under our necessary calamities ; of that spiri-
tuality of mind and acquaintance with Heavenly
things, which is the purest pleasure a man can
meet with here, and the necessary introduction to
still purer and brighter happiness hereafter.   But
in Himself God needs us not ! had we never been
born, our songs would never be missed in the full
chorus of angels ; and, were we all now to perish,
He could raise up from the dust beneath our feet
a better and a worthier race of creatures than we
are.   Who then are we, and what are our good
deeds, that we should venture to praise them in
His presence ?

But further, all these things in the performance
of which we pride ourselves are, after all, no more
than our duty.   We are commanded to do them ;
we are threatened most severely if we neglect
them.   All the good deeds which we have done

2

are, therefore, in fact, nothing more than so many
instances in which we have not done evil; and who
shall say that our not deserving hell, supposing it
to be true, would be, in itself an equitable claim on
such a vast reward as Heaven: or that our best
actions, being such as they are, would not be over-
paid by the life and health and happiness of a
single day, though we were immediately after to
sink into dust and be forgotten? Who then can
hope that such good actions as we can perform
can reasonably be placed in the balance against
our many evil deeds, or free us from the punishment which these last so loudly call for?

For this is another and a still more aweful reason for disclaiming all human merit, and placing
our only hopes of pardon in the great mercy of God,
by which also the publican in the parable sought
and found it. It is not merely the worthlessness
of our good deeds, but the number and greatness of
our evil deeds, which should fill us with humility
and fear in the presence of God; and lead us, instead of claiming reward, to acknowledge ourselves
worthy of the severest punishment. We have all
sinned, it is in vain to seek to hide it from ourselves, we have all sinned most grievously; if not
in those particulars, which the pharisee of whom
we have read mentioned, yet in many others which,
if less thought of by mankind, are no less strictly
forbidden by the Almighty; we are all God's
debtors to an infinite amount; and being so, it is
surely fitter far to cast ourselves on His mercy

altogether, than to set off our own pitiful balance
of good deeds, or supposed good deeds, as a reason
why judgement should not be passed on us.

But further, it may not be useless to remark the
disguises under which pride and self-conceit will
sometimes enter into our hearts ; and the manner
in which men are led to form high thoughts of
themselves, while they suppose that they are giving
the glory to God alone, and ascribing to Him alone
all the work of their salvation.   The pharisee was
ready enough to confess that it was of God alone
that he was less wicked than other men.   And I
have met with many serious persons who not only
acknowledged this, but affected to lay an exceeding stress on the doctrine, who yet were strangely
proud of their own supposed place in God's favour
as His elect, His chosen, His brands plucked forth
from the burning, and no less ready than the pharisee to make comparisons between themselves and
other men, and bless God that they were more
strict in their lives, more holy in their hearts, than
such or such poor lost creature, who never attended
church or meeting, or who was altogether unin-
formed or unconvinced of certain doctrines in which,
whether truly or falsely, they placed the sum and
substance of Christianity.

How offensive such conduct must be to God, a
moment's consideration will convince us.   " What
hast thou to do with thy neighbour's guilt or innocence ?"   Who art thou that judgest another man's
servant ?   To his own master he standeth or fall-

eth ¹." " Yea he shall be holden up if he acknowledges his sin and endeavours to forsake it; when
thou, with all thy greater advantages and greater
proficiency, mayst mourn, perhaps too late, thy own
presumption and want of charity."

There is a history told in one of the eastern writers which, for the moral which it affords, is here
not unfit to be mentioned, of a certain youth who
gave himself up to severe devotion, and passed
whole nights in the study of the Scriptures and in
prayer. " Behold," he said to his father, " how
these have forgotten their God, while I alone am
waking to His word and to His service!" " Alas,
my son," was that wise father's reply, " it were
better that thou hadst slept till the day of judgement than that thou shouldest thus wake to trust
in thyself that thou art righteous, and to speak evil
of thy brethren." He was a Mahometan who spake
thus; but from him it were well if very many Christians would learn that, do all they may, it is not
for them to institute comparisons with the weakest
and most unhappy of God's creatures.

Yet a few words to the occasion for which we
have many of us, I trust, during the last week, been
making preparation. Do we come, like this pharisee, trusting in ourselves? Do we come, like this
pharisee, inclined to condemn our neighbours? Or
do we come in the deep sense of our own weakness,
in the sorrowful recollection of our own misdeeds,

¹ Romans xiv. 4.

in the earnest desire to forsake our evil ways,
and in the hope, a sure and certain hope, that on
us who acknowledge ourselves sinners, the Lord
will show abundant mercy ? We have a more painful knowledge than even the publican described by
our Lord could possess of the danger of sin, and
its great offensiveness in the eyes of our Maker;
inasmuch as we know, which he could not, that to
obtain pardon for the sins of the world, it was necessary that God Himself should give us His beloved Son to be offered as a bloody sacrifice. We
have a more certain and blessed hope than this penitent publican enjoyed; inasmuch as that atonement, which he only knew through figures and
prophecies, we have known and felt as a historical
and spiritual certainty; so that not only by the
blood of bulls and of goats, but by the pure and
sinless blood of the blessed Jesus, we look to have
our sins done away, and our pardon sealed, and a
more blessed strength to be hereafter given us to
the forsaking of every evil way, and the purifying of
our conscience towards God.

Let us only not be wanting to ourselves; let us
only seek His grace through its appointed channels, and bending low before His altar, and receiving with deep humility the pledges of His peace, let
us renounce all hope but in Him alone, and cry
out each of us in our hearts to Him who is ready
to hear and to save, God be merciful to me a
sinner!

SERMON IX.

THE GOOD SAMARITAN.

[Preached at Delhi, Jan. 2, 1825.]

St. Luke x. 36, 37.

Which now of these three, thinkest thou, was neighbour unto him
that fell among the thieves? And he said, he that showed
mercy on him. Then said Jesus unto him, Go, and do thou
likewise.

THE discourses which Christ delivered to the people in the form of parables, may be classed under
three descriptions. Some of them are short and
simple stories intended for our example only, or to
explain His doctrine. Such is the parable of the
unjust judge, which has no hidden meaning, and is
merely introduced to illustrate the force of continued prayer. In some again, such as those where
He likens the kingdom of Heaven to a marriage
supper, a vineyard let out to husbandmen, and a
sower scattering seed, He describes in obscure language, and under the form of an allegory, His own
dealings with mankind, and the future fortunes of
the Christian Church. Thirdly, there are some
which partake of both these kinds; they contain an
inward and doctrinal meaning, which refers to the

faith of Christians, and a practical lesson, if they
are taken according to the letter, which is a guide
and example to their lives.   In both these ways the
parable of the good Samaritan affords us valuable
instruction.   If taken according to the letter, it is
a beautiful example of charity ; and if we go further into its meaning, and see, as I shall presently
explain, the Son of God represented by this benevolent traveller, we then are taught to derive our
love for mankind from the love which Christ has
shown to us, and His example is enforced by our
gratitude.

One of the teachers of the law of Moses, the
same order of men who are elsewhere called scribes,
had endeavoured to ensnare our Saviour by the solemn question, " what shall I do to inherit eternal
life [1] ?"   How this question was to ensnare does not
immediately appear; it might be to draw from Him
something contrary to the law of Moses, or offensive to the prejudices of the people ; it might be
accompanied by an insulting tone or manner, as if
to say, " what are these mighty discoveries which
prophets and kings have desired in vain ?"   At all
events, it was asked from motives of ill-will, and in
the hope to injure Christ.   Our Lord, in His answer, refers him to the passage in Deuteronomy
which, from his office, he read publicly every Sabbath.   " What is written in the law ?" are His
words, " How readest thou ?"   The lawyer replies,

[1] St. Luke x. 19.

" Thou shalt love the Lord thy God with all thy
heart, and with all thy soul, and with all thy
strength, and with all thy mind, and thy neighbour
as thyself.   And He said unto him, thou hast answered right; this do, and thou shalt live[1]."

But though the scribe had answered right, there
were reasons why our Lord's reference to this passage of Scripture was very unpleasing to him.   Not
only was it so wise and so true, and so conformable
to the law of Moses, that no accusation or slander
could be built on it, and all his malice and insult
was retorted on his own head; but his conscience
could not but inform him that he was openly condemned by his own law.   How could he boast of
loving his neighbour, who was even then laying
snares for the life of Christ; who with the deepest
malice and subtlety was asking a solemn question
in the hope of ruining his teacher.   He felt, it may
well be, that his words had judged himself; and to
escape this application of them, (as the Scripture
says, " to justify himself,") he caught at the cap-
tious distinctions of the Jewish doctors, and de-
manded, " who is my neighbour[2]?"   Jesus, instead
of answering as He might have done, " I, Jesus,
whom thou persecutest," is contented with a milder
method of instruction in the beautiful parable which
follows, and which is too well known to need repe-
tition.

The scenery and circumstances of the story

---

[1] St. Luke x. 26—28.   [2] Ver. 29.

were familiar to all who heard them, and were
such as might happen daily.   The road between
Jerusalem and Jericho is now, and always has been,
dismal and dangerous.   Is is through a deep and
barren valley, without grass, or water, or inhabitants, except savage bands of robbers, whose cruelties were so frequent that the road was generally
known by the name of the bloody way.   Any Jew,
therefore, who heard our Lord's discourse might
have fallen, himself, into the peril which is here
described, and the story, if we take it in its plainest
sense, told them, more forcibly than ten thousand arguments, to do unto others as they would
wish that others should act by them.   But this
was not the only, nor the main intention of the
parable, which, as it applied to the lawyer, was to
prove the claim which Christ had to his love and
gratitude, and to show the total insufficiency of
the law of Moses to rescue human nature from its
miserable condition.   The unfortunate plundered
traveller is, then, a representative of all mankind.
They, like him, have departed from Jerusalem, the
city of God, His favour, or the light of His countenance; and set their face towards the pursuits
and pleasures of this world, those temptations
which are represented under the name of Jericho,
a town which, as you will read in the book of
Joshua, was accursed of God, and devoted to everlasting ruin[1].   And, like this traveller, by their

---

[1] Joshua vi. 17.

departure from Jerusalem, they have fallen into a valley of blood, into the power of the worst of thieves, and the most cruel of murderers, the devil and his angels. And now stripped of his raiment of righteousness, wounded to the very death, and his wounds festering in the face of Heaven, man is left in the naked misery of his nature, without hope, or help, or comfort. A certain priest comes down that way ; by him are signified the sacrifices offered for sin in the earlier ages of the world, the offerings of Melchisedek, Noah, and Abraham. But to help this wretched object the blood of bulls and of goats was vain ; it could not cleanse his conscience, nor heal the wounds inflicted by his spiritual enemies ; the sacrifice passes by on the other side. A Levite next appears ; the representative of the Jewish law given by Moses, himself of the tribe of Levi, and administered in all its ceremonies by the Levite family. Moses is, indeed, represented as aware of the extent of the evil, and the miserable condition of mankind; he approaches, he looks on the sufferer, but will not, or cannot help him ; no ceremonies, no outward form of holiness are here of service ; he passes by on the other side.

But " a certain Samaritan," (do you not remember how the Jews had said to Jesus, " thou art a Samaritan, and hast a devil[1] ?") " A certain Samaritan," saith our Lord, using their own lan-

---

[1] St. John viii. 48.

guage, and the insults which they had thrown out
against Him, " as he journeyed, came where he
was ; and when he saw him he had compassion on
him, and went to him, and bound up his wounds,
pouring in oil and wine, and set him on his own
beast, and brought him to an inn, and took care of
him[1]." Do you not perceive, my Christian friends,
do not your own hearts inform you how truly this
parable represents our blessed Saviour ? He, when
no other help was found, when neither sacrifices
nor ceremonies could have saved us from perishing miserably in our sins, He came to us; He
bound up the wounds which the malice of the devil
had inflicted ; He expended His own provision,
His own life and blood to heal them ; and bore us
safely and tenderly to the ark of His holy covenant,
which is here represented as an inn, under whose
shelter all the sojourners of this world were to be
received, of every nation and caste, and however
wide had formerly been their wanderings.

Nor does His care stop here ; on the morrow
when He departed, for how short alas ! was the
stay of God among men ! though He is constrained
to leave the sufferer, he commits him to kind and
careful hands, with sufficient supplies for his present
necessity, and a promise of ample payment at his
second coming for all the good that should be done
to the least of these his brethren. And so closely
do even the smallest circumstances of the parable

---

[1] St. Luke x. 33, 34.

1

agree with this explanation, that the ancient doctors and fathers of the Church are of opinion that by the two pieces of silver, (which are in our version rendered pence, though their value was, in fact, much greater) by these two pieces of silver are represented the sacraments which are left for the support of Christians, till their good Samaritan shall return again, and which are committed to the care of the clergy who are represented here as hosts of Christ's inn, and dispensers of His spiritual provision and bounty. " Which now of these three," continues our Saviour, " was neighbour unto him that fell among the thieves?" Was it the priest with the sacrifices of blood? Was it Moses the Levite in whose law thou trustest? Or, lastly, was it I whom the Jews called a Samaritan? " He," the lawyer was compelled to answer, " he that showed mercy on him." Then said Jesus, " As I have loved you, even so do ye also love one another;—as far as the difference between us will admit, imitate my example—go and do thou likewise[1]."

The doctrine, then, contained in this parable may be stated in a few words ; that mankind by the malice of the devil were robbed of God's grace, and brought into a state of misery, and into the shadow of death, from which neither sacrifices, nor ceremonies, nor any effort which man could make, nor any revelation which God thought proper to

[1] St. Luke x. 36, 37.

declare before the Messiah's coming, were able to
recover them; and that (in the words of our Church
service,) " there is no other name given to man
through whom we may receive salvation, but only
the name of our Lord Jesus Christ."

The practical lessons to be drawn from it are
also of the most exceeding consequence to our salvation.   First, from the example here given us by
Christ, we may learn to "go and do likewise;"
to consider all mankind as our neighbours and
brethren; and to do them all the good in our
power.   And that this love and desire to do
them service is not to be confined to those only
whom we know, or with whom we are connected;
for the traveller described in the parable, was a
perfect stranger to the Samaritan, and no otherwise connected with him than as he wanted his
help.   But further, the Jews and Samaritans were
bitter enemies, hating each other as unclean and
unholy.   Yet this good man flings from him, at
once, we see, all former hate, all remembrance of
ancient injuries, and recollects only that the miserable wretch who is bleeding before him is a
man and a brother.   And shall we presume to let
our party feelings, our prejudices, or our own poor
resentments interfere with the commands of God,
or the duty which we owe to our brethren! When
our fellow-creature is perishing for lack of our
help, shall we plead that he is a stranger, that he
is nothing to us, that he has used us ill formerly,
and can expect nothing at our hands?   " As we

have therefore opportunity," are the words of the apostle, "let us do good unto all men [1]!"

But, secondly, we must not show our love in common expressions of pity, or excuse ourselves from doing nothing on the pretence that little is in our power. Some men will tell us gravely, that they cannot give to every beggar that asks, and therefore they shut their hearts against all. But if this Samaritan, because he could not build a hospital, because he could not give up his time to watch on that dangerous road for the many other wretches who were stripped and wounded there; if on these pretences, for I cannot call them reasons, he had left this man to perish, whom it was in his power to save, what should we have said or thought of such cruel prudence? Be not deceived; impossibilities are not required of us, but as far as we can, we must be merciful; and that our means of doing good may reach the farther, we must learn from this kind traveller. He went himself on foot that he might assist the dying man with his horse; he with his own hands bound up his wounds, and laid out on him the oil and wine which he had prepared for his own journey. In like manner we should keep a watch over our little useless expences, and deny ourselves some unnecessary luxuries or comforts, that we may have to give to them that need. Blessed is he who is frugal, for he is able to be generous.

[1] Gal. vi. 10.

Thirdly, we may draw from this parable very useful instruction as to the duty both of the clergy and of those committed to their care. We see that the wounded traveller, who represents mankind, was not immediately restored to health and vigour, but was to remain under cure till the second coming of his deliverer. And during this time, the ministers of the Gospel, as hosts of Christ's inn, and distributors of His Sacraments, are to view themselves in no other light than as patient nurses of a sick and feeble world.

Happy are they among our number, whom the Lord, when He cometh, shall find so doing; and woe, everlasting woe to those who neglect their duty! But you, my friends, you are also called upon to shew your gratitude to our good Samaritan, the Redeemer of our souls, by submitting to the advice and government of those in whose care He has left you. You must not murmur uncharitably at our imperfections, or seek unadvisedly after new doctrines, or new spiritual medicines. You must not leave the sound word of God to pamper your appetites with change; nor wander lightly from the shelter of the Church into the howling wilderness which surrounds it. It is your business and your duty, by a patient use of the regular means of grace, by devout hearing of the word of God, and diligent and faithful attendance on His Sacraments, to perfect the cure which Christ has begun in your hearts; and it is the business and duty of all, in whatever station they may be placed, by praying for each other, helping each other and bearing each other's burdens to fulfill the law of Christ.   This is His first and His last commandment, the beginning and the end of the Christian faith, that as He has loved us so should we love one another.   To Him we can give no worthy honour; our praise, our service, our gratitude are without power to reward the Almighty; but all He asks and all He requires as a return for His help and mercy, is that we should " Go and do likewise!"

SERMON X.

LABOURERS IN THE VINEYARD.

[Preached at Bombay, May 22, 1825.]

St. Matt. xx. 16.

So the last shall be first, and the first last ; for many be called,
but few chosen.

The parable which these words conclude, was
spoken by our Lord in correction of a little natural vanity in which St. Peter had indulged, when
contemplating the sacrifices which he and his brother apostles had made in the cause of the Messiah.
A certain young man of ample property, and of
dispositions favourable to religion, had been honoured by Christ, either as a test of his faith, or as
a mark of approbation of his virtues, with a call to
His ministry, and to the number of His chosen disciples. Dismayed, however, at the danger and self-
denial by which such a life was menaced, encum-
bered by his affection for the world, and by the
comforts and luxuries of his present condition, he
shrunk back, though sadly and unwillingly, from

the offered boon, and " went away sorrowful, for he had great possessions[1]." On this our Lord took occasion to remark, as may be seen in the preceding chapter, on the fascinating nature of worldly wealth, and the absolute necessity of a more than common dispensation of celestial grace, to enable the rich man to break the chain of pleasure and of pride, to resist the many and peculiar temptations with which his path in life is strewn, and to resign, if it should become his duty, his rank, his fortune, and his ease, in the service of that God from whom he has received them.

While He was thus speaking, and thus, as it should seem, lamenting the dangerous wealth of the young man who had just gone away, it is easy to perceive what was passing in St. Peter's mind. " If the sacrifice of wealth would have been so precious in the eyes of God, then, surely, the self-devotion of the poor must, at least, be equally well pleasing to Him. I and my fellows had, indeed, somewhat less to resign, but what we had, we gave up for Christ ; the comfort of a settled home, the security of peaceful labour, the endearments of our kindred, the implements of our toil, and all those numberless and nameless ties which bind the poor man, even more than the rich, to the scenes of his childish sports, the recollections of his earliest love, the limits of his humble ambition,—all these we resigned, and we resigned them cheerfully."

[1] St. Matt. xix. 22.

" Behold we have forsaken all and followed Thee! what shall we have therefore ?"

The answer of our Lord is more than usually impressive and beautiful. While assuring His ardent and affectionate disciple of an ample and overflowing recompense, He replies to his thoughts as well as to his words, and cautions him against supposing that all who now seemed comparatively backward in the cause of the Gospel, should remain for ever idle and indifferent; or that none but those who were the first and immediate companions of the Messiah, should be admitted to their proportionate share in the toils and honours of His kingdom. " I say unto you," are His words, " that ye which have followed me in the regeneration, when the Son of Man shall sit on the throne of His glory, ye also shall sit upon twelve thrones, judging the twelve tribes of Israel. And every one that hath forsaken houses, or brethren, or sisters, or father, or mother, or wife, or children, or lands, for my name's sake, shall receive an hundred fold, and shall inherit everlasting life. But many that are first shall be last, and the last shall be first [1]."

As if He had said, " Doubt not, Peter, that thou and thy companions will receive from a bountiful God a rich return for all your labours in His cause; doubt not that whatever sacrifices are made, for my sake, of present ease, of present possession, of present and worldly affections, will be all no less duly

[1] St. Matt. xix. 28—30.

and mercifully appreciated by Him, who will not
suffer even a cup of water given in His name to
pass without its recompence. But deem not yourselves so secure of my love by the sacrifices which
you *have* made as to relax in your future services.
Judge not those who stand idle now, for the time
of their labouring may come. Of you who have
been my earliest followers there is one who shall
betray his Lord; and another, even thou thyself,
shalt basely and shamelessly deny me. And there
is one whose name ye know not, and who is now
my bitter enemy, one Saul of Tarsus, to whom I
shall, hereafter, make myself known, who, having
received my faith, shall labour more abundantly
than you all, and come not a whit behind the
chiefest of my earlier Apostles." " For the kingdom of Heaven," our Lord proceeds to say, " the
kingdom of Heaven is like unto a man which is an
householder, which went out early in the morning
to hire labourers into his vineyard; and when he
had agreed with the labourers for a penny a day,
he sent them into his vineyard. And he went out
about the third hour, and saw others standing idle
in the market-place, and said unto them, go ye
also into the vineyard, and whatsoever is right I
will give you; and they went their way. Again he
went out about the sixth and ninth hour, and did
likewise. And about the eleventh hour he went
out, and found others standing idle, and saith unto
them, why stand ye here all the day idle ? They
say unto him, because no man hath hired us. He

saith unto them, go ye also into the vineyard, and
whatsoever is right, that shall ye receive.   So when
even was come, the Lord of the vineyard saith unto
his steward, call the labourers and give them their
hire, beginning from the last unto the first.   And
when they came that were hired about the eleventh
hour, they received every man a penny.   But when
the first came, they supposed that they should have
received more ; and they likewise received every
man a penny.   And when they had received it,
they murmured against the good man of the house,
saying, these last have wrought but one hour, and
thou hast made them equal unto us which have
borne the burden and heat of the day.   But he
answered one of them, and said, Friend, I do thee
no wrong ; didst not thou agree with me for a
penny ? take that thine is, and go thy way ; I will
give unto this last, even as unto thee.   Is it not
lawful for me to do what I will with mine own ? is
thine eye evil because I am good ?   So the last
shall be first and the first last, for many be called
but few chosen."

Is there any here who can impugn the justice of
such an expostulation ?   Is there any who does
not perceive that, when the earliest labourers had
received their stipulated hire, they had no colourable ground of murmuring against their employer
for giving an equal sum to any other whom he
chose to favour ?   Can we fail to recollect that of
all these labourers the necessities were the same,
though their opportunities of earning a supply had

not been equal; that the same kindness which called them in when so little remained to be done, might naturally be expected to prompt a liberal employer to proportion his bounty to their wants rather than to their merits ; and that he who might unblamed have relieved those wants without exacting any labour at all, was equally justified in exacting no more labour than the approach of night enabled them to apply effectually ?

Though, therefore, (as we have seen from the circumstances under which the parable was spoken) its primary application was plainly to the hope and reward of the Christian ministry, and its intention was to rebuke the self-exaltation of Peter, and to prepare both himself and his fellow apostles for the reception of future teachers of the Gospel and future participants in glory ; though this was, I say, its primary meaning, yet its principle is obviously capable of a far wider and more important application, as illustrative of the general dealings of the Almighty with mankind, and of the manner, more particularly, in which, under the Gospel, mankind in general are admitted to mercy and salvation.

I do not mean, as some have mistakenly supposed, I do not mean, that this parable can be fairly said to convey the doctrine (which is not very consonant with reason, and which is directly opposed to many positive assertions of Scripture) that the condition of the blessed in another world is to be alike to all ; and that, whatever their ex-

ertions in the cause of God, they are not to differ
from each other in glory.   Such a supposition is
opposed to the express declaration of our Lord
that in His " Father's house are many mansions ;"
it is opposed in a no less striking manner to the
memorable parable of the talents [1]; it is opposed
by all which we are told in Scripture of that celestial hierarchy of angels, whose fellow citizens we
ourselves hope to become ; it is opposed by the
specific promise which our Lord had just made to
His twelve that *they* should sit on twelve thrones,
in sovereignty as well as in dignity, exalted over
the tribes of believing Israelites.

But, in truth, those enquirers may do worse than
lose their labour, who seek in the illustrations and
parables of Scripture a detailed as well as a general
likeness of the objects which they are intended to
explain, and are discontented with the portrait if
they miss the minutest feature of the original. For
no purpose of instruction can such an accuracy of
circumstances be required ; on no principle of poetry
or eloquence is such servility of adaptation desirable.   When a lion is held up to the imitation of a
warrior fighting for his native land, shall this be
gravely received as a recommendation to contend,
like the lion, with the weapons only which nature
has furnished ?   When the sluggard is sent to the
anthill for instruction, did the wise king of Israel
intend him to scoop his dwelling in the ground ?

[1] St. John xiv. 2.   St. Matt. xxv. 14—30.

What would become of Esop and Bidpai, if their apologues were expounded by the same minuteness of allegory ?   Or what renders it necessary to suppose in the present instance, that the rewards of Heaven will, necessarily, be all on an equality, while we refuse at the same time, which we must refuse, to suppose that envy, murmuring, and an evil eye will be found among the spirits of just men made perfect ?

All, therefore, which the spirit of the parable necessarily implies, and all which it can be supposed to imply, (when coupled with the circumstances under which it was spoken, and compared with other passages of Scripture) is an assertion of the absolute sovereignty of God over His works, and the absolute freedom of His bounties to them ; a declaration that the rewards of another state of existence are not a matter of debt, but of grace and mercy, and that, in the distribution of these rewards the Almighty will be guided by a reference to the necessities of mankind as much as to their virtues ; and more particularly that those virtues so far as, for Christ's sake and in His name, they can be taken account of at all, will be sometimes estimated by proportions entirely distinct from the length of our Christian course, and the amount of opportunities afforded to us.

I will endeavour to explain myself, and in so doing to vindicate, by His help, the mercy and justice of the Most High.   It is, in the first place, certain from the whole tenour of the Gospel, and if

direct testimonies were wanting, it might be in-
ferred from the present parable, that no man can
either enter into a state of grace, or work out the
salvation once begun by God's Spirit, in his heart,
except by the preventing and supporting grace of
that blessed Spirit alone.   It is God's gift that he
is called.   It is God's vineyard in which he is pri-
vileged to labour ; and the power and opportunities
of doing good are, like tools for the day, supplied
to him by God alone.

In thus maintaining God's absolute sovereignty,
I am not maintaining the doctrine of absolute de-
crees.   I cannot conceive that God ever uses His
sovereignty in that manner ; though grace is free,
it will not follow that it is employed irresistibly ;
and, for all which appears to the contrary in the
present parable, the labourers who were sent into
the vineyard might, as well as the guests who were
invited to the marriage supper, have refused to go,
and have preferred their previous idleness, or the
service of a different master.   But with such as
accept the call, with such as persevere in their
labours, with such as, on account of these labours,
have reason to expect everlasting life from their
Heavenly Father, with all such the calling has been
of God ; and for that calling, and all its blessed
consequences, they owe to God unbounded thankfulness, and have reason to ascribe to His goodness
alone even the covenanted rewards which they receive from Him.   But it is obvious that His goodness to them, being thus free, cannot be lessened

by the fact that He shows to certain of their brethren a greater goodness still ; they are, themselves,
paid beyond their deserts ; and it is envy alone, of
all evil passions the worst and basest, which can
find pain in the happiness of another. Yet even in
this dispensation of our God, as represented to us
in the present parable, is nothing capricious or unintelligible, inasmuch as other considerations innumerable, besides the duration, or even outward success of our Christian course, must have their weight
with the Alljust and Allwise.

One believer, for instance, is placed by His providence in a distinguished and, outwardly, an arduous station of duty. He bears the burthen and the
heat of the day ; he rides in the foremost ranks of
the armies of His invincible Lord ; he carries the
banner of the cross where it is assailed by the po-
tentates of earth, and the princes of the power of
the air; and he fights, through a long life, the good
fight of faith successfully, being encouraged and
supported, in part it may be, by the very conspicu-
ousness of the sphere in which he moves, and still
more and more, undoubtedly, by that secret influence of the Most High, which hath girded his loins
with strength, and covered his head in the day of
battle.

The pilgrimage of another is of an obscurer kind;
his walk is through the secret paths of life, unknown, unpraised, perhaps reproved and slighted.
He has no converts to show ; he has had no splendid opportunities of evincing his love of God and

2

his dauntless faith in his Redeemer. His warfare
has been within; and in weakness and fear, in solitude and silence, he has struggled with the defects
of an imperfect education, with the discouragement
of unsuccessful labours, with the infirmities of a
peevish and distrustful temper, with the unkindness
or neglect of men, and with the indescribable terrours of those powers of darkness which are most
potent with the weak and melancholy. Yet, though
he has trembled, he has not yielded; yet, though
he has done little, he has endeavoured all he could;
yet, though he has been encompassed with darkness and dismay, from the deeps he hath called
upon God; and his eye, from the midst of the
valley of the shadow of death, has been bent on the
heavenly Sion! And of these two candidates, these
martyrs of different descriptions, which best may
claim the palm? I know not; who but God can
know! But the men are both gone to their reward; and I am convinced that the more illustrious
and distinguished servant of Christ would be neither
surprised nor grieved to find his weaker brother set
beside him!

It is the same with every exercise of the graces
and virtues of Christianity. A man is judged, and
if judged then surely recompensed, according to
that which he hath, not according to that which he
hath not. This man, we will suppose, has an
ample fortune, and uses that fortune nobly. He
supports missions, he founds hospitals, he relieves
the bodily and spiritual wants of hundreds. This

other is himself but little, if at all, elevated above
the condition of an object of charity; yet he steals
from his own repose to watch by the sick-bed of a
neighbour; he defrauds his own scanty meal to
share it with those who are yet more necessitous.
The one is a mighty river, which bears wealth and
fertility to many provinces; the other is a little
mountain spring, whose rills are but sufficient to
nourish a drooping flower, or to offer a cup of cold
water to a fainting traveller. But is the widow's
mite forgotten? or who shall doubt that, under
circumstances of which God alone is the fitting
judge, it may be, when the river and the spring
have alike rolled their waters to the ocean of eternity, that the one may, in proportion to its course
and its quantity, have been as valuable as the
other!

The same observation will apply to a longer and
a shorter life, or, to approach more closely to the
particular circumstances of the parable, to the
strongest case of all, of an earlier or later conversion to the faith and practice of Christianity. It is
a great and blessed thing when a man has, from
his youth up, been faithful; neither transgressed
in any considerable respect, the will of his Heavenly Father. For such a one a crown of glory is
laid up; for such a one the promise abideth sure
that he shall dwell in the presence of God for ever!
How many dangers does he not escape who, from
the beginning of his course, has never widely wan-
dered! How many fears, how many bitter sorrows,

how many struggles against habits of lengthened
evil, how many agonies unspeakable of repentance,
of shame, of doubt, of terrour and despair, has he
escaped, which must be assuredly undergone by
him who at the third, the sixth, or, still more, at
the eleventh hour, is awakened to a sense of his
condition.   Yet even of this last, whose day is
drawing to a close, the case, though most perilous,
is not altogether desperate.   His heart may yet be
touched ; he may yet seek the face of the Lord sincerely, humbly, penitently ; and that gracious Lord,
before whose angels there is joy on the conversion
of a single sinner, that Lord who bare with Him
from the cross the spirit of the penitent thief to
Paradise, will not disdain even the offering of a
single and a last hour, nor shut the gates of Heaven
against repentance under any circumstances.   But
can he regain his lost ground in the race ?   Can he,
beginning late, yet equal his earlier competitors ?
that must depend on ten thousand different circumstances ; but it must, under all circumstances to a
certain degree, depend on himself.   His task will
be the harder, too hard I own for a dying man ; and
for an old man, unassisted by an extraordinary measure of Divine grace, beyond the reach of possibility ; yet much may, in the strength of the Most
High, be done ; and if he sanctifies his few remaining years to the service of God, with a livelier faith
in proportion as his end is nearer, a deeper sorrow
in proportion as his sense of guilt is keener, a holier
fear in proportion as his danger is great, and an

unbounded love in proportion as the mercy shown
to him is unbounded, it may be that some of those
who have in past life accounted him reprobate,
may to their surprise, but in Heaven surely not
to their envy, hear the sentence, " I will give unto
this last even as unto thee !"

The sum of all is this, that the most experienced
Christian has great need to fly from confidence ;
and the most dispirited penitent no reason for indulging in despair.   The first, even in his most
prosperous course, will do well to take heed, lest
those, whom he has left far behind, should, through
his carelessness, be gaining ground on him ; and
he should learn to think more comfortably and
hopefully of many whose present condition appears most estranged from God, inasmuch as we
know not but an acceptable time may yet be
found, in which they may be called of God, and
hear His voice, and gladly and successfully become
His labourers.   The second may be emboldened
to a more excellent zeal and a warmer piety, to improve to the best advantage whatever time remains
to them, by the assurance that for those who labour
well even a single hour, a reward may be in store,
at which even their associates in glory may be
astonished.   But let all men beware how they suffer precedents of this sort to withdraw them from
a timely care of their salvation, as knowing that
whenever they are last called is the eleventh hour
to them, that the later our repentance is deferred,
it must needs be the more arduous and sorrowful ;

that neither youth nor middle age are exempt from
the accidents of mortality ; that though life should
be granted, it does not follow that grace will return ; and that he who commits his soul to the
chance of an evening which may never arrive, and
a warning which may never be granted to him,
may learn too late the consequence of his unspeakable folly, when the vintage is ended and the night
is come, and the steward of the vineyard shall descend in His Father's name to recompense their
deserts alike to the profitable and unprofitable
servant !

SERMON XI[1].

THE CONVERSION OF THE HEATHEN.

[Preached at Bombay, on Whitsunday, May 22; at Colombo, September 18; and at Calcutta, on Advent Sunday, November 27, 1825; in aid of the Incorporated Society for the Propagation of the Gospel in Foreign Parts.]

Acts ii. 38, 39.

The promise is unto you and to your children and to all that are afar off, even as many as the Lord our God shall call.

On the nature and certainty of that illustrious event which we are assembled this day to commemorate ; on the personality and divinity of that mighty Spirit whose advent has been now re-

---

[1] This Sermon is published agreeably to a promise made by his Lordship to the several Archidiaconal Committees formed upon its delivery. It is printed exactly as it was originally preached at Bombay. The body of the Discourse was substantially the same when delivered at Colombo and Calcutta, the introduction only, which relates to the day of Pentecost, being altered as the several occasions required. It was the intention of the Bishop to deliver it again at Madras on his return from his visitation of the Peninsula. It is unnecessary to relate the sad event by which this intention was frustrated.—*Calcutta Editor.*

N

corded; of the manner in which His testimony confirmed the truth of our Saviour's mission from the
Father; and on the blessed support, consolation,
and protection, which the universal Church, and
each individual member of it have since continued
to receive from Him; on these natural and usual
topics of discussion on the day of Pentecost, on
which it is reasonable to suppose the majority of
Christians informed, and on which I have abundant
reason to believe my present audience well instructed, it is not now my intention to address you.
There is another consideration, less obvious, or less
frequently insisted on, but which arises no less naturally from the circumstances under which the Holy
Ghost was given; and which, in connection with
those circumstances, I shall endeavour to impress
on your conviction; I mean the diffusive and universal character of the revelation of God's will
through His Son; the interest which every nation
under Heaven possesses in the Christian covenant;
and the obligation which rests upon every believer
to assist and forward, in his station and according
to his ability, the extension of that knowledge
whereby he is himself made wise unto salvation,
the communication of those spiritual riches which
he has himself received so freely.

That the message of mercy brought by Christ to
mankind was the common heritage of all who partake in our human nature; that to the Shiloh who
should come, the gathering of the nations was to
be; and that, in the promised descendant of Abra-

ham's loins all the tribes of the earth were to be called blessed, are truths so broadly stated in Scripture, and so universally received by those who defer to scriptural authority, that it seems needless, at this time of day, and among those who are not professed unbelievers, to prove that the religion of His Son was designed by God as the religion of all mankind; that it was the will of the Most High that His knowledge should cover the earth as the waters cover the sea; and that the false systems and false divinities of former ages should be consigned, by the disclosure of a holier and sublimer creed, to the custody of oblivion, of neglect and scorn; to the moles of their consecrated grottos, and the bats of their dark and deserted temples.

In conformity with these principles, and with innumerable passages in the ancient prophetic writings, in which these principles are developed and confirmed, we find our Lord, while on earth, announcing to his Jewish disciples His anticipation of other sheep of a different and distant fold; we find the same Lord, when already risen from the dead, sending forth His disciples, so soon as they should have received power from on high, to preach the Gospel to every creature; we find the promised Comforter, in the miraculous glory which He shed forth, and the miraculous gifts which He communicated, assuming a form and confirming a faculty, of which the one was without meaning, and the other without utility, except as symbols and instruments of diffusive light and knowledge; and

we find, lastly, in the counsel given by St. Peter to
his alarmed and conscience-smitten countrymen,
that the promise, consequent on baptism, of re-
mission of sins, and the gifts and comforts of God's
Spirit, was not only to them and to their children,
but to as many as God should call from the
furthest regions of the earth, and the nations previously most estranged from the knowledge and
worship of Jehovah.

It may be thought, indeed, that on this avowed
intention, and these repeated injunctions of the
Most High, the duty of endeavouring the conversion of the heathen might rest with sufficient security even abstracted from every other consideration of charity to the heathen themselves, and the
desire, which is natural to every well constituted
mind, of imparting to others those blessings which
we ourselves most value.

That man would be no dutiful servant, that man
would be any thing but an affectionate son, who,
even without a positive command, and with no
more than a bare intimation of the wishes of his
father or his lord, should hesitate to employ the best
exertions in his power to fulfil his blameless desires, and perform his righteous pleasure ; and
still less are the express injunctions of a parent or
a superior to be slighted, because we ourselves do
not at once perceive the expediency of an order,
or apprehend, without having made the trial, its
entire success impossible.   When David expressed,
though it were but a transient wish, to drink of the

fountain which welled up beside the gate of Bethlehem, his valiant men rushed forward, at once,
sword in hand, to forestall his commands, and
brought back from the thickest of the enemy, in
their helmets, that blood-bought water which their
sovereign had barely longed after. And the history
of every age is full of illustrious examples of obedience and loyalty, in which the severest labours
have been undergone, and the most appalling dangers encountered, in execution of commands, the
motives of which have been but imperfectly known,
or the policy of which has been even more than
doubted. Let but the professed followers of God
and His Son entertain the same desire to please
their Lord which was displayed by Abishai and
his comrades; let but the professed believers in
Christ exhibit the same trust in His wisdom and
deference to His authority, which is claimed by
every public man from his soldiers and subordinate
functionaries, and we may be assured that the attempt to communicate a knowledge of the truth to
the Gentiles will be no longer neglected or opposed as an unauthorised or chimerical labour.

If, indeed, that be true, which no professing
Christian will gainsay; if the religion of Christ be
acknowledged as that form of doctrine which most
of all represents God as He is, and in that sublime
and amiable character which the aweful Judge, the
mighty King, the most merciful Father of all,
maintains with His subjects and His offspring; if it

teaches men to reject all erroneous and degrading
notions of God, and to serve Him in the manner
most worthy of and most acceptable to Him ; it is
really hard to say, by what process of self-deception
a man can be led to suppose that he himself loves
and honours the Almighty, who yet is indifferent
or averse to the vindication of His name and attributes among his fellow-creatures. Of this feeling
we are all abundantly sensible where our own
honour, or the honour of any person whom we
really value is implicated. And I appeal to all
who hear me, whether, if even a tenth part of
those absurdities and abominations were asserted
of an earthly friend, an earthly parent, an earthly
sovereign or benefactor, which the heathen around
us, in their ignorance and superstition, assert and
believe of God Most High, our best and most persevering endeavours would not be employed to do
justice to the misrepresented friend, and undeceive
the blinded calumniator.

Nor is this obligation weakened by the objection
which is frequently brought forward, (sometimes
against the truth of the Christian doctrine itself,
and sometimes against the necessity of proclaiming
that doctrine to the Gentiles), that if God were
really displeased with the varieties of religious faith
which exist among mankind, or if He were really
so desirous as we suppose Him to be, for the universal adoption of any one religious system, He
has means in His hand for at once accomplishing

His purpose, without waiting for the tardy feet of those human agents, whose office it is to bear the good tidings of salvation.

Of this objection, as employed against the truth of Christianity itself, I know not that, in the present place, I am bound to take any notice. It is not my present business to discuss the evidences of our faith ; and, while addressing a congregation of Christians, I am justified in reasoning on Christian principles only, and taking for granted the data on which all Christians are agreed, that our religion is true, and that it is the best and most perfect which the Almighty has ever made known to His creatures. But as the notion to which I have alluded is at the bottom of very much of the avowed or lurking infidelity which we meet with, I may be excused for observing, that the objection against the Divine origin of the Gospel, which is taken from the pretended narrow limits within which the Gospel has been yet received, is alike unfortunate both in the facts which it assumes and in the arguments which it founds on them.

The adducers have, in the first place, misrepresented or misconceived the general purport of our Saviour's prophecies, in which, though the final triumph of His cause is often foretold, its immediate reception or rapid progress among men is never so much as intimated. The direct contrary is, indeed, implied in all comparisons of His Church and its privileges, to treasure hid in the ground which escapes the search of careless or superficial enquirers; to leaven buried in a bushel of meal, whose secret and pervading influence should make itself felt at length, and by degrees, through the whole of the mass which concealed it; of corn sown in a field, over which many moons must wax and wane ere first its green and tender shoots, its golden ears next, and lastly, its overflowing and manifold harvest, alleviate the anxiety and reward the labours of the husbandman. The contrary is, lastly, implied in the many predictions of our Lord while on earth, which prepare His disciples to encounter opposition, persecution, and contempt from the world in which they were to labour; and that many generations of offence, of dissension, of opposition, yea, and of apostacy, were to intervene before the Tabernacle of God was to be finally erected among His people, and the knowledge of the Lord should cover the earth as the waters cover the sea. Nor can it be accounted reasonable to object to the claims of a prophet to Divine inspiration, that the sect which He founded has not met with a more favourable fortune upon earth than He Himself, in the first instance, promised and foretold.

Nor is this the only fact connected with Christianity which has been ignorantly or wilfully misrepresented. Its actual progress among men, and the number of its external professors have been almost systematically depreciated and diminished, while, by an opposite mistake, the probable amount of the Mussulman and Gentile inhabitants of our

planet have been exaggerated in a five-fold proportion. But, if assuming the latest and most accurate
estimate which I have met with, (and that from no
friendly hand) of the comparative population of
the different sects among mankind, we estimate
the amount of those who at present are called by
the name of Christ at 200,000,000, or a fourth part
of mankind; if we recollect that, within these
limits are included all the most improved and im-
proving portion of the world, the most powerful in
arms, the most skilful in arts, the most distinguished
in every branch of moral and natural philosophy,
the most industrious, the wealthiest and the wisest
among the sons of men ; if we bear in mind that to
them the entire old world is immediately or indirectly tributary; and that, in the new world, to
which their genius has led the way, they have
found an almost vacant, and a little less than
boundless field for the occupation and dominion of
an innumerable and believing posterity; if we consider that, however slow the progress of Christianity
may have been, it is now and has been always progressive ; it may seem that the enemies of our
creed have been somewhat rash in their exultations
over its failure. It may require no mighty measure of faith to believe that " the Lord is not slack
as men count slackness ;" that the word which
hath gone forth from His mouth shall in no wise
return unto Him empty ; and that He who hath
thus far conquered will go on to fresh conquests
still ; till the kingdoms of this world shall become

the kingdom of God and His Christ; till His Church, afflicted first and militant still, shall become universal, and at length triumphant; and till the material world itself shall make way for a nobler and happier creation, and a great voice shall be heard of much people in Heaven, saying, " Alleluja, for the Lord God Omnipotent reigneth."

Those objectors, indeed, who would revile the Christian faith, because in the course of 1800 years it has not yet converted the world, have forgotten the analogy between the moral and material universe, and how universally, in the latter, those changes which are beneficial, are, in comparison, slow and gradual. The desolation of a province by an earthquake or a volcano, may be the work of a single hour; but months, and years, and ages have been necessary, ere the gradual deposition of alluvial soil has clothed the rocky valley of the Nile with the harvests and fertility of Egypt, or produced Bengal from its parent Ganges. And those who infer that God does not will the eventual triumph of His name, and the eventual and complete felicity of His creatures, because His providence works by the agency of secondary causes, and through the imperfection of human labourers, may as well reason from the existence of vice that God does not delight in virtue, and are blasphemers against the religion of nature, as well as against that of revelation and prophecy.

The honour, then, of God, and His will as declared in Scripture, are of themselves sufficient

7

reasons to engage the zeal, the affections, the faith, and energies of Christians in the endeavour to disseminate His truth among those who still sit in darkness.   Now, if much remains to be done ere the victory of the cross shall attain its full completion, if many nations still dishonour, by superstition, the glory of Him who made us all, and if the mightiest, and wisest, and best of beings is still unknown or misrepresented among the greater proportion of those who bear His image, the result on our minds should be no other than a greater ardour of exertion, in proportion as its necessity is greater, a more exalted zeal for His name, in proportion as that name is ignorantly dishonoured.

But it is not our duty to our Maker and Redeemer alone which should urge us to the dissemination of His Gospel; our love of man no less constraineth us to communicate to our neighbours and brethren the same inestimable blessings, which we have ourselves freely received from the Giver of all good things.   It was not for the glory of God alone that the Son of God descended from on high, but in order that peace and good will to man might be manifested in that illustrious condescension.   And it must be, to say the least of it, either a very inadequate notion of the nature and extent of the benefits conferred on mankind by a knowledge of and belief in Christianity, or a very lamentable coldness and indifference to the happiness or misery of our fellow creatures, which can make us backward, much more averse, to lend our aid, to

our power and in our proper station, to the progress
of the true religion among the heathen.

For, let us recollect, that it is not wisdom alone,
it is not the more perfect knowledge of God and
His nature and attributes, it is not a mere freedom
from idle or injurious superstitions, it is not a pure
and holy law of life and morals only; nor yet the
many and various advantages of a civil and political
character, the improvement of the human intellect,
the extension of secular knowledge, the acquisition
of fresh fields of enterprise and mental enjoyment,
and the perfection of those many arts and sciences
which an enlargement of the understanding brings
with it; it is not the advancement of social life,
the more enlarged and accurate notions of truth
and justice, the corroboration of every civil and
every domestic tie, the restoration of the other sex
to their natural place in society, and the many
blessed effects which flow to our own sex, from
that restored society and influence; not the wisdom,
the wealth, the peace, the civil liberty, which,
wherever Christianity has appeared, have uniformly
followed in her train, and which every nation has
enjoyed more purely and perfectly in proportion
as the system of Christianity which it has received has been purer and more perfect; these are
not the only, nor the greatest blessings which our
backwardness or indifference would deny to our
uninstructed fellow creatures. These, or any one
of them, would be an object worthy of the utmost
exertions and ardent desires of a benevolent mind;

and to accomplish which, in any considerable degree, the labour of a man's whole life would be a
cheap and easy sacrifice. Who is there among us
who would not rejoice, by all safe and peaceable
means, to introduce a greater reverence for truth,
a greater purity of language, a better founded and
more consistent veneration for the obligations of
justice and integrity among those with whom we
dwell, to whom is entrusted the daily care of our
persons, our property, and our children, and
through whose agency and evidence alone, those
among us who bear rule must provide for the public peace and security? Who is there who calls to
mind the wretched follies by which men, naturally
as acute and intelligent as ourselves, attempt to
escape from the burden of sin, and to appease
the anger of offended Heaven, without desiring to
substitute repentance and a faith in that great Victim who died for the sins of the world, in place of
the vain washings, the unprofitable self-mortifica-
tions, the abominable obscenity, the hideous cruelty,
the ashes, the torturing irons, and the torturing
flame, which engross the time, and delude the understanding, and destroy the happiness of the
Indian aspirant after holiness? Who, lastly, that
has either witnessed or heard but a small part of
the wonderful and horrible things which, in the
name of religion, are perpetrated and daily perpe-
trating around us, but must desire, (by the same
mild and persuasive arguments which only suit our
cause) to quench those funeral flames to which love,

strong as death, is now consigned by interested
priestcraft; to abate those murders which pollute
the stream of Ganges, and add a darker horror
to the hideous features of Juggernâth ; and to still
those innocent cries and dry up that infant blood,
which day and night mount up from Central and
Western India, as a witness against us, to the God
and Parent of all men ?

But more is yet behind ! These are not the
only nor the most awful considerations which im-
pel us to labour in the dissemination of the Christian faith. The souls of men are implicated ! It
is not, indeed, necessary for my argument, and it
is far, very far, from my inclination, to determine
rashly of the final state of those that are without,
and who must stand or fall to that great Master
only, whose throne is established in righteousness
and judgement. But whatever mercy may be shown
to those that offend in ignorance ; whatever benefits may emanate (through the uncovenanted bounties of our God) from the death of Christ, towards
those on whom the light of the Gospel has not
shined ; yet, doubtless, (if we would not resolve
the privileges of the Gospel into a nullity,) a faith
in Christ must be the entrance to a more certain
and excellent salvation ; the gifts of the Holy
Ghost, which the regenerate obtain, must not only
enable them to a more genuine holiness, but conduct them to a brighter glory; and, in whatever
sense the Living God is the Saviour of all men, the
same text, on which we ground this hope, assures

us, that, in a more pre-eminent and particular
sense, He is the Saviour of them which believe.
Nor is this all ; for if murder, if uncleanness, if
fraud, if falsehood, be breaches of that law which
is written in the heart of every man, and that natural light whereby even the heathen are left inex-
cusable ; yea, if idolatry itself be a practice, (as we
find it described both in the prophetic and the
apostolic writings), no less offensive in itself to
God, no less subversive of the morals of men, and
no less a criminal breach of the law of nature, than
it is inconsistent with the dictates of natural reason,
and with those notions of the Almighty which even
the visible creation inculcates ; it is impossible to
contemplate the spiritual state, and spiritual prospects of very many of those by whom we are surrounded, without a painful apprehension of the
issue of such errors, and a very earnest wish and
prayer that the knowledge and sanctifying grace
of the Gospel may be in time communicated to
them.

Nor can it be maintained with reason that feelings like these, and the exertions consequent on
such feelings, are exclusively incumbent on a peculiar order of men, on the ministers or missionaries of Christianity. On us, no doubt, there
is an additional and aweful obligation ; a woe is laid
on us if we preach not the Gospel ; and He who
hath sent us forth into the world to proclaim His
truth to every creature, requireth of us, beyond a
doubt, our utmost endeavours,—where means of

personal exertion are afforded—and our utmost liberality, where we have to aid the personal exertions
of our brethren.   But to all, and not to the clergy
only, the honour of God should be dear.   On all,
and not on a small minority of God's servants, the
obligation is imposed of desiring the happiness and
promoting the salvation of their brethren.   And it
is as much the duty of every Christian, in his
proper sphere, and according to the means which
he possesses, to lend his help in turning the sinner from the errour of his ways, and delivering the
blinded Gentile from the accumulated danger of his
condition, as it would be to pluck his brother out
of the fire, or to prevent him, by timely warning,
from walking down a precipice.

" Still," it has been said, " for such feelings and
exertions there is ample scope at home. There are
thousands in our native land who, no less than the
heathen, need instructing and reclaiming, and on
whom it were wiser and better to expend our missionary energies, than to intrude them on a race
with whom we have no concern, and who may re-
sent the intrusion in a manner dangerous to the
dearest political interests of our nation."

For the first of these objections there might perhaps be more plausibility, if the promoters of missionary exertions abroad were indifferent to the
condition of their erring countrymen, or if they did
not also labour, at least as diligently as their opponents, in the support of schools, in the distribution
of the Scriptures, and in every other channel of

benevolent exertion and expenditure, which can
reclaim the wretched from the errour of his ways,
and instruct the ignorant in his duty. But to maintain that the danger of those who are already in
possession of the means of grace, is to occupy our
mind so entirely that we can spare no pity to those
who have no means of grace at all, that the progress of God's kingdom is to be suspended so long
as there remains, in those countries over which it
has a general empire, a perverse and unbelieving
remnant, is to maintain that which, if it had been
held by the apostles, would have excluded us, who
are now assembled, for ever from the knowledge
and blessings of which we are partakers; inasmuch
as while a single Jew remained unconverted, it
would have been an offence, on this principle, to
offer the kingdom of God to any single Gentile.
And who does not see, that the existence of misery
and vice, and ignorance in our own land, is no
argument whatever against endeavouring, in other
lands, to diminish the amount of vice and ignorance, and misery, and that we are bound by every
tie of reason, and compassion, and piety, to render
honour to God's name wherever we may ourselves
be thrown, and, as far as we have means and opportunity, to do good to all men without distinction.

But can it really be maintained, with any semblance of truth, or reason, or humanity, that the
nations of this country, our neighbours, our domes-
tics, our fellow-subjects, our fellow soldiers, who
toil for us; who shed their blood in our defence;

whose wealth contributes so largely to the prosperity of Britain, and their valour (their faithful
and invincible valour and allegiance,) so essentially
promotes our security and renown; that these
men, with whom we live and converse, distinguished
by so many estimable and amiable qualities of intelligence, of bravery, of courteous and gentle demeanour, are devoid of a claim on all the good
which we can render or obtain for them, on our
affections, our bounties, our services, and, I will
add, our prayers? Can we petition their Father and
our's that His glorious kingdom may come, without
desiring, if we think of them at all, that they may
be partakers in it with us? or can we forget that
such prayers and desires are no other than a
mockery of God, unless our actions follow our lips,
and we endeavour, in God's strength and help, to
forward that triumph of His mercy for which we
profess ourselves solicitous.

To the plea of political danger I must not be supposed insensible. We have no right, as Christians,
to attempt a good work in a manner which is likely
to be attended with an immediate and preponderant
evil; we are bound, as Christian subjects and citizens, so to temper our zeal with discretion, as not
to disturb the peace of the land wherein we dwell,
and the government from whom we receive protection. And even setting aside all secular considerations and secular duties, we shall err most grossly
against that pure and peaceable wisdom, whereby
only we can attain the conversion of the heathen,

if we assail their errours with any other weapon than mild and courteous and unobtrusive argument, or do any thing which can array their angry passions against those opinions which we seek to recommend to their acceptance.

But in the system which only has been tried by the members of our communion, and which only, so far as my advice or authority can reach, shall ever, by God's blessing, be attempted in India; a system studiously distinguished from and unconnected with government, yet studiously kept within those limits of prudence and moderation which a wise and liberal government has prescribed; a system which, while it offers our faith to the acceptance of the heathen on the ground of its spiritual blessings, disqualifies no man, on account of his contrary opinions, from any civil or political advantage; a system which, by the communication of general instruction and general morality, imparts a knowledge and feeling which, whether they become Christians or no, must be highly valuable to them; a system which puts them in fair possession of the evidences of our creed, leaving it to themselves and their own unbiassed choice to determine between light and darkness; in such a system, so long as it is steadily adhered to, and patiently and wisely pursued, there is not, there cannot be danger.

They are their own learned men who are our teachers, our correctors of the press, our fellow-labourers in the work of instruction; they are their

own countrymen, yea, and they themselves who are
benefited by the large expenditure which our system occasions amongst them; and even our missionaries, as associating with them more, and speaking their language better, and occupying themselves
with their concerns and the promotion of their real
or apprehended interests, are, (I have reason to
believe, by what I have myself seen and heard in
no inconsiderable part of India,) among the most
popular Europeans who are to be found in their
respective neighbourhoods. Yea more, I have had
the happiness of witnessing, both in the number of
converts which have already been made in Hindus-
tan, in the general good conduct of those converts,
and in the good terms on which they in general
appear to live with their Gentile neighbours, both
how much good may be done, and how little offence
will be occasioned by a course of well-meant and
well-directed efforts to enlighten the inhabitants of
India.

Of all the various bodies of professing Christians,
who, with more or less of light, and with greater or
lesser zeal and providence, have been our precursors, or are about to be our emulators in this great
and illustrious enterprise, it becomes me to speak
with respect, and if I know my own heart, I shall
never think of them with hostility. Every sect will
naturally seek to diffuse those religious notions
which they themselves esteem most agreeable to
reason and religion; and any mode of Christianity,
even the modes least distinguished by its peculiar

and most blessed characteristics, must be in itself,
so far as it extends, a happy change from idolatry.
But, while we rejoice that Christ is preached, even
by those who hold not His faith in our own unity of
fellowship; while we are content that the morality
of the Gospel should be disseminated, even by
those who rob Christ of His Godhead and mediato-
rial attributes; it is surely our duty to be no less
anxious than they for the support and preaching of
those forms which are associated with every recollection of early and ancestral reverence, those doctrines which we feel and know to be our surest
sanction of morality in this world, and our only
ground of hope in worlds beyond the grave.   Every
man, and every sect, must act for themselves, and
according to the lights which they have received;
but let no man teach a doctrine which he does not
believe, because it is likely to be popular, or sup-
press a truth which he holds most sacred, because
he fears that it will not be well received by those
whom he seeks to benefit.   God, we may be sure,
has revealed nothing to men which it is not highly
desirable for men to know; and the man who encourages the circulation of an imperfect creed, in the
hope that its adoption may lead the enemy to that
which he himself professes, is at once dealing untruly with himself, his neighbour, and the Most
High; with himself as seeking after God's glory by
means which God has not sanctioned; with his
heathen neighbour, as offering him a religion of
which he holds back the most essential portion;

and with his God, as concealing the honour which
God has given to His Son, and being ashamed, (for
what else is it but shame or cowardice which with-
holds a truth through fear of offending ?) being
ashamed before men of the divinity and cross of his
Saviour.   In what I have said, I seek to dissuade
no man from propagating the truth which he pro-
poses, but I desire to impress on those who profess
the same truth with myself, that on the support and
munificence of the members of the Church of England, the institutions of that Church have a paramount claim, beyond those of any other sect or
society.

Of that Society, and that particular Institution
for which I am now anxious to interest your bounty,
it may be said in few words, that the Society for
the Propagation of the Gospel in Foreign Parts,
has, since its establishment in the year 1701, been
sedulously and successfully labouring, with the approbation and under the guidance of the venerable
fathers of our Church, and of some of our most
distinguished statesmen and philosophers, in supporting a line of missionary stations, (above 100 in
number), in some of the wildest and most neglected
portions of the British empire, in the Scilly Islands,
in New South Wales, in the wildernesses of Africa
and America.   Having been encouraged by recent
events, and by an increase of funds derived from
the contributions of a liberal public, it has extended,
within the last ten years, the range of its labours into
Bengal, where it now maintains three episcopally

2

ordained missionaries, (one more is on his way
hither), and is the chief contributor to an institution in which all the three presidencies are equally
interested, the establishment of Bishop's College,
Calcutta,—of which the avowed and appropriate
objects are to superintend and forward the translation and publication of the Scriptures in the languages of India, the education of youth, both native
and European, (and selected in equal proportions
from Bengal, Madras, Ceylon, and Bombay), in
such a manner as to qualify them, as schoolmasters,
for the diffusion of general knowledge among the
natives, and, as missionaries, to impart that saving
knowledge, without which the value of human ac-
quirements is small indeed.   It is on these grounds,
and with a more immediate view to the present
unfinished state of this establishment especially, (as
an institution of no foreign or distant interest to
those whom I am addressing, but which only wants
your bounty to enable its conductors to do that
of which they are most desirous, and extend its
operations to this very neighbourhood, and to every
part of the Western as well as the Eastern coast of
this vast peninsula), that I respectfully but with
confidence appeal to a bounty, to which appeal has
never yet been made in vain.

And, as you desire the glory of God, and that
the truth of His Son should be made known to
every creature under Heaven; as you covet the
happiness of mankind, and that innocent blood
should be no longer shed amongst us; as you long

for the salvation of souls, and that those who serve
and love you here should feel a yet purer and
stronger affection for you in Paradise ; as you love
your own souls, and would manifest the sincerity of
your grateful faith in that Saviour by whom you
are redeemed, I exhort, I advise, I entreat, yea, in
the name of my Master and yours, in the name of
Jesus, Son of God Most High, I demand, in this
cause, your assistance and your offerings.

The Son of God, indeed, must reign, be the
people never so unquiet ! The Gospel will finally
triumph, let us neglect or oppose it as we may !
But woe be in that day of God's power to those
who have set themselves against His Church's
infant weakness ! and woe be to those minor or
more timid sinners who have not lent their hand
to His harvest ! " Curse ye Meroz," said the angel
of the Lord, " curse ye bitterly the inhabiters thereof, because they went not forth to the help of the
Lord, to the help of the Lord against the mighty !"
But of you, my brethren, I am persuaded better
things ; and, both as knowing your liberality, and
as desiring that your bounty may be made beneficial to your own souls and to those interests which
you seek to forward, let me entreat you to devote
those good works to God and His Son alone, by a
lively faith, by a more excellent repentance, by a
fervent prayer—that while you build an ark for
others, you may not yourselves be shut forth and
perish—and by a participation, let me add, in the
blessed body and blood of Him by whose merit

alone we obtain, either that our alms-deeds or prayers can be remembered or accepted before His Father.

And, O Merciful God, who as at this time didst teach the hearts of Thy faithful people by the sending to them the light of Thy Holy Spirit, grant us, by the same Spirit, to have a right judgement in all things, and evermore to rejoice in His holy comfort, through the merits of Christ Jesus our Saviour, who liveth and reigneth, with thee, in the unity of the same Spirit, one God, world without end. Amen.

SERMON XII*.

THE OMNIPRESENCE OF GOD.

[Preached August 5, 1825, on the Consecration of the Church of
Secrole, near Benares.]

GEN. xxviii. 16, 17.

*And Jacob awaked out of his sleep, and he said, surely the Lord
is in this place; and I knew it not. And he was afraid, and
said, how dreadful is this place! this is none other than the
House of God, and this the gate of Heaven.*

THIS was the natural and touching exclamation of
the patriarch Jacob, when, in his lonely and perilous
journey from Canaan to the land of the Chaldees,
the God of his fathers appeared to him in a dream

---

* This Sermon was published at Calcutta, with the following
dedication :

TO WILLIAM AUGUSTUS BROOKE, ESQUIRE, SENIOR JUDGE,
&c. &c. &c., SIR FREDERIC HAMILTON, BART. COLLECTOR,
WILLIAM JOHN SANDS, ESQUIRE, SECOND JUDGE, AND THE
OTHER CIVIL AND MILITARY OFFICERS OF THE CITY AND
DISTRICT OF BENARES, THE FOLLOWING SERMON, PRINTED
AT THEIR REQUEST, IS MOST RESPECTFULLY DEDICATED,
AS AN ACKNOWLEDGEMENT OF THEIR MUNIFICENT ZEAL
FOR THE INTERESTS OF TRUE RELIGION, AND THEIR
FRIENDLY AND GRATIFYING ATTENTIONS TO THEIR MUCH
OBLIGED AND FAITHFUL HUMBLE SERVANT, THE AUTHOR.

to confirm him in his faith and service, and to encourage him in his wanderings with the assurance
of an unseen and Almighty Protector.

At that time an outcast, in some degree, from
the tents of his father Isaac, and a fugitive from
the anger of a justly offended brother; a forlorn
and needy wanderer, he had laid him to sleep on
the sands of the wilderness, his head supported on
a pillow of stone, and his staff and scrip his only
riches. But in his dream he saw Heaven opened,
and " behold a ladder set up on the earth, and the
top of it reached to Heaven, and behold the angels
of God ascending and descending on it. And, behold, the Lord stood above it, and said, I am the
Lord, the God of Abraham thy father and the God
of Isaac; the land whereon thou liest, to thee will
I give it and to thy seed; and thy seed shall be as
the dust of the earth, and thou shalt spread abroad
to the west, and to the east, and to the north, and
to the south; and in thee and in thy seed shall all
the families of the earth be blessed. And, behold,
I am with thee, and will keep thee in all places
whither thou goest, and will bring thee again into
this land; for I will not leave thee, until I have
done that of which I have spoken to thee. And
Jacob awaked out of his sleep, and he said, surely
the Lord is in this place, and I knew it not! and
he said, how dreadful is this place! this is none
other but the house of God, and this the gate of
Heaven !"

In this memorable history are many circum-

stances which might afford us useful lessons, and
any one of which would be a sufficient and copious
subject for our morning's meditation.   The first
and most striking, perhaps, is the strange and aweful difference which frequently is found between
the manners in which the same persons are accounted of by man and by God ; and how little
the Lord seeth as man seeth, in His estimate and
choice of those whom He delights to favour.   Who
that had seen the forlorn son of Isaac in his journey
over that desolate land, unsheltered, unattended,
on foot, and struggling with fatigue and hunger,
" a Syrian ready to perish" in the waste howling
wilderness, would have guessed in this unhappy
wanderer the founder of a mighty nation ?   Who
that had known the circumstances of fraud and
meanness which had compelled his flight would
have expected to find in the supplanter Jacob, an
Israel, " the prince of God," to whose descendants,
above all the earth, the knowledge of the true God
should be entrusted ; and from whose loins that
Saviour was, in His mortal nature, to arise, in
whom not the tribes of Israel alone, but all the
nations of the world were, in after days, to be pronounced blessed ?

Yet thus it is that the wisdom of the wise is
often put to shame ; that God, even in the affairs
of this world, should seem, on certain occasions,
to delight in lowering the mighty and raising the
humble on high ; and that the riches of His grace
are, sometimes, most abundantly shown in calling

sinners to repentance, and choosing out for great
and glorious ends, the most contemptible and unworthy instruments.   These things should make
the proud man humble, and they should keep the
humble man from despair.   They should warn the
first on how slender a thread his own power or
eminence depends ; and how little reason he has
to think those beneath him, who, notwithstanding
their present and outward inferiority, may be, in
truth, of higher estimation in the eyes of God than
himself, and designed by God to far greater usefulness here, and hereafter to far more exalted glory.
The second may learn from them, that however
insignificant he may feel himself in the eyes of
men, however unable to render God worthy service, or to contribute, in any perceivable degree,
to the amendment or happiness of His creatures,
yet, if he perform with good will what little is in
his power, that little may, by God's blessing, in its
effects be infinitely multiplied ; while, at all events,
so far as he himself is concerned, the very least of
his endeavours is not lost in the sight or memory
of the Most High, nor will be forgotten in that day
when the widow's mite and the believer's cup of
water shall in no wise lose their reward, and when
he " who has been faithful in a few things," shall,
by the Judge of Heaven and Earth, be " made
ruler over many things."

Another observation which we shall be naturally
led to make in considering this passage of Scripture,
is the constant reference and connexion, which the

promises of the Old Testament maintain with that
great and glorious event, to bring us to which the
Old Testament itself is only, as it were, " a School-
master."   To a wanderer like Jacob, it would have
been a promise sufficiently comfortable to have
been assured, by a heavenly vision, of the protection of God in his journey, and of a safe and prosperous return to the land which he left against his
will, and constrainedly.   It would have seemed an
almost superfluous blessing to be told of the future
greatness to which his descendants should be advanced, or to be reminded of the grant to the seed
of Abraham of the land which he was now forsaking.   But with neither of these points is the Heavenly promise terminated; not only is his family
to become as numerous as the stars of Heaven, but
through one of their number, all the nations of the
earth are to be blessed; and for his seed is reserved the glory of reconciling God to man, and opening to penitent sinners the gates of a better Paradise than that which Adam had forfeited.

Nor need we wonder that this constant connexion should be found between worldly and spiritual privileges in the promises made by God to
the family of Abraham.   It had the effect of serving three very important purposes.   In the first
place, the prophecies of the Messiah were more
listened to and better remembered by a gross and
carnal people, from being thus, as it were, inseparably bound up and linked with promises of earthly
power and greatness.   Secondly, when the former

part of the prophecy was fulfilled by the increased
multitude and extended power of Jacob's descendants, those descendants were naturally inclined to
pay greater attention to and place more trust in
the remainder, of whose fulfilment in the course of
time they had thus received, as it were, the earnest.
And above all, amid whatever disappointments and
adversities might in the present life befall them,
the constant and recorded renewal of such promises, together with all the different manifestations
of God's power and protection, would serve to remind the pious Israelites that, however the possession of an earthly Canaan had failed to preserve
them free from those calamities which are the common inheritance of mortals, there remained yet
another and a better rest for the people of God,
to which the Saviour who was promised to arise
from the seed of Abraham, when He came, should
open the way.

Nor can we, " on whom the ends of the world
are come," whose lot is fallen to play our parts in
the last great scene of nature, the concluding mystery of redemption, fail to perceive from this constant reference to the coming of Christ in the older
records of God's Providence, how noble and excellent are the privileges which we enjoy; how important in the eyes of God are those blessings, the
knowledge of which is now opened to our gratitude;
and how great a necessity is laid on us to employ,
to the furtherance of God's glory and our own salvation, those lights which the patriarchs saw dimly

and from far, those mysteries which so many prophets desired to understand, but desired in vain!

Nor is this all. For, secondly, we may learn,
from the union which I have noticed as universally
observable in Scripture between the promise of
worldly blessings and the opportunity of Heavenly
graces, that the former of these are, in the eyes of
the Allwise, only so far valuable as they are means
of conducing to the latter; and that whatever
wealth, whatever power, whatever personal or men-
tal·or worldly advantages the Most High may in
His wisdom extend to us, are not blessings in
themselves, but as a way to greater blessedness,—
as gifts by the use and improvement of which we
are required by our God to serve the cause of His
Son, and entitle ourselves, (if I may venture to use
the expression,) entitle ourselves, through faith, to
a more illustrious reward hereafter.

If the Israelites were endowed beyond the nations of mankind, with wise and righteous laws,
with a fertile and almost impregnable territory,
with a race of valiant and victorious kings, and a
God who, (while they kept His ways) was a wall of
fire against their enemies round about them; if the
kings of the wilderness did them homage, and the
lion banner of David and Solomon was reflected
at once from the Mediterranean and the Euphrates;
it was, that the way of the Lord might be made
known by their means upon earth, and that the
saving health of the Messiah might become conspicuous to all nations.

My brethren, it has pleased the Almighty that the great nation to which we ourselves belong, is a great, a valiant, and an understanding nation : it has pleased Him to give us an empire in which the sun never sets, a commerce by which the remotest nations of the earth are become our allies, our tributaries, I had almost said our neighbours ; and, by means (when regarded as human means, and distinct from His mysterious providence,) so inadequate, as to excite our alarm as well as our wonder, the sovereignty over these wide and populous heathen lands.

But is it for our sakes that He has given us these good gifts, and wrought these great marvels in our favour ? Are we not rather set up on high in the earth, that we may show forth the light by which we are guided, and be the honoured instruments of diffusing these blessings which we ourselves enjoy, through every land where our will is law, through every tribe where our wisdom is held in reverence, and in every distant isle which our winged vessels visit ?

If we value then (as who does not value ?) our renown among mankind ; if we exult (as who can help exulting ?) in the privileges which the providence of God has conferred on the British nation ; if we are thankful (and God forbid we should be otherwise) for the means of usefulness in our power ; and if we love (as who does not love ?) our native land, its greatness and prosperity ; let us see that we, each of us in our station, are promot-

ing to the best of our power, by example, by exertion, by liberality, by the practice of every Christian justice and virtue, the extension of God's truth
among men, and the honour of that holy name
whereby we are called.

There have been realms as famous as our own,
and, (in relation to the then extent and riches of
the civilized world,) as powerful and as wealthy,
of which the traveller sees nothing now but ruins
in the midst of a wilderness, or where the mariner
only finds a rock for fishers to spread their nets.
Nineveh once reigned over the east; but where is
Nineveh now? Tyre had once the commerce of
the world; but what is become of Tyre? But if
the repentance of Nineveh had been persevered in,
her towers would have stood to this day. Had the
daughter of Tyre brought her gifts to the Temple of
God, she would have continued a queen for ever.

There is yet a third lesson to be drawn from the
vision of God at Bethel, and the exclamation which
I have noticed of the patriarch Jacob; I mean the
unseen and pervading presence of the Most High,
" who is about our path and about our bed, and spieth
out all our ways;" of whom, not in the field of Luz
alone, but wherever our footsteps carry us, it may
be said, that " surely God is in this place;" to
whom the whole firmament of the skies is as a tent
to dwell in, and the universal earth His footstool;
and in whose sight and through whose favour it is,
let our pilgrimage lie where it will, that *every where*
is the gate of Heaven!

This notion of God as an Almighty, All-present, All-seeing and Unseen Existence, who " is not far from any of us, and in whom we live and move and have our being," is, unquestionably, a strange and aweful subject of thought, and one which cannot be agitated in our minds without a deep and almost a painful and terrifying sense of our own weakness and dependance. Even to a good man, and to one who is, on good grounds, assured of the protection and favour of his Maker, this presence not to be shunned, this power not to be resisted, this aweful eye for ever bent on our ways is, at times, oppressive as well as surprising. " Whither," said the Psalmist, " shall I go then from Thy spirit, or whither shall I go then from Thy presence? If I climb up into Heaven Thou art there. If I go down into hell Thou art there also. If I take the wings of the morning and remain in the uttermost parts of the sea, even there also shall Thy hand lead me, and thy right hand shall hold me. If I say, peradventure the darkness shall cover me, then shall my night be turned to day. Yea, the darkness is no darkness with Thee, but the night is as clear as the day ; the darkness and light to Thee are both alike !"

We are lost in the meditation of such greatness. In this sea of glory our powers, our wisdom, our life, appear to sink into nothing. What is man, (we are apt to say) that God should condescend to regard him ? and what are the thoughts, the words, and works of man, that they should be able to en-

dure the constant inspection of a Judge so wise, so
great, so terrible ?

But if even good men, if even the best of men,
must be thus at times affected by the sense of God's
unseen and continual presence ; if they too must,
at times, find the place dreadful where they thus
stand before Him ; how grievous must this recollection be to those who live without God in the
world ; who are conscious that by their daily sins
they have drawn on themselves His heaviest anger,
and that they have done before His face, and under
the beam of His indignant eye, such actions as they
would have been afraid or ashamed to have fallen
into in the presence of a mere mortal bystander ?

It is a dreadful thing, when conscience reckons
up her catalogue of secret guilt, to remember that
every one of those crimes which were most hateful
to God and to man were done with the knowledge,
and in the presence, of the Judge, the severe and
upright Judge of men and angels. A dreadful thing
it is to know that He from whom nothing is hidden
while doing, and by whom nothing is forgotten
when done, was there in the midst of our foulest
lurking-place, in the assembly of our guilty friends
and accomplices, His eye bent on our deeds, His
anger kindled by our wickedness, and His arm,
perhaps, upraised to strike us down to death and
hell, if His mercy had not interfered to afford us
a little longer time for repentance. A dreadful
thing it is to say, " surely God was in this place,
when I cast my eyes so carefully around and flat-

tered myself that my uncleanness, my robbery, or my fraud was hid in darkness and solitude. God was in this place, when I deformed His image with drunkenness, and when my mouth was filled with the words of lust and blasphemy. God was in this place, when I called on His holy name to obtain credit for my falsehood, and challenged His power to punish me if I dealt untruly with my neighbour. And God is in this place, and beholds my present hardness and impenitent heart; He knows and sees my lingering fondness for the sins which I am pretending to abandon; and He is waiting, perhaps, even now, for the conduct which I shall now adopt, the resolution which I shall now follow, to determine whether my lot shall be hereafter among the children of light, or whether His Spirit shall be withdrawn from me, (it may be,) for ever!"

Surely, my friends, the presence of our Creator, our Saviour, our Judge, and our King, is to all of us a matter of deep and serious concernment! If the Almighty were at this moment to make Himself visible to our eyes; if we beheld, like the Israelites in Horeb, His glory as it were a consuming fire, shining forth from amid the darkness of the cloudy firmament; if we beheld Him, like Isaiah, on His throne exceeding high, with the many winged seraphin around, exclaiming Holy, Holy, Holy; if we were caught up, like St. John in the Revelation, to the open gates of Heaven, and beheld in the midst of its sea of glass, and beneath

its rainbow canopy, that seat on which He who
sitteth is in brightness as a jasper and a sardine
stone ; or if that vision were shown to us which
came to Daniel, when the Ancient of Days did sit
on the cloud with His ten thousand times ten
thousand angels, when the fiery stream went forth
before Him, when the judgement was begun, and
the books of life were opened ;—should we not be
led in this case to cry out with the Israelites, let
not God speak with us lest we die !—should we not
say, with Isaiah, woe is me for I have seen the
Lord the God of Israel !—or what posture of body
should we think sufficiently humble ; what form of
behaviour too strict, too cautious, too reverent, in
such a presence ?   How should we endeavour to
restrain our lips from evil, our thoughts from wandering, and our inclinations from whatever might
offend Him ?

Alas, have we forgotten how thin a screen that
is which separates us from this glorious and aweful
spectacle of Jehovah's Majesty !   Let but the word
go forth from His mouth, let but one of His innumerable ministers cut the thread of our days, and
set our spirit free from the curtains of this bodily
tabernacle, and in a moment we should perhaps be
introduced to that very scene of which the thought
is so dreadful to us.   In a moment our soul would
find itself introduced to the vast world of invisible
beings; would behold, it may be, the angels of
God ascending and descending as ministers of His
will between Heaven and earth ! and our Maker

Himself in His boundless glory, and our Redeemer standing at His right hand! This moment, while I speak, this prospect is offered for the first time to many who, in the different nations of the world, are passing from life into eternity ; this moment it may be offered to any of us who are here assembled. Surely the Lord is in this place, and we know it not, how dreadful is this place! This place may to each of us become, according as we are prepared for the passage, the gate of hell or Heaven!

The practical effects which considerations like these should produce in our lives and actions, are too plain to need my pointing out to you. If these things are true, (and their truth is proved, not only from revealed but natural religion) what manner of persons ought we to be in holiness and pureness of living? But if there be one time or place more than another where the feeling of this presence of God should possess and govern us, it must be when we are avowedly assembled for the purpose of acknowledging His presence by prayer and praise in these holy buildings which are called after His name, and which the usual and decent reverence of mankind has concurred to set apart from profane and secular purposes.

This separation, indeed, by some outward mark of reverence, of things devoted to the service of God from those which serve the ordinary uses of the present life, is a practice, which seems enjoined by nature itself, and which has been observed

by all nations and by almost all religious sects or
parties.

It is, indeed, most true, (and I have laboured in
vain if I have not brought the conviction home to
your minds,) it is true that the earth is the Lord's
and all that is therein ; that the open field, the
private dwelling, the ship, the house of merchan-
dize, the highway, the forest and the fell, are, each
of them, on proper occasions, a suitable scene of
prayer; and each and all of them, as scenes of
God's pervading presence, should be hallowed by
our unending duty, by our aspirations ever bent on
Heaven, our innocency of heart and of life, our
submission of every word and thought to the go-
vernance and glory of the Most High.   But such
is the weakness of our mortal state, that a religion
thus widely diffused would infallibly become weakened and diluted, unless there were some certain
rallying points of attention and of reverence, in
which our hearts should be more closely drawn to
God, and our thoughts composed to a stricter sense
of His neighbourhood.

We find it in the institution of the Sabbath, (an
institution which, if it were of human authority
alone, would, for its practical wisdom and utility,
deserve the praise and imitation of all who give
laws or set examples to mankind,) we find how
needful it is that the love and service which we
ought to render every day, should, if we would have
them paid at all, be on some days paid more strictly.
And, if we desire to remember God on the ocean

and in the field, if we desire to bear His image with us through the crowded and busy walks of life, and to recollect effectually that the universe is His temple, it is well that some portions of this vast whole should be divided and set apart in our ideas, as associated with customary piety, and unprofaned by secular mixtures.

Accordingly, even in the heathen world, " secernere sacra profanis," was accounted the duty of a king, while kings were yet the priests as well as leaders of their people. The rude stone altars of the ancient patriarchs, yea the very pillar of Luz, which this Jacob reared in memory of his glorious vision, were, by solemn prayer and by the pouring on of oil and wine, devoted to the thoughts of an invisible world and the service of the God of Abraham. The tabernacle first, and afterwards either temple, had their solemn feasts of dedication ; and even in the latter days of the Jewish covenant, and when the temple of God in Jerusalem was so soon to be given up by its Heavenly King to that common destruction which chastised His rebellious subjects, we still see the Son of God, all gentle and gracious as was His usual character, aroused to a sense of wrath by the indignities offered to His Father's shrine ; and on this provocation, and in this quarrel only, assuming to Himself the power of an earthly king, and inflicting on the corrupt guardians of the sanctuary the terrours of an earthly chastisement.

The God of the ancient patriarchs, the God of

the Jews, the God and Father of Him whose name
we bear, is the God of the Christians still ; human
nature is still the same, and in us, no less than in
them, it requires these outward appliances and asso-
ciations, which attune the mind to a solemn and
serious harmony, and enlist the senses on the side
of the soul and its everlasting interests.   The temple of God, which was soon to perish, was holy notwithstanding ; and, while it lasted, the house of
prayer, and of prayer only.   The Church of God,
which is to endure for ever, does this demand a less
reverence at our hands ? or is it not meet that these
buildings, where that Church assembles to plume
her wings and prepare her flight for her everlasting
and Heavenly habitation, should, as the instruments
of a more illustrious covenant than that of bulls and
goats, receive at our hands a still humbler and more
constant reverence ?

It is for this cause, and fortified by this great example, that in the primitive Church, and in the
humble but golden days of Christian zeal and courage, the tombs, the caves, the lowly and secret cells
where the scattered congregations assembled to
sing hymns to Christ, bear witness by their inscrip-
tions, remaining at the present day, with how deep
reverence they were approached, and with how solemn services they were appropriated to the honour
of the Lamb, and to the memory of His saints and
martyrs.   It is for this cause, and encouraged by
so vast a cloud of witnesses, that the more recent
Church of Christ has continued to call down an

appropriate blessing on those temples which national or individual piety has reared to such holy
purposes; and for this cause it is, and to no superstitious end, and, as we trust, from no presumptuous principle of will-worship, that we have this day
offered the work of your munificence, in a public
and solemn manner, to Him from whom we have
received all things!

Let not him assume the name of Christian who
is wilfully or willingly wanting in his token of respect to even the building thus hallowed by its
destination; let not him lay claim to the character
of a devout and rational worshipper, who forgets
that, though God is every where, His blessing may
be more largely given in one place than in another;
and that no places can with greater propriety have
hope of such a privilege, than those temples which
are called after His name, and which have been
repeatedly distinguished as the scene of His mercies!

Yea, rather, let the sense of the high privileges
of which we are or may be partakers here; the
communion with God which we here enjoy; the
union with His Son, which through His body and
blood we are not afraid to aspire to; the gift of the
Holy Ghost, which our accepted though imperfect
prayers may here obtain from the Giver of every
good thing; inspire us to a reverence not only of
the body but of the mind, a submission of ourselves
to His holy will and pleasure, and an ardent long-
ing after those celestial habitations where, not

through the dark glass of faith, or the long and dim perspective of hope deferred, but in the flesh shall we see that Lord, who now, though unseen by mortal eyes, is present to reward or punish us.

Where two or three, said Christ, are gathered together in my name, there am I in the midst of them! " Surely God is in this place, though we behold Him not! How dreadful is this place! This is none other than the house of God, and this the gate of Heaven!"

SERMON XIII.

SIN AND GRACE.

[Preached at St. Mary's, Madras, March 4, 1826.]

ROMANS vii. 24, 25.

Oh wretched man that I am! who shall deliver me from the body of this death! I thank God through Jesus Christ our Lord!

A VERY touching and natural complaint is expressed, and a very seasonable and efficacious consolation afforded in the former and latter parts of this passage of Scripture, which contains, indeed, in very few words, a comprehensive and forcible view of the necessities and the hopes of a Christian. The natural misery of man is expressed in the heaviness of that sorrow which, when abstracted from the consideration of redemption through Christ, made St. Paul declare himself most wretched; and the merciful deliverance of man is no less warmly and gratefully acknowledged in that noble burst of rapture wherein he magnifies the favour bestowed on him, and thanks his God for his escape, through his crucified Lord and Saviour, from the body of death.

Without these distinct yet blended feelings; with-

out a sense, and a mournful sense, of the natural
weakness and forlorn condition of mankind, and
more particularly of his own condition; and without an earnest and thankful hope of God's help and
mercy through His Son, it is hardly too much to
say that no man can be a genuine Christian.   If
he is deficient in the former of these feelings; if,
not acknowledging his own helplessness, he trusts
in himself that he is strong, he cannot ask the aid
of Christ, nor will that blessed and mighty aid be
offered to him.   If he is deficient in the latter, he
must also want that love for his Redeemer which
arises from a sense of His benefits ; he must want
that reliance on his God, which only can save us
from despair.   It shall, therefore, be the aim of my
present discourse to lay before you, shortly and
clearly, the nature and the grounds of both these
mental habits ; and, at the same time, to point out
and illustrate the tenour of the apostle's reasoning
in that remarkable passage of Scripture from which
the words of my text are taken.

    The Epistle to the Romans, it is always neces-
sary to bear in mind, was addressed, in the first instance, to individuals of the Jewish nation, who,
though they had so far believed in Christ as to acknowledge Him for their Messiah, were very far
from a right understanding of the nature of His
errand among men, or of the blessed and wonderful effects of His merits, His intercession, and His
sufferings.   They denied, in fact, that truth in
which the main secret of the Christian system lay,

the forgiveness of sins by His one sacrifice of Himself once offered; or at best they confined the necessity of such an atonement to the blinded Gentiles alone, without admitting that the race of Israel required any further aid than was supplied by the law of Moses.

To those who were led by that glorious light which, in the wilderness, rested on the mercy-seat of the ark, and in subsequent ages shone with a different, but not less clear and miraculous illumination, in the writings of so many prophets, what room, they argued, was left for further knowledge? By those who had the divinely imposed seal of circumcision, and were themselves the kindred of Christ, what further proof of God's favour was required or could be looked for? And, by those who walk after the whole and perfect rule of God's commandments, could any condemnation be feared, could any further atonement be needed?

To cure this lofty opinion of themselves is St. Paul's scope through the greater part of this Epistle; and the principles on which he reasons are, perhaps, of matchless ingenuity and clearness. He begins by proving that which, indeed, the best informed among the Jews have themselves allowed, and of which the experience of the world affords abundant and melancholy evidence, that the Gentile and the Jew were alike transgressors before God. He shows that the circumcision on which they so much relied, was in itself a badge of their profession, a distinctive mark of God's favour to

1

those who kept the law, but no more to be pleaded
as an atonement for the breach of the law, than
the uniform of a soldier is an excuse for his transgression of those articles of war, which that very
uniform enhances his obligation to keep inviolate.
The question of the law itself he treats in a more
elaborate manner, by urging, both that the publication of a law contains in itself no atonement for
its transgression; and still further, that such a law
could do no more than show men their danger,
without furnishing the means of escape, and thus
would leave them more wretched than it found
them.

The argument thus brought forward is obscure,
perhaps, though just and subtle. A familiar illus-
tration may explain it. If I see my neighbour
riding furiously towards the brink of a precipice, I
do well, indeed, to cry to him to stop his horse;
but if his horse have the mastery, no benefit will
arise from my warning. If I tell a man who is
tempted to commit adultery, that the consequences
of such a crime will be infamy here and everlasting
ruin hereafter, I tell him, indeed, a sad and dismal truth; but, if his passions so enslave him, that,
while acknowledging the goodness of my counsel,
he professes himself unable to follow it, it is plain
that such advice has only the effect of enhancing
his folly, and rendering his sin more exceedingly
sinful.

Now this was the case with the law of Moses;
and it must, from the constitution of our nature, be

the case with every law and every rule of conduct which can be given, unless there be given at the same time a power of keeping the law; a mastery over those passions, the indulgence of which is prohibited; and a pardon and atonement for the transgressions of which we have been previously guilty. Now as the former of these was in no degree supplied, and the latter in a very imperfect manner supplied, by the moral and ceremonial law of Moses; it followed that the law of Moses by itself fell short of our necessities, and that neither the Gentile nor the Jew could stand upright in the sight of God, without the preventing grace and atoning sacrifice which our Lord brought to light in His Gospel.

It is thus that St. Paul, with admirable precision of dexterity, avoids the necessity of ascribing to the law an efficacy which it did not possess, while he admits, in the fullest terms, that praise and excellence of the law for which the Jew was chiefly anxious; its Divine original, its inherent purity, its adaptation to the happiness and virtue of mankind.

Every commandment of God, he allows, was just and holy. But those commandments (which were, in truth, only declarations of God's displeasure against particular sins) gave their hearers, indeed, a sufficient warning as to the danger of indulging in those sins, but conferred no power to overcome the force of passion, no opening of escape from the temptations by which they were surrounded. " We know," observes St. Paul, " that

Q

the law is spiritual, but I am carnal. I am a mere
fleshly being, weak and easily tempted, sold unto
sin, the bondslave of my evil passions and my evil
habits." " For," he adds, shortly afterwards, " I
delight in the law of God after my inward man."
My reason, my soul, the spiritual part of me acknowledges the excellence of the commandments
of God; and, as a rational being, I sincerely desire to conform to them. " But I see another law
in my members, warring against the law that is in
my mind." I perceive my mere animal propensities
contending against, and overpowering that line of
conduct which reason acknowledges to be the
best, and " bringing me into captivity to that law
which is in my members, those sinful habits which
are inherent in my body, and in the indulgence
of which alone my animal nature finds delight.
" Oh, wretched," therefore, " wretched man that
I am! who will deliver me from the body of this
death," this mortal and deadly nature which thus
presses down my soul to sin and to the grave, and
clogs her flight to that Heaven which is her proper habitation ?

   This, doubtless, is a state of exceeding terrour
and misery, and one which fully justifies the pas-
sionate exclamation of St. Paul, inasmuch as no
danger is so dreadful as that which we incur with
our eyes open; no sufferings so keen as those
which we bring on ourselves, no state so degrading
as subjection to the blind caprice of a madman, or
an irrational animal.

It is related of a bloody tyrant in ancient times, or it was the fiction of the poets to describe the excess of tyranny, that it was his frequent and horrible pleasure to bind the living to the dead, to condemn his lingering victims to endure for days and nights the cold embrace and loathsome touch of some swollen and rotting carcase, which they themselves were ere long to resemble, and with whose wretched dust their own was to moulder away. Such may be thought the bitterest dregs of human misery; yet hardly inferior, perhaps, to the reasonable soul of man, is the bondage and burthen of that mass of fleshly appetites, whose earthly bands restrain its every nobler aspiration; whose increasing corruptions pollute while they destroy; whose propensities tend downwards to their native clay, and whose heritage are the grave and hell!

Nor must this hideous picture be regarded as the creature of imagination; nor is it of his own case only that St. Paul is speaking; though he, like other men, had felt the bondage which he mourns, and, happier than many men, had been greatly and gloriously rescued. It is a complaint in which every man must sympathize, who has examined seriously his own heart and conscience, who has ever sought to forsake a single sinful practice, or attempted to cleanse his soul from the stain of a single unholy desire. Wickedness is often called blindness, and, as it should seem at first, with sufficient reason; since a course of wickedness is so

utterly contrary to the visible interest of man, that
none but the blind, it might be thought, would
court their ruin.   But if wickedness proceeded
from blindness only, should we so often find, as we
are unhappily doomed to do, that they who have
eaten most largely of the tree of knowledge, are
often the furthest removed from the tree of life? And
that they who, of all men, best know their duty
and interest, are often of all others the most backward to follow either ?   The profligate whose
vices are dragging him to an early grave, will tell
you, perhaps with tears, that he knows but cannot
escape his danger ; and many a man of lofty spirit
and lofty understanding has mourned in secret
over those pursuits by which his outward attention was engrossed, and exclaimed with one of our
poets,

> " Why was I born with such a sense of virtue,
> With such keen horrour of debasing guilt,
> And yet a slave to such impetuous passion ?"

The complaint, I repeat, is as old as the world
itself, and as familiar as our daily rest and nourishment ; nor is it a misfortune of which the Jew or
the Christian have alone been rendered sensible.
" It may seem," said Araspes to Cyrus king of
Persia, " that there are at once two souls, an evil
and a good, within me, between whose opposite
counsels my will hangs wavering and irresolute,
and which, as either gets the better, determine me
to vice or to goodness [1] ;" but of these alas ! how

[1] Xenophon Cyrop. vi. 1. 41.

greatly is the evil spirit superior in natural strength
to that which is wise and holy!

The enquiry would be too long and too meta-
physical; it is, perhaps, too hopeless to attempt,
with our imperfect knowledge of the ways of God,
to give a reason why things are suffered thus to
be, or to trace to its source that mighty strife
between good and evil which is coeval with all
created things, in which the angels first, and afterwards our parents fell; and which, crushed as the
serpent's head has been by Christ, continues still,
and, till the final triumph of our Redeemer, must
continue to shake with its convulsive struggles the
pillars of the universe. It is enough for us to know
that we are by nature sick unto death, but that we
have a great Physician at hand to heal us. It is
sufficient for us to recollect that we must not com-
plain of evils for which a remedy is provided; and
that the apostle himself, who would seem to plunge
us in despair by the picture which he draws of our
natural condition, bursts forth, immediately after,
into a noble exclamation of thankfulness to that
God who hath delivered us through Jesus Christ
our Lord!

Of the means whereby this great deliverance was
effected; of the dreadful ransom which the Son of
God has paid for our souls; and how, by His own
dying agonies, He stopped the jaws of that death
which else had gaped insatiably for all, I need not,
as I am addressing Christians I surely need not,
proceed to treat more largely. I shall, therefore,

only observe, that the two points in which that deliverance consisted were, precisely, those which,
according to St. Paul's argument, could not be
supplied by any human code of morality, nor even
by the Jewish law itself and the commandments
given from Mount Sinai.   These points are pardon
and grace ; pardon for past offences, grace to enable
us to lead new lives, and to make us less unworthy
inhabitants of that Heaven whither Christ is gone
before.   The one restores us to the same degree of
favour with God which our nature possessed before
its fall ; the other supports us against those temptations under which we must else, of necessity,
again have fallen ; and thus, by the Christian covenant, are boasting and despair alike excluded ;
boasting by the sense of our natural inability to
please the Most High, and despair by the knowledge that the Most High Himself is on our side,
and that if we fall not away from Him, we may in
security look on the assaults of our spiritual and
fleshly enemies.

From all which I have said, the following practical conclusions may be drawn.   First, since our
condition is by nature so perilous   since our passions are so strong, and our flesh so frail and prone
to evil, what constant vigilance do those passions
and propensities require, of which St. Paul com-
plains so heavily ?   If we were shut up in the same
den with a wild beast ; if we were opposed to an
armed enemy ; if we were steering a vessel through
an unknown sea, amid the dash of waves and the

1

glimmering of breakers, we should need, I apprehend, no admonition to be watchful and diligent.
Alas! my friends, our own hearts are wilder than
the savage of the woods; our own hearts, uncon-
trouled, are more formidable than the deadliest adversary; our own hearts are more changeable and
deceitful than the winds, the waves, the depths, and
shallows of the ocean. Watch, then, and pray,
lest ye enter into temptation. Watch and pray!
Without prayer to God "the watchman waketh
but in vain [1];" and without an answerable watchfulness and care for our souls, displayed in the usual
tenour of our lives and actions, our idle prayers
will be only an offence to God.

Nor should the difficulty of the task hold us
excused from attempting it; seeing that what is
necessary to be done, it becomes us, at least, to
try to do; and what God commands, we may be
sure that He will also give us strength to accomplish. Of ourselves we can do nothing, but we
can do all things through Christ that strength-
eneth us; and the same glorious Being who commanded the lame to walk, gave his limbs, at the
same time, ability to perform His bidding! So far
indeed from the weakness of the flesh being able to
destroy the hope of the sincere and industrious
Christian, "My grace," saith Christ, "is sufficient
for thee [2]:" and the triumph of that grace is shown,
not only in enabling the reasonable soul to subdue

[1] Psalm cxxvii. 1.   [2] 2 Cor. xii. 19.

the body wherein it dwells, but in sanctifying that
body into a temple of the Holy Ghost, and raising
it hereafter from the grave to be a palace of unspeakable glory, wherein the pure and spotless soul
shall, through all eternity, reside, to the praise of
Him " who shall change our vile body that it may
be fashioned like unto His glorious body, according
to the working whereby He is able even to subdue
all things unto Himself[1]."

But in the promise thus held out of this gracious
gift to men (the gift, as the beloved disciple has
stated it, " of power to become the sons of God[2];")
in that promise itself is implied a due recurrence to
the external means of grace, those instruments, if
I may so speak, of God's overflowing bounty to
man, whereby we draw near to our Maker's throne,
and lay hold, like Esther in the Jewish annals, on
the golden sceptre of His pardon, His support and
favour.   It is needful not only to believe in Christ
with our hearts, but to confess Him with our lips
unto salvation ; not only to endeavour to glorify
Him in our lives, but devoutly to seek, through the
channels of prayer, of hearing the word and of
study of the Scripture, and through the ordinances
which He has left behind, that help from on High
by which alone we are more than conquerors. To
such of you as have not yet renewed, in your own
persons, that solemn and blessed covenant, which
in your infancy was contracted for you by your

---

[1] Philip. iii. 21.   [2] St. John i. 12.

sureties, an opportunity will be on Thursday next held out both to profess before men, in express and solemn terms, your faith in your crucified Saviour, and to solicit for His sake, and in the manner which His holy apostles have appointed, the gift of the Holy Ghost, the Comforter.

And all who are religiously and devoutly disposed, all who feel the burden of their sins, and desire in future to live less unworthy of their calling, all who seek for help and life through the blood of Christ alone, and all who are in charity with their neighbours, forgiving those who have done them wrong, and desirous to make amends, so far as their power shall reach, to all those, if such there are, whom they have injured, all such are invited on the next Lord's Day, to partake with us in the solemn commemoration of the greatest and saddest mercy which ever was shown to man, and to draw forth life and health to their souls from the body and blood of their broken and bleeding Saviour.

May the days which intervene be to all of you, my brethren, a period of diligent self-examination, of frequent study of the Scriptures, of frequent and earnest prayer. And not for yourselves only let those holy prayers be offered; but for us who watch for your salvation; for those young plants, of faith whom we are seeking to train up in the ways of peace and pardon; and for those heathen multitudes, whose eyes are bent on us for good or evil, in all the dealings of our lives, and all the cere-

monies of our religion, and of whose souls one day
a strict account must be rendered by all whose
example has made the way of truth be evil spoken
of, and all who have not employed to the good of
their fellow men, and to the glory of the Most
High, the abilities, the influence, the leisure, and
the abundance which the wise and good God has
entrusted to them.

SERMON XIV.

ON THE LOVE OF GOD.

[Preached at Cawnpoor, October 11, 1824.]

St. Matt. xxii. 37—40.

Thou shalt love the Lord thy God with all thy heart, and with all thy soul, and with all thy mind. This is the first and great commandment. And the second is like unto it, thou shalt love thy neighbour as thyself. On these two commandments hang all the law and the prophets.

This beautiful summary of duty, even before the time of Christ, appears to have been proverbial among the Jews, as the statement of those objects which the law of Moses was intended to secure and illustrate. But whoever was its original author, (something like it, though not the very words themselves, may be found in the Psalms, and in the prophet Micah a still nearer approach to its import[1]) yet as thus solemnly adopted by Christ it becomes entitled to the acceptance and obedience of every Christian, and an adherence to its rule as among the surest pledges which any Christian can

---

[1] Micah vi. 8.

offer of his continuance in the faith, and that his
faith is such as may hereafter profit him.   A sense,
indeed, of God's goodness, and a desire to render
ourselves acceptable to Him, is the only principle
of action which a wise and gracious God can be
supposed to regard with pleasure.   We are God's
children, not His slaves; and it is our love which
He requires, as much as, and still more than, our
obedience.   If this last were all which He sought
for, He might have compelled it by an overruling
necessity, or have accompanied His commands
with such resistless and miraculous influence, as
should prevent even the possibility of rebellion.
But He demands a reasonable service, a warm and
affectionate energy which shall urge us, not only
to fly from hell, but to evince our gratitude for
the hopes of Heaven; by kindness, therefore, and
long suffering, He endeavours to excite our love;
and even when His menaces or His judgements
rouse us to a necessary perception of our weakness,
our guilt and our danger, His assurances of mercy
never fail to accompany His terms.

Accordingly, though in the nature of the Mosaic
law, and in the leading circumstances of its pro-
mulgation, His immediate purpose was rather to
display His justice than His mercy; to set forth in
fiery characters His anger against sin; and, by a
wholesome and searching severity, to prepare men's
hearts for the healing dispensation of the Gospel;
yet, even here we find, through the Scriptures of
the elder covenant, the mercy of God more fre-

quently insisted on than either His justice, His might, or His majesty. We find ourselves invited to " praise the Lord for His goodness ;" " to taste and see how good the Lord is, and how great are His tender mercies on them that call upon Him [1]." Jehovah too sometimes condescends to reason with His unthankful people, and to appeal to the men of Judah themselves, whether more could have been done than He had done for His vineyard [2]? And in that dreadful moment when God Himself came down to give forth His laws to men, and by a discovery of that holiness which He requires from His servants, to open men's eyes to their own guilt and their need of the promised Intercessor ; even then, from the midst of thunderings and darkness, and surrounded with every circumstance of majesty and terrour, the Almighty makes His strongest appeal to their love, and not to their weakness, and He lays claim to their obedience as their Deliverer and their Friend, " the God who brought them out of the land of Egypt, out of the house of bondage [3]."

And since, by the Jews themselves, the principle of love and thankfulness, the love of God, and, for God's sake, the love of our neighbour, were recognised as the sum and substance of the law ; since these were the two commandments which its other precepts, and its external ceremonies, served only to defend and illustrate ; and since these were in a still more conspicuous manner enforced and con-

---

[1] Psalm cvii. 8. xxxiv. 8.   [2] Isaiah v. 3, 4.

[3] Exod. xix. 16—19. xx. 2.

firmed by the Messiah, we might, perhaps, from this admitted truth alone, establish the truth of our Lord's declaration, that He came to fulfill and not to change the precepts of the ancient covenant; to make its promises more blessed and its duties more easy by a clearer discovery of those hopes and privileges which were dimly shadowed out before ; and by replacing with stronger motives and more powerful spiritual assistance, those sacrifices and ceremonies on which the ancient Israelite relied for the expiation of his sins, and the constant recollection of his duties.   Yet still, and now more than ever, the claims of God are founded on our love and thankfulness.   He expects them, indeed, no longer from a single favoured race, as the God who had broken their chains, who had led them from a land of slavery, and loaded them with many temporal advantages ; but He has laid on all the nations of mankind a more precious and extensive obligation, as their Maker, their Redeemer, and their Sanctifier, their Deliverer from that fear of death under which all nature, till His coming, had languished ; and from that bondage of sin which is ten thousand fold more terrible than the fetters of an earthly tyrant.

It is thus that the message which the Only Begotten brought into the world was proclaimed both by Himself and His angels to be " good tidings of great joy [1]."   It is thus that the nature of the Al-

----

[1] St. Luke xi. 10.

mighty is described in the New Testament as love, in its fountain and original; and that we are called on to behold and return that regard which He has shown to mankind in that, while we were yet sinners, He gave His only Son to die for our salvation.

This obedience, indeed, of affection, this freewill offering of ourselves is, so far as we are able to judge, the most material distinction between the best and the worst, the happiest and most miserable among the creatures of God, the angels who have kept their first estate, and those spirits for whom everlasting fire is prepared. Those guilty and most unhappy beings have faith, we know, for they " believe and tremble[1]." We know likewise that, when in the exercise of their malice towards mankind, they were checked by the commanding voice of the Messiah, they too could pray to Him for a little longer forbearance of punishment; they too made haste to relinquish their victims at a word, and yielded to the injunctions of their conqueror an immediate and terrified obedience.

But they are not prayers like these, they are not services of this description which, in the nature of things, can be well pleasing or acceptable to the Almighty. Which of you would choose such obedience in a servant? In a son, which of you would endure it? The fear of God is indeed, in the words of Solomon, " the beginning of wisdom[2]." Of

---

[1] St. James ii. 19. [2] Prov. i. 7.

knowledge and of faith it is the first fruit, and the
primary foundation of active and habitual holiness.
But if our knowledge and our faith bring forth no
further increase; if our holiness advances no higher
in its Heavenward progress, so far will be such a
faith from availing to our salvation, that better had
it been for our souls had we never known nor believed!

Nor is it only as affording a noble and more acceptable principle of action than fear, that the love
of God is thus valuable in God's eyes, and thus indispensable to those who call themselves His servants. Those actions which proceed from love,
however powerless in themselves (as powerless all
our actions must be) to contribute to the happiness,
or augment the glories of Him whom the angels
serve, and whose praise all creation shouts forth
with her ten thousand voices, have yet in the
nature of things, and judging from the analogy of
the visible world, a claim on Him to whom they
are offered. We feel ourselves that the affection
of a servant or a child, endears to us and renders
valuable in our eyes, even the poorest and humblest
effort by which that affection is expressed or manifested. Nor can we doubt that infinite as is the
distance between man and his Maker, yet by Him
to whom all His works are known, the love even of
His weakest servant must be regarded with a similar
complacency, and that the affection which we feel
within ourselves towards our unseen and Almighty
Benefactor is reflected back from Him towards

ourselves with an intenseness so much greater than our own, as God excells us in the clearness of His views and the benevolence of His nature. It is faith which enables us to contemplate God, but it is love which diminishes the distance between God and ourselves; and it is love alone which, under Christ, can bring us to Heaven, or, when we are entered there, can make Heaven a place of happiness.

But enough has been said to show the necessity and value of a genuine love for God ; and I would now proceed to point out, to the best of my ability, the most probable and efficacious means of awakening such a .love within ourselves ; as well as the effects which it may be expected to produce on our thoughts, our tempers, and our daily and hourly actions. And to obtain a knowledge of these, little more, perhaps, is necessary than to examine the causes which produce and increase in us an affection for earthly objects ; inasmuch as, notwithstanding the mysterious nature of many of God's dealings with us, and more particularly of that spiritual and sanctifying influence which He exerts over our minds, and without which, it must never be forgotten, no amiable or holy principle can be generated in our breasts ; yet in this love, whensoever derived, there is in truth nothing mysterious; and the love which we feel for God can differ from the love which we feel for an earthly parent in nothing but the intensity of its obligation, and the infinite worthiness of its object.

Examine then your hearts, all you that have parents, and ask them why you love your father and your mother ? why you delight to serve and please them ? why you obey their wishes from affection, not from fear ? why you esteem all which you can do but too little to promote their happiness, and rejoice to incur inconvenience yourselves so it may evince your attachment towards them !

You love them, you will doubtless answer, because they have first loved you; because from them you derive your life and all its chequered series of interest and enjoyment; because they nursed you when you were weak, instructed you when you were ignorant, endured you when you were froward, trained you up, it may be, to distinction and prosperity in the life which now is, and taught you to look forward to everlasting happiness in the life to come. For these and similar reasons you love your father and your mother. You do well! Continue to love them more and more, for they well deserve your best affection! But know, children of God, your Heavenly Father hath done for you greater things than these ! But do you not also find that this feeling of filial love is increased and strengthened by a frequent recollection of the benefits which you have received from your parents; and that your hearts have grown warmer towards them the more you lived in their society ; the longer and oftener you conversed together; and the more and greater the acts and evidences of mutual kindness which passed

2

between you ?   Is it not, unhappily, most true, that
long absence and habitual disregard will always
greatly damp and often entirely extinguish that affection which ought to exist, and under other
circumstances, would naturally have existed between the members of the same family ?   Beware,
then, how you neglect that species and degree of
intercourse with your Heavenly Father, to maintain which His mercy permits and His word invites,
and His grace, if you make use of it, enables you!
Beware lest, by thinking of Him but seldom, but
seldom addressing Him in prayer, and seldom hearing His voice in His Holy Scriptures and His public
ordinances, you estrange yourself, by degrees, entirely from His love, and allow the pursuits and
pleasures of the world to establish an empire in
your heart left empty of holier affections!   It is
by daily prayer and daily thanksgiving, by patient
study of God's word, and by patient meditation on
our own condition, and on all which God has done
and will do for us, that a genuine and rational love
for Him is kindled in our hearts ; and that we become unfeignedly attached to the Friend of whose
kindness we have had so much experience.

It is, indeed, to be expected, and it therefore
should by no means be allowed to discourage the
inexperienced Christian, that at first, and in the
earlier stages of our approach to God, we should
experience but little of that ardour of devotion,
those pleasures of earnest piety which are, in this
world, the reward of love as well as its most con-

vincing evidence. Our prayers at first will often
be constrained; our thanksgivings cold and formal;
our thoughts will wander from our closets to the
world, and we shall have too frequent occasion to
acknowledge with shame and sorrow the imperfection of those offerings which we as yet can make
to our Benefactor. A religious feeling, like every
other mental habit, is slowly and gradually acquired.
A strong and lasting affection is not ordinarily the
growth of a day; but to have begun at all is, in religion, no trifling progress; and a steady perse-
verence in prayer and praise will, not only, by
degrees, enlist the strength of habit on the side of
holiness, but will call down, moreover, and preserve to us that spiritual support and influence,
without which all human efforts must be vain, but
which no one will seek in vain, who seeks for it in
sincerity and by the appointed channels.

But though the absence of fervour be not the
produce of permitted and habitual sin, undoubtedly
it must be ruinous to every well-founded hope of
acquiring a genuine love for Him who is of purer
eyes than to behold iniquity. In disputes between
men we are taught by every day's experience that
it is hard to love those whom we have injured; and
that the more we feel ourselves in the wrong, the
more inclined we are to view with dislike as well
as apprehension, the person who has cause to be
offended with us. And thus it is that every additional act of transgression indisposes our hearts
the more to a faith in the gracious offers of our

King, and to an acceptance of them ; and the more impossible it seems that we should be pardoned, the more sturdily and desperately do we proceed in courses of which we know that the end is death, but the dereliction of which, as we apprehend, would be now altogether fruitless.

Such a state of mind, of all others to which a sinner can be reduced on this side the grave, is surely the most terrible. It is one, however, which is more common among men than the generality of mankind imagine ; and it is a danger which cannot be too often or too earnestly represented to all those who dwell carelessly, lest their habitual offences should shut the door against reconciliation ; and not only so grieve the Holy Spirit as to deter Him from returning, but, even if He should vouchsafe to return, render their hearts insensible to all the ordinary methods of His mercy.

An amendment of life, indeed, and a conduct conformable to the will and word of the Most High, is the only mark I know of to distinguish a genuine love of Him from those vain and enthusiastic flights of fancy which have their origin in the fancy alone ; which are consistent with indulgences the most impure, and passions the most unrestrained and unconverted ; in which the devil would gladly persuade the sinner to rest contented through life, but the vanity of which will be made apparent in that season when the axe will be laid to the root of all false pretences and unfounded hopes, in the hour of death and in the day of judgement. And it is happy for us that a point of such importance is one on which the sincere enquirer can scarcely by possibility deceive himself, inasmuch as the effects of a genuine love are such as can hardly be counterfeited, and are such, indeed, as without the inspiration and assistance of Him whose name is love, the nature of man is unable to bring forth to perfection. And among these the following are some of the most conspicuous.

In the first place, he who really loves God, will be content to depend on Him, and acquiesce with cheerfulness in all His dispensations of severity or mercy. That we do, in fact, depend on God for all which we receive, and all which we hope for, will be recognized by the decision of reason alone ; and it is a truth which even an unregenerate heart may admit with fear and trembling. But a contented and hopeful dependance on God, a cheerful acquiescence in all which He determines, a frame of mind which converts into an unceasing source of pleasure our recollection of that strength on which we rely, that wisdom which is conspicuous alike in every instance of good or evil fortune ; such a feeling as I have described can proceed from love alone, and I can hardly admit the existence of a genuine love of God without it.

A sense of weakness and dependance without love is always miserable. But where love is, even in the imperfect attachments of the nether world, the recollection of such dependance is never oppressive or melancholy. It is any thing but painful for a

child to cling to the embrace, the support, the
comfort and provident kindness of a tender and
most dear parent. It is any thing but painful to
unbosom our griefs, our trials, and our difficulties
to a kind and experienced and powerful friend,
who shares our thoughts, who sympathizes with
our sorrows, and whose hand we trace in all the
more conspicuous comforts and advantages of our
situation. By the favours of those whom we love
and venerate we are elated, not humiliated. We
are proud, not ashamed, of the obligations laid on
us by a gracious sovereign, or a wise and discrimi-
nating patron, because we delight in his benefits as
evidences of his regard, and identify ourselves, in a
certain degree, with the excellencies of him who
honours us with such a friendship. And even so
in the child-like leaning of a Christian on his God,
not only is fear in a great measure cast out as
knowing on whom we depend, but enjoyment is
enhanced for His sake, by whom all our enjoyments
are bestowed; and all which we love becomes more
lovely in our eyes when we say in our hearts,
" And this also is my Father's bounty !"

If, on the other hand, He who hath given should
take away, however we may feel the smart (and
there is certainly no charm in religion which can
make us impassive or insensible) a real love for
God will be our best and most efficacious comfort.
It will recall to our minds all the blessings which
we have received, and all the far greater blessings
we look for ; it will silence complaint by the recol-

lection of past kindness ; and withdraw our attention from present suffering by the anticipation of
future and more abundant mercy. We shall deduce
from our own love for God a confidence that this
love is mutual, an assurance that His chastisements
are mercies in disguise, and that the clouds under
which our nature shudders, will, ere long, burst
over our heads in blessing. " Perfect love," said
he who of all men most loved Christ, and whom
more than all other men, Christ in the time of
His humiliation loved. " Perfect love casteth out
fear ;" or if this painful but wholesome and necessary intruder must yet at times return, and be
our occasional companion through our earthly pilgrimage, it will be a distrust of ourselves, not a
doubt of God ; it will be mingled with a trembling
joy for the continued sense of His mercy and forbearance ; by the recollection of our weakness it
will bind us closer to His strength, and make the
blessing of His presence more precious in our eyes,
by the possibility that we may, hereafter, by our
own faults, deprive ourselves of that blessing.

Such lives as these are, in themselves, a continued
act of prayer and thanksgiving; yet even such a life
as this would not excuse us from that which is
another evidence of the love, for whose good all
things are made to work together, " a frequency
and regularity of private and public prayer, and a
diligent perusal of the Holy Scriptures." It is in

[1] 1 St. John iv. 18.

such acts as these that the soul draws nearer to its
Maker; it is then that we speak to Him and hear
His voice again; and that love would be a mere
mockery of the name which should shun the conversation and neglect the correspondence of the person whom we most affected to esteem and honour.
As the practice then of prayer, of praise, and the
study of the Scriptures is the most availing and necessary course to kindle a love of God in our hearts;
so is, on the other hand, a cheerful continuance
in the same habitual piety the certain effect and
the necessary evidence that the flame thus excited
is alive and yet glowing within us.

Another necessary proof of this love is the light
in which we look on sin. I need not repeat what
I have already urged against the incompatibility of
any gross and habitual transgression with the existence of genuine love for the Almighty. But if we
take pleasure in the recollection of foregone, or the
imagination of future or possible evil; if we feed
our fancies with acts which we dare not perform,
and witness with indifference or with unholy pleasure the transgressions of those who live around us;
if we feel a regret for the indulgences which we are,
by our situation in life, compelled to forego, and
condemn as fanatical or enthusiastic all endeavours
after a more rigid and excellent piety, a moment's
consideration will show how little the love of God
can dwell in us! It is a necessary part of affection
to like and dislike the same objects with the person
to whom we are united; and in truth, in that

particular species of affection which I am now dis-
cussing, it is scarcely possible for any one, with a
true conception of the causes which led to Christ's
death, to read once attentively the details of that
aweful sacrifice, without experiencing, for the time
at least, a loathing and horrour of those sins which
it was necessary to visit so severely on the guiltless ;
and something like a bitter indignation against
himself as one whose offences, amid the great
mass of the foreseen offences of mankind, added
sharpness to the thorny crown of Him who died to
save us !

The last, however, and of all others the most
decisive symptom of God's love residing in our
hearts is, that the love of our neighbour also holds
its dwelling there. It would occupy too much time
(indeed I feel that I have already encroached too
largely on your patience) were I to go through all
the different bearings and details of this second
great commandment : I would therefore merely
direct your thoughts to the close connection which
exists between the two, and to the utter impossibility of keeping the one while we transgress or
neglect the other.

Though it were possible, (and it is a possibility
which can only be supposed for the sake of argument) though it were possible, that all the other
proofs of loving God should be found apart from
this last and greatest, yet would this one deficiency
give all the rest the lie : " He that loveth not his
brother whom he hath seen, how can he love God

whom he hath not seen [1] ?"   Where our affections
are so selfish and so cold as not to throw a kindly
warmth around the little circle of our friends and
neighbours, the kindred of our blood, and the poor
who are always with us, how can their feeble rays
extend to the depth and heighth and breadth of invisible and infinite existence, of Him who is seen
by the eye of faith alone, and who reveals Himself
only to the pure in heart and to the merciful?
How can we love our Father while we hate His
children? How can we love our Redeemer, while we
are indifferent to the welfare of those whom He
died to save, and lives again to intercede for?

He then who loveth not his neighbour as himself
is never, whatever may be his other pretensions to
sanctity, a sincere and genuine lover of God.   But
the opposite assertion is also strictly true, and he
who loveth not God most of all, will never love his
neighbour as he ought to do.   He wants, as we
have seen, the only motive of action which is either
acceptable with God, or availing against the snares
of our mortal condition, the only principle which
can encourage us to look for the further gracious
assistance of that Spirit through whom we are conquerors.

It is, indeed, no difficult task to be liberal of fair
words to others.   It is, thank God, no uncommon
thing where wealth is abundant, and avarice despised, and liberality held in honour, to find men

_____

[1] 1 St. John iv. 20.

who, by no stretch of charity, can be supposed to
care seriously for God, who yet are not insensible
to the calls of kindness and of pity, and not un-
willing to dispense some portion of their superfluities for the relief of their necessitous brethren.
But of that charity which is self-denying as well as
kind ; of that charity which is solicitous for the
souls as well as for the bodies of men ; of that charity which can labour long and suffer much, as well
as contribute largely; of that charity which " is not
puffed up; doth not behave itself unseemly,—hopeth
all things, believeth all things, endureth all things[1]."
I wish to God the instances were more frequent
than my experience leads me to believe them ; and
I am sure, so far forth as that experience extends,
that no single instance has been found in which the
philanthropy was not engrafted on some species of
religious feeling.

The truth is, that our practice of the two great
commandments can only be effectual and progressive where they reciprocally foster and increase
one another. The more we grow in love to God, the
more love we shall feel for His children ; and the
greater real kindness we cherish and practise towards
mankind, the greater and warmer thankfulness we
shall be inspired with towards Him, by whom the
world has been created, preserved and pardoned ;
to whose goodness we owe the comforts of society,
the endearments of kindred and the blessings of

---

[1] 1 Cor. xiii. 4, 5. 7.

friendship; who hath in His mercy ordained men to be helpful one to another, and who has graciously made the discharge of this most necessary duty a source of the purest earthly happiness.

But of these two commandments, the love of God stands first; first in order, first in object, first in dignity; where this is really found, the other parts of holiness will, almost of necessity, follow; but where this is not sought after, their progress must be small who stumble on the threshold of religion.

Be it then your endeavour, brethren, to acquaint yourselves with all which God has done for you, with your own undeservings and His great and unfailing mercies. Be it your business to wait on Him in prayer, to converse with Him in the Scriptures, to renounce in your thoughts and actions whatever is displeasing to Him, and to practice towards His creatures, and for His sake, that mercy and meekness, that forgiveness and bounty which you hope yourselves to find from Him.

Nor fear, if you act thus, but that you will soon begin to love; fear not, if you love thus, but that you will be surely loved in return by Him who is the centre of your hopes, your imitation, and your affection. Yea, if you love thus, be sure that God already loves you; that the seed which He has sown in your heart is the first pledge and promise of His affection; and that He has already taken possession of that temple wherein, unless we cast Him forth, He hath purposed to dwell for ever.

" If a man love me," said the Son of God, " he
will keep my words, and my Father will love him,
and we will come unto him, and make our abode
with him [1]."

Amen, Amen! Even so, come Lord Jesus. Even
so, Father of all, for Thy Son's sake descend on us,
and by Thy Spirit sanctify our hearts, that they
may be filled with Thy invisible presence in this
dark and evil world, so that, in the world to come,
we may see Thee as Thou art, and be in Thee and
with Thee everlastingly.

[1] 1 John xiv. 23.

SERMON XV.

[Preached at Calcutta, Christmas Day, 1825.]

St. Luke ii. 14.

Glory to God in the highest, and on earth peace, good-will to-wards men.

This is the hymn with which the angels celebrated the incarnation of our Blessed Saviour, and to us, whom the authority of our national Church, the precedent of early antiquity, and the example of the great majority of believers in every age and country invite, as at this time, to give thanks for the same illustrious display of Divine mercy, no fitter subject of devout meditation can be found than the words in which the spirits of Heaven announced that mercy to mankind.

And of the topics of reflection which the words in question offer to the mind, the following are among the most striking. In the first place, the fact itself of that sympathizing joy which the angels are represented as feeling in the event which they announced with so much celestial pomp and splen-

dour, must needs excite in us a powerful apprehension of the greatness and illustrious nature of the
benefit thus extended to our race, and may convince
us both that those evils are very grievous from which
the coming of the Son of God was to free mankind,
and those blessings are even greater than our familiarity with them leaves us always able to estimate, which could move beings, so much superior
to ourselves, to express such a lively and unusual
interest in them.   And the inference, I think, will
follow both that, in the birth of the Messiah, the
spirits of Heaven recognised something far more
remarkable than the birth of a mere earthly prophet, and that something far more valuable than a
new and more perfect revelation of God's will was
anticipated by them in their song of peace and
good will to the sons of Adam.

Of earthly prophets and earthly heroes the birth
had been announced, and announced by angels, in
former and well-known instances.   Isaac and Ishmael had each had his Heavenly harbinger, and the
mother of Sampson was comforted in her lonely
prayers by the promise of a distinguished offspring [1].
But in none of these instances was there the like
promise displayed, in none of them was the like
ardour of exultation and congratulation manifested
which now brake the slumbers of the shepherds
on the hill of Bethlehem; and which chaunted, this
one time, in mortal ears, that harmony which swells

[1] Gen. xvii. 16. xvi. 11. Judges xiii. 5.

the choirs of Paradise. A celestial visitant, in form
as a man, and suspected only to be more than man
from the unmoved and terrible beauty of his countenance, a messenger indeed to mortal clay, but a
messenger of too high a rank and too far removed from
mortal pursuits or passions to mingle sympathies with
that which was but the child of a day, or to occupy
himself more or longer than his errand required with
the fallen inhabitants of our planet, such was the
form whose touch consumed to ashes the offering
of Manoah and his wife; such he who came to Agar
in the wilderness, to Zacharias in the temple ; and
such the three (though with respect to *one* of these
a yet further mystery belongs) who reproved the
incredulity of Sarah, and received the homage and
hospitality of Abraham beneath the oak of Mamre[1].
The time had been when God Himself came down
to speak, in the form of God, with man, in might
and majesty beyond a doubt, but with no tokens
of gratulation, no songs of jubilee. On Sinai was
a thick and lonely darkness, a mountain smoking
like a furnace, which neither man nor beast could
approach, save Moses only, and which Moses himself drew near in exceeding fear and trembling.
No angel shapes broke through the gloom, no angel melodies were heard in the pauses of the thunder ; but the trumpet alone waxing louder and
louder, and the voice of God, of which they who
heard it said, " Let not God speak with us lest we

[1] Judges xiii. 20. Gen. xvi. 7. Luke i. 11. Gen. xviii. 1.

S

die ¹ !" How different were these sights and sounds
from the glory of the Lord, from the herald angel, accompanied by a multitude of the Heavenly
host, and the hymn which, while it ascribed fresh
glory to the Most High, spake of peace restored
between Heaven and earth, and renewed good will
from the Creator to His creatures.

If, however, we look back to what the angel had
announced to the shepherds, " unto you is born
this day, in the city of David, a SAVIOUR ;" if we
recollect that this birth was the first thing executed
on earth towards reconciling mankind to God;
that it was the first step towards the overturn of
that evil spirit, who is the enemy and accuser of
angels as well as of men; that it was the noblest
instance of mercy and condescension which even
Omnipotence could show, and the more noble in
proportion to the wretchedness and manifold de-
merits of those in whose favour it was exerted, we
shall not wonder that the happy and benevolent
inhabitants of Heaven felt joy in the extension to
other worlds of those blessings in which they themselves partook without measure ; that the far-seeing cherubims beheld with delight and wonder a
display of wisdom, of power, and of holiness which
surpassed their most elevated contemplations, and
that the seraphs loved, with augmented ardour, that
good and gracious Lord who had pity on the least
worthy of His creatures.

¹ Exod. xx. 19.   ² St. Luke ii. 11.

The reason, then, assigned for the exultation of the Heavenly host, is that Christ was born " a Saviour." And if we desire to ascertain in what peculiar sense the Lord Jesus was a Saviour beyond all the prophets who went before Him, we shall find, or I am much mistaken, a very considerable difficulty (on every hypothesis of His nature and functions but that which we call the orthodox one) in finding an adequate reason for the eminence and peculiarity of the title thus appropriated to Him; for the exultation expressed by the angels while thus appropriating it; and for the vast and lavish display of wonder, of prophecy, of vision, and of miracle, by which the birth, and life, and death, and resurrection, and ascension, and destined return of the Messiah, both have been and will be illustrated. Were these honours paid to Christ as to a mortal man, but taught of God and endued with an unexampled degree of God's spiritual assistance, the chosen instrument of bringing to light a more perfect and holy law of life and morals, confirmed with stronger sanctions than the law of Moses, and with that strongest sanction of all which arises from the resurrection of the dead and a future life without end? God forbid that I should underrate the benefits which, even according to this imperfect view of the Christian faith, will appear to have been conferred on man through Jesus of Nazareth. I admit that, though we were to consider Him as a human prophet only, " He spake

s 2

as never man spake[1];" I admit that a fuller stream
of grace and wisdom has been poured on Him
than on the most favoured sons of Adam, who had
gone before or were to succeed Him; I admit that
no dictates of human wisdom, no previous lesson
taught by God's prophets to mankind, can equal
the simple and sober majesty of the sermon on the
mount, the touching softness of the parable of the
lost sheep, and the returning prodigal, or the thrill-
ing union of awe and tenderness which is inspired
by His picture of the last judgement; I admit that
neither Socrates, nor Moses, nor David, nor Isaiah,
have left us any thing which can equal in purity
and pathos His conversation during His last supper, and when bidding adieu to His disciples; I
admit that the doctrine of a life after death, though
intimated in many passages of the Mosaic law, and
more largely dwelt on by the prophets; though
deducible, in a great degree, from the dictates of
natural reason, and actually deduced from those
dictates by more than one distinguished heathen
philosopher; though forming a part of the popular
tradition of almost every nation of mankind, and
though received, above all, by the great majority
of the Jewish nation in its fullest extent, and with
almost all the circumstances of awe and majesty
with which even Christians are accustomed to
clothe it; I admit that this life after death, and a

---

[1] St. John vii. 46.

future state of reward and punishment were never so authoritatively declared, or so forcibly represented, or so experimentally proved, as they have been to us who believe in the doctrine and resurrection of Jesus. But I maintain that all these points of difference between Christ and the preceding prophets are not enough to account for that difference which I have remarked in the honours paid to Him, and the display of Divine power and angelic praise by which His birth and person were, above all other prophets, distinguished ; and I maintain, above all, that in none of these respects, nor in all of them taken together, is His claim made good to that title which, of all prophets, is given to Him alone, and which constituted the specific ground of those congratulations which the angels bore to their fellow-creatures of mankind, the illustrious title of " Saviour."

Is it from the fear of death that the world is delivered by our Lord? And is this end accomplished by the spectacle of His own glorious triumph over the grave, and over them that had the power of it? Alas, are we ignorant that to the sinner (and who is there among men that sinneth not ?) his fears are but the more increased by the clearness of this discovery ! The same great Moralist who hath taught us by His words, and proved to us by His own example, that the grave is but the gate to a new and eternal state of existence, hath taught us also that there is an everlasting fire prepared for the workers of iniquity,

and we must escape from the burden of our manifold offences before the resurrection of Christ can
be to us any other than a savour of death everlasting!

Can, then, a pure and holy law of life be sufficient to save mankind from their sins ?   Verily, if
a law could have been given which was competent
to produce this effect, salvation would have been
by the law of Moses!   But it is evident that so
long as we are ourselves carnal and sold unto sin,
the more spiritual and pure any rule of life may be,
the less likely we shall be to comply with it ; and
it is no less evident that where Moses and the prophets had failed to produce repentance, not all the
terrours and hopes of an invisible world, no nor, if
Christ is to be believed, the very spectacle of one
returning from the dead would be sufficient, without some further help, to alarm the sinner from the
errour of his ways, or to confirm the wavering soul
when tossed on the storms of temptation.

But be this as it may, and even supposing us in
time to come to avoid the crimes of our previous
life, yet without some deliverance from the consequences of our former sins, this late repentance,
though it might prevent our increasing their number, could not of itself rid us of apprehension.
Repentance cannot make the past not to be ; that
we have not continued to act foolishly is of itself no
reason for freeing us from those burdens which our
folly has already incurred ; and we must find out
some atonement for sins past, as well as some pre-

servative against sins future, before the people of God can lay claim to the blessed hope of being saved from those sins whose guilt defiles, and whose consequences terrify them.

Nor is more needful to show the entire conformity of the Messiah's character and office, as understood by the great majority of His disciples, with the name by which He is best known among men, and by which the angels of the Most High proclaimed Him, who was clothed with our nature that He might reconcile us to God, who lived for our instruction, who died for our sins, who rose again for our justification, and who, from His Father's right hand, both intercedes for our infirmities, and sends forth His Spirit of holiness to prompt, and help, and sanctify our sincere, though imperfect services.

What then remains but that, thus mightily delivered, we should show forth in all our words and works a constant and becoming thankfulness ; that, thus mightily aided, we should labour more abundantly in promoting our Master's praise ; and that, united with the Godhead, as our nature is through Christ, we should the more aspire to emulate in diffusive goodness that God who maketh His sun to shine on the just and the unjust, and is kind to the unthankful and the evil.

The present season is one in which, by a natural and laudable association of ideas and feelings, the great majority of the Christian world have been accustomed to express their thankfulness for the

blessings bestowed on them, by imparting in a
fuller measure than at other times the marks of
affection and tenderness towards their fellow-creatures, by calling in, either literally or figuratively,
their neighbours and brethren to rejoice with them,
and by providing that, while they themselves exult
in the bounty of the Almighty, the widow's heart
should by their means be also made to sing for
joy, and the blessings of him who was ready to perish, should mount up on their behalf an acceptable
offering to their Maker.   And here in Calcutta, in
a city which, God be praised, may be honourably
distinguished among the cities of the world for the
extent and splendour of its public and private charities, the custom has long prevailed, in pursuance
of which I yet further crave your attention, while
recommending to your bounty the most ancient,
and (I may be allowed to say), the most useful and
necessary of all our humane institutions, that which
alone administers to the pressing wants, alone alle-
viates the distress, the hunger, the nakedness, and
the ignorance of the unhappy Europeans, and descendants of Europeans, who abound in the crowded
dwellings and obscurer streets of this great and
luxurious city.   The necessity of such an institution is too obvious to require enforcement; but that
necessity may be, perhaps, less known or less ad-
verted to by those who are only occasional resi-
dents here, or who, immersed in public duties, or
elevated above the access of petitioners, are but
partially aware of the amount to which relief is

given, and the still greater degree in which it is needed.

Of the great body of Europeans of every nation and class of life who come out annually to seek their fortune in the flattering land of India, it is obvious that a small number only can hope to succeed in attaining even a livelihood; and that there are very many who are labouring at this moment under severe distress, and who are only kept here by the same poverty and want of friends which at once prevent their thriving, and prohibit their return. Nor is misfortune confined to these alone; in a country where speculation is so tempting, and where without speculation so little can be accomplished even by industry, not only are many humble but promising fortunes shipwrecked by undertakings which, if not strictly prudent, are under the circumstances of this country rendered almost necessary; but, where a prouder fabric of fortune and enterprise is shipwrecked, there are always many humbler barks whose fate depends on it, and whose industry and talent can rarely find another field till the assaults of famine, and the advances of disease, and the agony of ruined hopes and utter brokenheartedness have made them, even if another situation could be found, too often unfit to discharge its duties.

Nor are they misfortune and disappointment alone which multiply the claimants on the vestry fund, nor are these the most necessitous or the most interesting claimants on our bounty. As in

no land under Heaven is death so sudden and so
frequent, so in no land that I have ever heard of is
the death of a parent, or a husband, attended with
such utter and immediate ruin to those who depend
on him, as with the description of persons of whom
I speak, it ordinarily is in Calcutta.   And when to
these we add the multitude of orphans, or worse
than orphans, whose existence and distress are alike
the evidence and aggravation of their father's
crimes ; when we consider that not Calcutta alone,
but the poor and populous colonies of Serampoor
and Chinsura are included within the natural limit
of our care ; and that whatever be the amount of
distress in all these districts, it is to Europeans
alone, under ordinary circumstances, the sufferer
can look for relief or sympathy ; it cannot excite
surprise that, large as the funds are which have
passed through the hands of those who manage this
good work, they are altogether insufficient to the
number of claimants who besiege them.   Yet if
those funds should fail, to what quarter must the
poor apply ?   Shall private and individual charity
suffice to feed so great a multitude ?   Let those
answer who are already wearied with a daily swarm
of petitions, and who may be assured that those
petitions would, without this institution, be augmented a hundred fold, and their doors be blocked
up by suffering Christians in every hideous shape
of hunger, disease, and nakedness, till their time
and means were engrossed by giving to those whose
cases they could not investigate, or their hearts

hardened against all by the apparent impossibility of relieving many. Nor can further arguments be required to prove the advantage of a common fund under the management of a few benevolent individuals, who are content to give up no small portion of their time to enquire into the cases submitted to them; and who, from their long familiarity with this work of mercy, are really enabled, at a smaller expense of time than would, under any other circumstances, be necessary, to ascertain with tolerable accuracy the character and condition of each individual claimant.

Of the labours of the vestry, and of the effects of those labours, though not myself a member, I have frequent occasion to hear something; and when I mention that I have known instances of females respectably born and educated, soliciting for the monthly allowance of paupers; that I have known strangers who must have perished in the street for lack of friends and shelter, had not the bounty of the institution intervened; and that the free school of Calcutta, which owes its chief support to this fund, has been, under God, the only means of rescuing from an early death, or a life which was worse than death, many thousand children of Christian parents who had either abandoned or could not educate or maintain them; when I state that in the vestry alms, no Christian in distress, of whatever nation or sect, is suffered to go unrelieved; and that in the free-school, though we naturally prefer the religious instructions of our own Church, yet

2

those inftructions are forced on no child whose parents are of a different persuasion; that Armenians,
and Greeks, and Romanists, and even Hindoos,
may be seen in our classes, their prejudices respected, and their progress and comforts no less
attended to than the children of our own people,
I shall have said enough, I trust, to establish the
claim of the institution, for which I now am plead-
ing, to the support of every man who wishes well
to his fellow-creatures, and who, without neglecting the prior claims of " the household of faith," is
desirous, according to his power, " to do good to
all men."

They were these claims, and claims like these,
appreciated by a heart and head, than which few
in the history of British India have been so warm
and so cool, so ardent in the relief of distress and
so calmly judicious in the choice of measures for
alleviating it, which procured for this institution
a more than common share of the attention and
liberality of that great man whose life was cherished
still, though his presence and counsels had been
withdrawn from these colonies, not by his private
friends alone, but by every well wisher to India;
by every one who had learnt to honour private
worth or public integrity and firmness; by the
guests who had drawn delight and improvement
from his conversation while they partook in his hospitality; and by the poor against whom his doors,
his attention, his indulgence, and his purse had
never been for an instant closed.   His loss, the in-

stitution which I am now recommending, laments in common with almost every other religious or humane institution in the city; but it may be well to state, in order to intimate the extent of our misfortune in losing him, and to incite those who hear me to the exercise of a similar liberality, that accessible as Mr. Adam always was to the petitions and personal applications, of the frequency of which I have spoken, there was no charity whose claims he felt so strongly as this the eldest of all; that, ample as the donations were which the world saw affixed to his name, those donations fell considerably short of the sums which he contributed anonymously; and that even when he had left India without an idea of seeing it more, he had determined that, while life was spared him, his charities should linger here still. In him, in that other benevolent and virtuous statesman, whom, at a yet more recent date, the will of Providence has called to his reward; in others of less exalted rank, but of zeal not inferior for God's good cause, and the relief of their suffering fellow-creatures, whom since I last addressed you, a year of unusual mortality has swept from our social circles, the cause of charity has lost much; but to replace the void is not beyond the scope of our own increased exertions and the exertions of those fresh labourers who have, during that time, been added to the vineyard. Only let it be our endeavour to bestow alms as of the ability which God giveth, and that God may bless our bounty to its objects and to ourselves, let us devote it in humble prayer

1

at His Altar from whom we have received all things, and from whose grace only it cometh that we can render Him any true or laudable service.

To Him the Father of the fatherless, the Defender of the cause of the widow, to Him who heareth the cry of the destitute, and whose Son is not ashamed to call the poor His brethren, to Him, with that blessed Son, and the Spirit of bounty and love, be accounted all honour, praise, and glory!

SERMON XVI.

NEW YEAR'S DAY.

[Preached in the Cathedral, Calcutta, Jan. 1, 1824.]

St. Luke ii. 21.

And when eight days were accomplished, for the circumcising of
the child, his name was called Jesus.

In reviewing those circumstances in the life of our
Lord, which it is the custom of the Church to commemorate on the first day of every year, there are
two observations which would seem to force themselves on our notice ; the one personal and respecting Christ alone, the other of a more general character, and relating to the institution itself to which
He thus, in great humility, became subject.   The
first is the apparent strangeness of the fact that at
His earliest entrance into the world, the Son of
God should be made liable to suffering; the other
the authority and sanction which, from the analogy
of the Jewish covenant, is afforded to the practice
of the general Christian Church, in not denying
baptism to persons of like tender years.

The first of these is a reflection of no inconsi-

derable importance, as it conduces, or should conduce, to our love and admiration of His goodness
who, being throned above all created things, endured the elements of the world to save us ; who,
being born before all worlds, became for our sakes
a suckling ; whose entrance and exit into life were
sprinkled alike with blood; and who, though Himself spotless and pure, thought it not unworthy of
His nature or His character to fulfill even the most
revolting forms of legal righteousness. It may teach,
too, that even the forms and ceremonies of religion
(particularly when those forms and ceremonies have
received the sanction of the Most High) are neither
to be neglected without abundant cause, nor dis-
pensed with by a less authority than that which
imposed them ; but that, in these outward signs, an
inward blessing dwells.   And that He who Himself
condescended to observe that law which was so soon
to vanish away, will far less hold them guiltless
who neglect or regard as trifling those rites which
are to endure till He shall return again ; of which
the one was the legacy of His death, and the other
the injunction of His triumph ; His " do this in remembrance of me," and His " go ye baptize all
nations [1]."   The second is a remark of a more con-
troversial, but of a scarcely less practical nature ;
it is a reflection which penetrates into the recesses
of every family, and which blends with the earliest
affection and the earliest duties which we can feel

[1] 1 Cor. xi. 25. St. Matt. xxviii. 19.

for, or extend to our offspring. And, in this region of India, it is a question the more seasonable, and the more obvious to our consideration from the numbers, the popularity and distinguished learning of those among our Christian brethren who have embraced a contrary opinion and practice. I am anxious, therefore, to offer (with as much brevity as the subject will admit, and I trust with as little violation of mutual charity as the infirmity of our nature suffers) a few of the many reasons which have induced the great body of Christians to apply the analogy of the ancient rite to that rite by which it was superseded, and to bring the first fruit of their infants' days to that merciful Saviour of all, who did not forbid the little children to come unto Him, and who, Himself, when a child, became partaker of the covenant of Israel.

That the intention and advantage of the federal rite of the Jews were in many, nay, in most particulars, very closely answerable to the intention and advantages of baptism, is an assertion which even a moderate acquaintance with the Old Testament and the writings of St. Paul might seem sufficient to convince us. In the first appointment of circumcision by the Almighty, it is represented as an expression of the faith of the person initiated in the power and promises of Jehovah. " I will establish my covenant between me and thee and thy seed, for an everlasting covenant, to be a God unto thee and thy seed after thee." " Every man child among you shall be circumcised," " and it shall be a token

T

of the covenant betwixt me and you."   " Abraham,"
saith St. Paul, " received the sign of circumcision,
a seal of the righteousness of the faith which he
had yet being uncircumcised[1]."   Nor was it of faith
only in the promises of God that circumcision was
expressive.   It was expressive also of a controul
over men's unruly appetites, a purification of the
inward man from every foul and sordid affection,
and a renunciation of the superfluities of the world
for the service of that God who is of purer eyes
than to behold iniquity.   And it is hard to deny,
when reading some of the later prophets, that the
same change in the inner man of which baptism is
typical, was betokened by and confirmed in circumcision ; that " the circumcision of the heart" must
have been something very like in its import to our
term of " regeneration ;" and that to them who,
under affliction and persecution, kept the law,
" circumcision verily profiteth[2]" in the only way
by which it could profit them, by purchasing the
praise not of men but of God, and a participation
in the benefits of those promises, the fulfilment of
which they did not in life receive, but in which they
died stedfastly believing.

    Nor am I aware that any thing further or greater
is expressed or received by the Christian in baptism than is attributed by St. Paul to circumcision
in the Jew; a declaration of faith, an assurance of
mercy, an admission into the privilege of God's

[1] Gen. xvii. 7, 10, 11. Rom. iv. 11.   [2] Rom. ii. 25.

elect people upon earth, and a renunciation of
those sins and vanities which unfit us for that
Heaven whither our hopes are tending. Nor can
any words, as I conceive, be devised, which, *mu-
tatis mutandis,* more accurately express the obligations and the benefits of a truly Christian baptism, which more strongly depict the danger of
holding the faith in unrighteousness, or of resting
contented with an outward sign while the inward
and spiritual grace is, in our heart, extinct and
buried, than the caution that " he is not a Jew
which is one outwardly, neither is that circumcision which is outward in the flesh ; but he is a Jew
which is one inwardly ; and circumcision is that of
the heart, in the spirit, and not in the letter [1]."

And here the question will naturally arise, " at
what period of their lives were men conceived fit
subjects for such engagements ? how soon or how
late were they called on by a public ceremony to
receive a seal of that righteousness which was by
faith, and whereby they, the Jews, were justified
with faithful Abraham ?" And when these enquirers
learn that, at eight days' old, the infant Israelite was
thus initiated ; that the period of his initiation was
thus fixed by God himself; and that at the same
early age the Son of God began in this manner to
fulfill the righteousness of the law, they may be led
to ask, perhaps with some surprise, what Christians
those can be who are insensible to the analogy of

[1] Rom. ii. 28, 29.

such a practice with that of infant baptism, who forbid us to dedicate our children to God at the same age when, by God's own appointment, the children of the Jews were dedicated ; and when the Son of God Himself, in His character of a Jew, undertook the burden and laid claim to the promises which belonged to the seed of Abraham ?

Let us examine the matter a little more closely. God is not mocked, neither is God a mocker of His creatures. He knows our misery too well to trifle with it, and He is as far from giving us the delusive comfort of a useless pageant, as He is from being Himself imposed upon by any pageantry of worthless ceremonies. But, if the baptism of children, as these suppose, is worthless and unmeaning, it is evident that the circumcision of children must fall under an equal censure. But this last is allowed, on all hands, to have been instituted by God Himself, and it will follow that the inconsistencies ascribed to the former practice must be more imaginary than real, and that we may well hope that God favourably alloweth this charitable work of ours in bringing these infants to His holy baptism.

I know it has been urged that circumcision was the seal of admission, not to spiritual, but temporal privileges, the possession of an earthly Canaan, the entrance into the visible sanctuary, the right of being numbered among the descendants of Abraham and the family of the future Messiah. I have already proved, I trust, that its privileges were not confined to these, and that its meaning, if regard be had to some remarkable expressions both of the prophets and of St. Paul, was exceedingly more extensive and more solemn. But, even if we were to admit the allegation, how would this destroy the analogy? In the first place, it is well known (so well known, indeed, as to admit of no dispute among Christians) that the civil institutions and temporal privileges of the Jews had all, likewise, a typical and mysterious character; that they were shadows of good things to come, and representatives of that spiritual blessedness which we seek after and obtain by a due recourse to the sacrament of baptism. But from the type to the antitype the inference is fair and obvious, and if a child might, by submitting to a certain ceremony, be made partaker of the advantages of the one, it is, surely, too much to deny that a child being, in another and corresponding ceremony, dedicated by its parents to God, might not, through God's favour, become partaker of the privileges of the other. Is God's arm grown short under the Christian dispensation? Is His mercy chilled and narrowed? or is not the promise of the glorious Gospel given to us and to our children, and to our children's children, no less than was to the house of Israel the promise of those elemental and external blessings which, in comparison with our own, St. Paul is not afraid to designate as " beggarly [1]."

But let the privileges conferred by circumcision

---

[1] Gal. iv. 9.

have been of whatever kind they may, those privileges, it is plain, were conditional on the performance, through life, of certain duties.   It was to the
Israelite a seal of the faith which he had in the
promises and power of the Almighty; it was a
pledge on his part of obedience to Jehovah that he
should have the Lord for his God, and none other.
If he broke this covenant his privileges were forfeited; his circumcision became uncircumcision; he
retained neither lot nor part in the federation of
the tribes, or was liable only to the indignation and
vengeance of their Heavenly Patron and Sovereign.
It was in fact a contract, no less than baptism is
now, between each individual Israelite and the
Most High.

But if the child of Jewish parents were capable
of entering into such a contract, who has forbidden,
or who shall forbid the Christian infant from, in
like manner, entering by his sureties into a similar
solemn engagement? Who shall doubt that though
the weakness and the tender age be alike in both,
the merciful arms of a gracious Lord are as open in
the one instance as the other?

And this presumption will gain yet further
strength, if we recollect that circumcision is, by
God Himself, called " a token of the covenant between Himself and Israel." Now for whose use
and instruction was such a token intended? for
which of the contracting parties? Did *God* require
a memento of His own gracious purposes? Did *God*
need that a bodily mark should be imposed on His

people, in order that He might know and distinguish them from the Gentiles among whom they were scattered? Or was it not rather designed for the instruction and comfort of the individual on whom it was affixed, to preserve in his mind the recollection of those hopes which were held out to his continued allegiance to God, those terrours which impended over his departure from the prescribed conditions? Was it not a pledge on the part of the parents and friends, that the infant whom they thus brought into treaty with the Most High should, in after years, be trained up by them in His faith and fear, and that Ishmael and Isaac should be taught, like their father Abraham, to know the Lord their God, and to look forward to his future Messiah? Or which of all these points is there which is not equally supplied to the child of Christian parents by his early dedication to our Great Master's service? He cannot, indeed, in the one any more than in the other instance, himself be at the moment made sensible of his new privileges, or the new obligations which are laid on him; but he has the prayers of his parents and of the Church, offered up in that manner and by that form to which the Almighty has promised a blessing. The ceremony which he undergoes is a pledge on the part of the Church that he shall be admitted to her external means of instruction; it is a petition addressed to the Almighty that those means of instruction may be blessed to his everlasting happiness; it is a solemn claim of that promise from

God, which He has made to all without exception,
and which, be it remembered, is a promise of free
grace and mercy only, to the fulfilment of which,
whether infant or adult, the applicant is alike inca-
pable of contributing any merits or strength of his
own, and for which the infant, no less than the
adult, has the plea of his natural weakness and his
natural misery.

The promise, I repeat, is made to all, and the
young as well as the old partake in it. " The
child," according to the ancient prophet, was under
the Gospel covenant, " to die an hundred years
old[1]." And who shall deny that those infants of
whom Christ himself declared that " of such was
the kingdom of Heaven[2]," have, no less than the
most aged saint, their proportional share in its happiness ? But, can any enter Heaven without the
sanctifying grace of Christ ? Or, if infants are fit
subjects for this grace, if they are really inheritors
of the kingdom of God, and partakers of those spiritual influences in this life, without which our
fleshly nature cannot see the Lord, then " can any
man forbid water that these should not be baptized,
which have received the Holy Ghost as well as we[3]?"
Surely, the more we examine it the more reasonable does the practice appear, as a seal of past mercies, as an engagement to future duties, as an admission to the external means of grace which the
Church can in this world supply, and as a solemn

---

[1] Isaiah lxv. 20.   [2] St. Matt. xix. 14.
[3] Acts x. 47.

petition to the Almighty, that His blessing may render those outward means effectual! Suffer, then, the little children to come to Christ and forbid them not, for of such is the kingdom of Heaven!

In this short view of a very interesting and important question, I have not had the opportunity, and circumstanced as I am, at this moment, with regard to books of reference, I have hardly had the means of bringing forward, in the manner which it deserves, the vast body of authority and precedent which the Talmudists and the ancient Fathers supply, both as to the circumstances under which baptism was administered by the ancient Jews, for the Jews had also their baptism, and of the admission of infants in the earliest times of the Church, to the privileges and pledges of Christians. Enough, however, has, I trust, been said to show, that in thus admitting them, we neither act irrationally nor unscripturally; that we neither mock the Lord our God with an empty and unauthorised form, nor mock our helpless offspring with an unavailing remedy for their natural corruption and misery. I will only add that the wisdom of our Church, and the merciful appointment of our Maker have added, in the ceremony of a confirmation subsequent to baptism, the force of a personal engagement to the blessing of an early dedication, and that the regenerate by water may be renewed by the Holy Ghost, if they seek Him in earnest prayer, and at the hands of His appointed ministers.

One observation yet remains as to the occasion which calls us together. It has been the devout and commendable custom of our Indian Church to assemble on the annual return of this day, for the hearing of God's word and of prayer, less, perhaps, with reference to the particular event in our Saviour's history which the service of this day commemorates, than for the sake of offering our thanksgiving to Him who has protected us through another revolution of the sun, and of beginning the new year with an act of solemn prayer, and an offering of ourselves to His service. Such a custom it would most painfully grieve me to see neglected, or passing into oblivion ; but that such a custom may be something more than an empty form, let me entreat you, my brethren, to make some part of this day a season of self-examination ; of enquiry into the present state of your feelings towards God, and the tenour of your past conduct before Him ; of making a solemn resolution for the amendment of your future life, and of earnest private prayer to Him, without whose help and guidance, even our best future resolutions will be as vain as those which have preceded them. The return of days like these are as milestones in our passage through the world, but they differ from such way-marks, inasmuch as they respect the past alone. They tell us how far we have advanced, but they leave uncertain how short a course we may yet have to travel. Yet one thing they teach us, that our journey cannot be long, that we have most of

us already passed too many stages to have many
yet behind, while a retrospect of those which we
have gone through, may assure us of the exceeding
shortness even of those months and years, and tens
of years, which, as we advance towards them, appear so interminable.

Under the mildest suns and the most temperate
climates of earth, our course must be short, and its
termination may, at any time, be immediate. But
here, where the lamp of life, even under the most
favourable circumstances, must burn so rapidly,
surrounded at every step with deaths and diseases,
and placed under the constant influence of the most
awful and destructive phenomena of nature, can
we yet hope to prolong our days for ever? can we
yet forget that God who only can defend us against
the sun by day, the moon by night, the arrows of
the sky, and the hand of the armed enemy? Here,
if any where, in the midst of life we are in death!
And of whom may we seek for succour, save of
Thee, Oh Lord, who, for our sins, art justly displeased! Yet, Oh Lord most Holy, Oh Lord most
Mighty, Oh Holy and Merciful Saviour, deliver us
not into the bitter pains of eternal death! So
teach us to number our days that we may apply
our hearts unto wisdom! And, Oh Lord most
Holy, Oh God most Mighty, Thou most worthy
Judge eternal, suffer us not at our last hour for
any pains of death to fall from Thee!

SERMON XVII.

EASTER DAY.

[Preached at Tanjore, March 26, 1826.]

Rev. i. 17, 18.

He laid His right hand upon me, saying unto me, Fear not; I
am the first and the last; I am He that liveth and was dead;
and behold, I am alive for evermore, amen; and have the keys
of Hell and of Death.

THESE were the gracious expressions of our glorified Lord to His faithful and most favoured disciple,
when, in the prison of Patmos and amid the solitary
devotions of a Christian Sabbath, the apostle St.
John was visited by "One like unto the Son of
Man." The features yet remained distinguishable
to the eye of ancient friendship, of Him whom he
had known on earth as the lowly and the poor,
whose afflictions he had shared, whose journeyings
he had followed, and who with His dying lips had
commended to his filial care the desolate old age
of His mother! But He was now arrayed in long
and kingly robes, His girdle was of gold, His eyes
gleamed as the fire, His limbs were bright as burning brass, His voice as deep and tuneable as the
sound of many waters. Seven stars were in His

grasp; before His face a flaming sword went forth;
and His countenance was as the sun when its light
is strongest. " Fear not," He said, as His ancient
follower sank down in terrour at His feet, " I am
the first and the last, I am He that liveth and was
dead, and behold I am alive for evermore, and have
the keys of hell and of death."

In these few words are expressed or implied all
the several and peculiar doctrines on which the
Christian builds his hope of a life to come ; and I
have selected the passage for our devout consideration this day, because I know few other passages in
Scripture which so concisely, so forcibly, and so
majestically express the belief by which we are distinguished from the Jews, the Mussulmans, and the
Heathen. The eternity of Christ, with which His
Divinity is closely connected, is expressly stated in
the opening member of the sentence. His death
and resurrection are no less explicitly laid down in
the assertion that He " liveth and was dead;" and
the concluding proposition, that " He hath the keys
of hell and of death," would be unintelligible on any
other principle than that it is by His power, and
through His merits only, that we are ourselves, in
like manner, to burst the prison-house of the grave ;
that it is by His power, and through His merits
only, that the resurrection thus obtained for us can
be a subject of hope and thankfulness.

Each of these distinct topics would afford abundant and useful matter for a sermon ; but it shall
be my endeavour at present to point out, so far as

the time allows, how they materially confirm and
illustrate each other, and more particularly connected with the blessed event which we are this
day assembled to celebrate, how much both of probability, of reasonableness, of religious and moral
consistency is derived, from a faith in the Divinity
and atonement of our Lord, to the doctrine of His
resurrection and our own.

It is certain that, unless the resurrection of Christ
be true, His religion is itself a lie.   This is the
alternative expressly admitted by St. Paul; " If
Christ be not raised, your faith is vain ; ye are yet
in your sins.   Then they also which are fallen
asleep in Christ are perished [1]."   The prophets had
foretold, not only that the Messiah should die a
bloody and painful death, but also that His soul
should not remain in hell, neither should His holy
person see corruption [2].   To this resurrection within
three days Jesus had repeatedly appealed, as the
fullest testimony of His divine commission, the
crowning and consummating evidence of His religion.   If, therefore, Jesus had not actually risen
again, the conclusion must have followed, both that
He had failed in one most essential and striking
characteristic of the predicted Christ, whose character He assumed ; and that, in expressly foretelling so remarkable an event, and foretelling it in
vain, He had proved Himself, beyond all shadow of
defence, to be either deceived or a deceiver.   It

[1] 1 Cor. xv. 17, 18.   [2] Psalm xiv. 10.

followed, that such who had grounded their hope of
a future life on His promise, had but reared a base-
less fabric; and that such as hoped for pardon of
their sins in confidence of His intercession, had
been treasuring up for themselves the bitterest disappointment, if there were indeed another world
and a day of dreadful retribution. Accordingly it
shall be my endeavour, in the first place, to lay
before you, in the least possible compass, some few
of those arguments which appear to me most convincing for the reality of that extraordinary event
which the apostles witnessed to the world, and for
the sincerity of those persons who so boldly and
constantly proclaimed it.

It is on this latter foundation, indeed, that the
faith of Christians reposes. The reality of Christ's
resurrection we receive on their testimony alone,
and a moment's consideration may convince us that
it is their sincerity only which can be called in
question. It was a point on which they could not
be mistaken. If their account be true, it was no
single nor transient visit which their crucified Master paid them after His resurrection. He was in
their company, at short and uncertain intervals,
during forty days; He ate and drank in their presence; He allowed them to examine His person
and His wounds; He discoursed with them in His
usual manner; and, when He departed from them
at length, He departed in the broad light of day,
ascending upwards before their eyes till the inter-
vening clouds prevented them from observing His

1

further progress. To say that they were unlearned
and superstitious persons, is to speak very widely
from the purpose. Unlearned and credulous persons are as competent judges of the facts for which
the apostles vouched, as the most skilful and cautious naturalist. It needs no physical knowledge
to use the hands and eyes ; it is not necessary that
a man should be acquainted with the laws of re-
fraction or electricity to enable him to swear to his
having seen, in broad day-light, the person of a
friend whom he had for three years together continually attended; and the circumstances under which
our Lord exhibited Himself were such, if they are
rightly described, as to render vain and impracticable all kinds of phantasmagoric illusion.

Let us see, then, what arguments the apostles
were enabled to advance to convince mankind that
they were not the preachers of a cunningly devised
fable, and to gain credit for a fact so extraordinary
as that a person, confessedly put to a public and
shameful death, had resumed His life, had returned
from His grave, and was at that time, under God,
the invisible Governor of all things.

And here it must not be forgotten that the very
improbability of this story, paradoxical as the assertion may seem, is, to a certain extent, a presumption of its truth. It is not like the invention
of a religious cheat, or of a man or body of men
(some of them, to judge from their writings of no
inconsiderable talent and attainment) who were
anxious, by a ready lie, to sustain the credit of a

ruined cause, and to save themselves from sinking into that insignificance from which the eloquence and renown of their Master had originally raised them. A less daring forgery might have been sufficient for such a purpose ; nor is it likely that, had they been impostors, and been anxious in the name of Jesus to carry on the imposture which He began, they would have ventured on a tale so wild as that of His actual re-appearance in the body, when a pretended interview with His ghost would have better suited the prejudices both of their own countrymen, and of the Gentiles. Nor is this all, since, as neither their countrymen nor the Gentiles had any pre-disposition in favour of their story ; since, on the other hand, the attributing such honour to a crucified man was the greatest stumbling-block which the new religion offered to the house of Israel; and since the bare mention of a resurrection from the dead was enough to excite the mockery of the Athenians, and to extort from Festus the exclamation that the preacher of such a doctrine was beside himself[1]; we might be, *à priori*, sure that such an assertion would never have been received as true by the many thousands who, on the apostle's preaching, did receive it, unless their testimony had been confirmed by some very remarkable proofs both of their sincerity, their sanity, and their divine commission.

We know ourselves, there is, perhaps, no country

---

[1] Acts xxvi. 24.

U

in the world where we have so good reason to know
it as in India, we know that it is no easy matter even
for the most popular talents and the most persevering zeal to persuade men into a new religion.
We know that this very article of Christ's resurrection from the dead is uniformly, at first sight, by
the heathen now, as by the heathen of old, regarded as folly and madness; and we may well
perceive the argument of Origen to be founded in
reason and probability, that those miracles must
have been great indeed, those arguments must have
been of a most convincing potency, which could
have obtained, in the first instance, even hearers,
far less believers for such a tale in the streets of
Rome, of Athens, and of Alexandria.   Accordingly,
though beyond a doubt the apparent disinterestedness of the first teachers of Christianity, the absence
of all worldly gains which might prompt them to
the continuance of such an imposture, and the un-
daunted patience and constancy which, even in
death itself, distinguished the witnesses of the resurrection, though all these must have had on their
contemporaries, as they still have on ourselves, a
powerful effect in gaining credit to their narration,
they are the marvels still more which they wrought
in Christ's name, and in attestation of His religion
to which, in their writings, the apostles themselves
appeal, and which they adduce as proofs of their
having been actuated by the Spirit of God.   And
it is more remarkable still that neither of Christ
nor His apostles are the miraculous actions denied

2

in those attacks on our faith which have come down to us from the earliest ages. The article of miracles was met by the Antichristian disputant with the allegation, not that the miracles were false, but that they might possibly be magical; and when driven from this strong hold, they appear to have had no excuse nor evasion but the pretence that, in their own temples, wonders of the same kind were not unknown, and an attempt to counterbalance the miracles of Peter and of John, by the tales of Vespasian with his blind man, and Apollonius of Tyana with his fountain genii.

The resurrection, then, of our Lord, as it stands on the testimony of the apostles, is confirmed by the impossibility that they could be themselves deceived; by the absence of any adequate motive which could induce them to impose on others; by the simplicity of their lives, their constancy in death, and the miraculous powers which, in the greatest and least credulous cities of the Roman world, obtained them hosts of auditors and converts. But one objection will yet remain both to the fact which they proclaimed, and to the miraculous facts by which they chiefly strengthened their testimony; an objection which has more influence among men than, I believe, is generally suspected, and which is at the bottom of much of that practical or professed infidelity which, in the present day, and in our native land, so frequently surprises and shocks us; I mean the doctrine of Hume, that no evidence can establish a miracle, inasmuch as there is more probability that the witnesses should deceive or be deceived, than that the ordinary laws of nature should be transgressed by the Almighty.

In this argument it is apparent that there is more than one *petitio principii.* The sophist assumes the existence of certain definite laws by which nature is tied; (which code, nevertheless, if he had been called to produce, it would have been very easy to anticipate his perplexity). He assumes that supposing such laws to exist, what we call miracles are breaches of them, whereas, for all he knew or could know, such visible interpositions of a superior intelligence may be, as indeed they are represented in Scripture, foreseen and necessary events in the great work of God's Providence, and no less constituent parts of a regular system than the movements of the comet, the hurricane, or the earthquake. But above all, he forgets that, if a sufficient reason can be assigned, the visible interference of the Maker of the world becomes no more than might be reasonably expected from His usual and provident care of His creatures ; while the discovery and attestation of truths infinitely important to mankind, can scarcely be denied to be a reason which might make a display of Almighty power expedient and natural.

And here it is that the great mystery of Christian redemption comes forward with irresistible force to overturn the sceptic's argument, and to convince every candid reasoner that no ordinary rules of probability will apply, where the analogy is so completely broken and dissolved by the greatness of the interests concerned, and the dignity of the persons implicated. The resuscitation of a corpse, if it were alleged to have taken place without any reason at all, or for a reason of minor expediency, might demand, indeed, a rigid enquiry into its circumstances, and a suspension of our belief, even if we failed to detect imposture. It is one of the many reasons which persuade me to withhold my faith from the pretended miracles of the Romish Church, that the interests of a convent, the honour of a shrine, nay the truth or falsehood of those minor differences, which have for so many ages disturbed the peace of those who acknowledge the same Creator and Redeemer, do not appear to me such sufficient grounds of miraculous interposition, as to induce me to expect that God would make bare His arm, or that the thunders of Heaven would muster in such a quarrel. And if the Socinian hypothesis with regard to Christianity were true; if Christ had been, indeed, a mere man of men, possessed of no further dignity than a prophetic commission from on high, and with no more aweful secret to disclose than that future life after death, which the majority of mankind believed already, I might, perhaps, have wondered at the strange prodigality of miracles with which His short continuance on earth was adorned and illustrated. I might have doubted the fitness of darkening the sun, because an innocent man was brought to an untimely end, and have

apprehended that it was hardly necessary to bring
back our Teacher from the grave to establish, by
that greatest of prodigies, the truth of the doctrine
which He had delivered. But when I learn that
the seeming man of sorrows was actually an incarnation of the Deity, I can understand at once, and
without difficulty, the reason and fitness that so
many and so mighty works should have shown
forth themselves in Him. When I learn that His
death was the ransom of a guilty world, I can
appreciate the sympathy which made the inanimate
creation tremble, which obscured the face of day,
and made the dead burst untimely from the womb
of their sepulchres.

I cease to wonder at His return from the grave,
when I know that it was " impossible that He
could be holden of it," that " He had power to
lay down His life and power to take it up again,"
and that He who was, for a time, " obedient to
the death on the cross," had life in Himself co-
eternal with the eternal Father. I cease to wonder at the high exaltation to God's right hand,
which He who " was found in fashion as a man,"
has attained to, when I know that the glory which
adorns Him now, is but the same with that which
He had before the world was[1]; but my hope is increased, and my deep thankfulness ten thousand
fold augmented, when assured that it was the First
and the Last who condescended to die for me ; that

[1] Acts ii. 24. St. John x. 18. Phil. ii. 8.

He is faithful who hath promised to send the Holy Ghost to quicken us to a perpetual remembrance; and that the keys of death and hell are in the merciful and mighty hands of Him who hath poured out His blood to save us from the one, and hath made the other the gate of immortality!

ADDRESS ON CONFIRMATION.

[Delivered at Trichinopoly, April 3, 1826.]

DEARLY BELOVED IN THE LORD!

You have been engaged this day in one of the most aweful and important transactions in which a created being can bear a part; the solemn renewal of your former covenant with your Maker, and the no less solemn claim of the stipulated mercies of that great Creator towards yourselves. In Christ's name you have drawn near to the Most High to tender to His service, in the terms of your baptismal engagement, the bodies which He has framed, the lives which He has given, the immortal souls which, through His Son, He has redeemed from misery unspeakable.

For God's acceptance of these offered services; for the spiritual strength which only can enable you to render them; for the merciful indulgence which, even when they are most diligently performed, they must still need at God's hand; and for the unbounded and eternal reward which His free bounty has promised to even the weakest efforts to please Him, when made in His Son's name, you have pleaded the merits of that blessed Son, by the confession of your faith in Him, and by the solemn prayer which we offered up together to the Throne of Grace, for the gift of the Holy Ghost the Comforter.

In reliance on these merits and on the precious promises of our Redeemer, I, lastly, as His servant and in His name, have prayed for you that your faith fail not. In His name and as His servant, and in imitation of His holy apostles, I have laid my hands on you and blessed you, as a sure token that our prayers would not return empty from the Lord of life, but that ye might receive the Holy Ghost whom ye had desired, and might partake henceforward, in a larger measure and by a daily increase, of that Heavenly grace which was, in part, bestowed on you in baptism.

And I doubt not, that so many of you as with faith unfeigned and fitting preparation of heart, have repaired to this holy ordinance, have been as truly and effectually, though not so conspicuously, sharers in that unspeakable gift whereby we are sealed to the day of redemption, as when the Heaven was opened over the congregations of the primitive Church, and He whose temples we are, came down in cloven flames, and hovered over the heads of His servants.

I doubt it not, because I dare not doubt the strength of prayer, and the promise of the Son of God, that His Father and ours, (for, by the spirit of adoption, we have permission to call Him so) that His Heavenly Father and ours will not refuse the Holy Spirit to them that ask Him! I doubt it not, because I dare not doubt the efficacy of an apostolic injunction, or that the petitions which we offer in the manner which those dearest to God enjoined and practised, will be acceptable with God and with His Son; and to us, as to those from whom we have received them, be the fountain and pledge of Heavenly strength and blessing. I doubt it not, because I dare not doubt the last words of our Lord upon earth, when He sent forth His ministers with a like commission to that which He had Himself received of His Father, and when, though foreseeing, as what did He not foresee, the lamentable degeneracy of those who should bear His name, He promised, nevertheless, to His Church, His invisible protection and presence till the kingdoms of this world should become the kingdom of the Lamb, and this same Jesus, which was then taken up from us into Heaven, should so come in like manner as He was seen going into Heaven.

Oh Master, Oh Saviour, Oh Judge and King, Oh God faithful and true! Thy word is sure, though our sinful eyes may not witness its fulfilment! Surely Thou art in this place and in every place where thine ordinances are reverenced, and Thy name is duly called on! Thy treasures are in earthen vessels, but they are Thy treasures still! Though prophecies may fail and tongues may cease, Thy truth remains the same; and though prophecies have failed and tongues have ceased, and though the Heaven and the earth are grown old and ready to vanish away, yet it is impossible but that when two or three are gathered together in Thy name, Thou also shouldst be in the midst of them! So continue with us Lord evermore, and let the Spirit, the Angel of Thy presence, be with us all our days, even as He hath this day been at hand to help, to deliver and to sanctify all who came to receive Him.

In assurance, then, my brethren, that our prayers have not been in vain, and that an effectual power to become the sons of God has been, even now, according to Christ's holy promise, communicated to those who sought it faithfully, it is my duty to call on you to give hearty and humble thanks to the Father and Giver of all good things, to the Son whose blood has bought for us these spiritual treasures, and to that Good Spirit who hath not disdained to dwell with men, and of whose indwelling and inspiration it cometh that we can either think or do such things as please Him. And that your hearts may be better fitted to retain this Heavenly guest, and that you may not, by a relapse into sin, resist and grieve the Holy Ghost as Israel did of old, and so increase your damnation by erring against a greater light, and flinging away a greater mercy, receive a few plain instructions by way of caution for the management of your hearts, and the improvement of that time and those opportunities of His service, which God may hereafter vouchsafe to you.

I will not do so much injustice to the well-known zeal and ability of your spiritual instructors, on the present occasion; I will not do so much injustice to the seriousness of deportment and apparent earnestness of prayer, which I have, with pleasure, remarked in most of you, as to doubt that you have been duly taught the nature and necessity of those baptismal engagements which you have now renewed; or that you are really sincere in the desire which you have expressed to be enabled to serve and please your God hereafter. Nor need I do more than recall to your recollections that truth, which is implied and acknowledged in the whole of this solemn ceremony, that this power to serve and please God is given us by His Spirit only; that in ourselves, that is in our flesh, there dwelleth no good thing; and that we are utterly unequal to strive with the many temptations which surround us, unless a Greater and Mightier than we vouchsafes to go forth with us to battle. The promise of this visitation and indwelling of the Holy Ghost, has, we trust, been now fulfilled to us; and it remains to enquire in what manner our hearts may best entertain their Heavenly Inhabitant, and how we may most surely keep, enjoy, and profit by the inestimable privileges to which we are become entitled, the favour, the fellowship, the help, and comfort of the Most High.

Of the things most conducive and requisite to this desirable end, the first is, evidently, a firm and lively faith in our Lord Jesus Christ, and in the redemption which He has wrought for us. That you are, at present, actuated by such a faith, that you are persuaded that the things contained in the Gospel are true, and that relying on their truth, you have come hither to ask a blessing, I should grieve if I were not persuaded. But be it borne in mind that a faith which is to save us must be in our recollection as well as in our knowledge; that it must be positively as well as potentially in our minds; that we cannot be said to believe in the God of whom we are not thinking, inasmuch as faith necessarily implies thought exercised upon an unseen object. And this may show the manner in which our faith may fail, and fail most ruinously for ourselves, without our ever actually entertaining a doubt of the truth of those things in which we have been instructed, inasmuch as if we do not believe them, or, which amounts to the same thing, do not think of them when the time of temptation arrives, it is of very little use that in Church, or when by some similar circumstance they are brought back to our memory, we again receive them with unabated conviction. Accordingly, not only the absolutely wicked are turned into hell, but the people who forget God lie under the same aweful menace [1]. And we have the authority of God's

---

[1] Psalm ix. 17.

holy word for maintaining that all the errours, all the superstition, all the hateful and hideous idolatry which the world has seen, arose from this single source, inasmuch as because men did not like to retain God in their thoughts, He gave them up to a strong delusion that they should believe a lie! So necessary is it by daily recollections of God, by daily study of the Holy Scriptures, and by a frequent reference to those works of devotion and instruction which the Church supplies, to avoid this dangerous and deadly downfall, and to keep the blessed Trinity in our minds, if we would have God to dwell in our hearts for ever.

The next thing requisite to a constant faith in God is a total dependance on Him, through the merits of His Son. This is, indeed, implied in a right faith, but it is a particular part of our faith which many are apt to feel and cherish but imperfectly. By a total dependance on God I mean a perfect sense of our own weakness; an entire renunciation of our own merits; a childlike leaning on the hand and help of the Most High, which claims to receive nothing but from free mercy, and hopes to perform nothing but in His name and by His power alone. So long as we resolve in our own strength, our resolutions will be worse than idle; so long as we are not daily and continually sensible of our own utter weakness, God will not help us and our prayers will be rendered vain.

Be careful, then, to accustom yourselves to this lowliness of heart; and that you may feel your own

weakness the more readily as it respects your
Maker, be the more careful to bear yourself humbly
and meekly towards those who are your fellow-
sinners and fellow-servants. If we love not our
brother whom we have seen, we know who has
told us that we cannot love God whom we have
not seen; and he, in like manner, who indulges
himself in haughtiness towards those with whom
he dwells, will seldom, if ever, be able to feel sufficient meekness towards Him who is visible by the
eye of faith alone.

A third and a still more important instrument in
preparing our hearts for the reception of the Holy
Ghost, is a habit of prayer. " Ask and ye shall
have," " Seek and ye shall find," is the constant
language of Scripture [1]. Without asking we shall
not obtain; without continuing to ask, what we
have obtained will not be prolonged to us. Your
hearts, as we trust, are now the temple of the Holy
Ghost. But a temple is a house of prayer; and if
we omit to serve the Deity we cannot hope that
He will continue in His shrine.

But woe be to us, then, when He, the Spirit of
God, forsakes us ! Woe be to our wretched souls
when that voice is heard concerning them, which,
when the measure of Israel's guilt was full, in the
dead of night resounded through the courts of
their sanctuary, " Let us depart hence," as from
our polluted dwelling. The Spirit of God, I re-

[1] St. Matt. vii. 7.

peat, will not always strive with man; and if His·
accepted time is despised or suffered to pass by
unimproved, the time may come in the which we
shall desire to see one of the days of the Son of
Man, and it shall not be shown unto us [1] !

A neglect of prayer, then, of morning and evening
prayer, (I name these times because a short prayer,
at least, is then in every body's power, and because
no times are so proper, none so natural for devotion as the moments at which we are about to
commit ourselves to a temporary death, or at which
we have just undergone a lively image of the resurrection,) a neglect of morning and evening
prayer, as it is always one of the earliest symptoms
of our falling away from God, so it is the certain
means of estranging ourselves entirely from Him,
and provoking Him to give us up to still farther
guilt, and to withdraw from us, it may be, even the
opportunity and power of repentance.

But even this daily prayer will of itself be insufficient, unless we honour the Lord our God in public
as well as in private, and on those solemn and
stated Sabbaths above all, which the practice of the
whole Church, the authority of the inspired apostles, the sanction of the Lord Jesus Himself, when
risen from the dead, and after His reception into
glory, have combined to consecrate from worldly
and ordinary purposes to the examination of our
hearts, the improvement of our minds, the rest of

---

[1] St. Luke xvii. 22.

those who toil for us, and a union with our brethren and fellow-servants in a more solemn and
conspicuous piety. I am but too well aware of the
difficulties which, in India, under many circumstances of life, oppose themselves to the due observation of Sunday. I know but too well the influence exerted by the surrounding heathen ; I know
but too well the necessities which are sometimes
felt, but oftener fancied, for invading the sanctity
and repose of an institution which, even if it were
a political institution only, would, from its wisdom
and mercy, well deserve the imitation of every law-
giver, and the observation of every friend to mankind. I know but too well that the habits of the
country are against us, and that of some of those
who hear me, the time may really not be altogether at their own disposal. But in India there are
many hours in every day which are at the disposal
of every one of us. These at least, if no more can
be obtained, let the servant, the soldier, and the
mariner hallow from each succeeding Sunday to
the service of Him who only can prosper or forgive
his labours ; and let all others, even the busiest, but
make the trial, and they will find, or I am greatly
mistaken, that they need leave no lawful business
undone by resting one day in seven ; and that it is
amusement after all, not duty, which leaves them
no time to spare for private and public devotion.

Sir Matthew Hale, himself no less a rare model
of successful diligence in a laborious profession,
than of exalted talents and distinguished attach-

x

ment to the liberties of his country, has left on record that, in the course of a long and active life, he
never failed to find that his weekly business had
been best and most prosperously performed when
he had begun the week by a more than usually
careful observation of the Lord's day. Under the
safeguard of his authority I shall hardly be suspected of superstition; and I confess, it seems to
me a thing very far from incredible or unlikely, that
our labours may indeed be then most prosperous,
when our minds have been refreshed and strengthened by one day devoted to the most composing
and encouraging of all meditations; and that we
may look, without presumption, for an additional
blessing from the Lord on those lawful pursuits
which we have not suffered to interfere with His
service.

One instrument of blessing yet remains, the
mightiest of all, and that to which the ceremony
you have now undergone is a fitting and necessary
introduction; the Sacrament of the body and blood
of Christ. Of the value of this institution as a
means of grace; of its natural, I had almost
said, its necessary effect on the human heart, to
compose, to purify and strengthen it; of the re-
freshment which our souls derive from duly receiving it, and of the evident peril of neglecting one
of the last and most solemn, as well as most easy
and delightful commands which He who died for
us has left us, I need not now speak, as I trust the
instructions which you have received are still fresh

1

in your memory. One thing, however, I would
earnestly press upon you all, that your attendance
on the table of the Lord be not only frequent hereafter, but that your first visit to it be delayed as
short a time as possible. That is a strange reluctance, and one for which it is by no means easy to
account on any rational or human motives, which
keeps back young persons, on the pretext of their
youth, from this comfortable and blessed ordinance;
as if their being young and comparatively innocent
were a reason which could make their prayers less
acceptable to God, or as if the strength of their
passions and the temptations to which they are exposed, were not an additional and most forcible.
reason for their seeking after spiritual help in that
way which is, of all others, the most prevailing. But,
let me entreat you, my young friends, to consider
earnestly with yourselves that there is no text in
Scripture which confines the necessity of the rite
in question to those who are advanced in life, or
sinking down with weakness and infirmity; that
youth has no privilege, any more than age, which
exempts it from sudden death; that if we are
unfit to receive the Sacrament, we must be still
more unfit to die and stand before the judgement
seat of the Almighty; and that, however imperfect
our lives may be now, yet if we never employ the
helps which God in His bounty has furnished, we
cannot reasonably hope that they will ever become
better! You fear your own unworthiness. And I
know you to be most unworthy, unworthy so much

as to gather up the crumbs under the Lord's table.
But it is not in your own worthiness that you
are invited thither, but in the worthiness of Christ,
in the mercy of God, and in the marriage garment
which His grace will supply to all that do not wilfully reject it. You fear your own weakness, and I
know you to be most weak. I know that you are
unable of yourselves to do even the least part of
those things to which you stand engaged. I know
that your present good resolutions, if left to themselves, will vanish like a morning dream ; and
therefore it is that I so earnestly call on you to
seek for spiritual strength where best it may be
found, and to renew these gracious impressions,
both speedily and often, in the temple of the Lord,
and kneeling on the footstep of His Altar! Let,
then, the time which intervenes between the present day and the next opportunity of receiving the
Sacrament in your respective Churches, be to you
a time of frequent serious thought, of prayer, and
study of the Scriptures ; and let not, I beseech
you, that first opportunity pass away without returning to the Mercy Seat of God, without renew-
ing the free-will offerings of yourselves, your souls
and bodies, to His holy will and pleasure, and in-
treating the continuance and increase of the grace
and comfort which has been now held out to you.

Finally, holy brethren! partakers of the spiritual
gift! Let this day be to you a day remembered
much and often thought upon in the stillness of
the night, in the languor of noon, in the loneliness

and inactivity of an eastern journey, whenever
your soul retires upon itself, and finds food in the
recollection of past scenes and past impressions.
Bind the promises which you have made, and the
hopes which have been held out to you as a crown
on your heads, and as a bracelet on your arms,
that they may never pass from your recollection,
but occur to you then when all holy recollections
are most needed, when the world menaces or the
flesh entices, or when the tempter whispers dark
things in your souls, and seeks to draw you from
that strength in which only you can stand safely.
Write down this day as a date to be much observed,
as a new æra in your spiritual existence, in some
one or more of those books of devotion which you
have studied, or with which, on asking for them,
you will be supplied most cheerfully. And remember, above all, that the great and proper use of
days like this is, not to sanction or counterbalance
your sins, but to enable you to leave off sinning;
that for this cause we call on you to pray; for this
cause to be baptized; for this cause to frequent the
Church; for this cause to receive the Holy Ghost;
for this cause to become partakers in the Communion, that your hearts may be changed and renewed from the corruption of a fallen to the holiness of a Heavenly condition; that you may be
purified to Christ, a peculiar people zealous of good
works; that you may imitate, so far as He enables
you, His blameless life in whatever sphere of action His Providence may have allotted you, and

lay down at length your tranquil heads in death in the sure and certain hope of a resurrection to eternal life, beloved and regretted by those who have witnessed your demeanour on earth, and welcomed by those angels who shall then convey your souls to the land of rest and thankfulness! And now farewell! depart in the faith and favour of the Lord; and if what you have learned and heard this day has been so far blessed as to produce a serious and lasting effect on you, let me entreat you to remember sometimes in your prayers those ministers of Christ who now have laboured for your instruction, that we who have preached to you may not ourselves be cast away, but that it may be given to us also to walk in this life present according to the words of the Gospel which we have received of our Lord, and to rejoice hereafter with you the children of our care, in that land where the weary shall find repose, and the wicked cease from troubling; where we shall behold God as He is, and be ourselves made like unto God in innocence, and happiness, and immortality!

THE END.

LONDON:

PRINTED BY R. GILBERT, ST. JOHN'S SQUARE.